THE HEALTH-LOVER'S GUIDE TO

Super Seafood

250 Delicious Ways to Enjoy the Ultimate in Natural Nutrition

BY TOM NEY
FOOD EDITOR
PREVENTION MAGAZINE

Rodale Press, Emmaus, Pennsylvania

~~~~~~~~~~~~~~~~~~~~~~~~~~~~~~~~

To Alice and Vince Ney, who charted my course.

Copyright ©1989 by Rodale Press, Inc.

Printed in the United States of America on acid-free paper containing a high percentage of recycled fiber.

Book design by Glen Burris
Illustrations by Janet Bohn

Recipe photograph on front cover: Baked Salmon with Island Jewels, page 97.

Library of Congress Cataloging-in-Publication Data

Ney, Tom.
    The health-lover's guide to super seafood : 250 delicious ways to enjoy the ultimate in natural nutrition / Tom Ney ; photography by the Rodale Press Photography Department.
        p.   cm.
    Includes index.
    ISBN 0-87857-778-5 hardcover
    ISBN 0-87857-950-8 comb
    ISBN 0-87596-272-6 paperback
    1. Cookery (seafood) 2. Nutrition. I. Title
TX747.N53   1989
641.6'92 - dc19   88 -7878
                                                          CIP

2 4 6 8 10 9 7 5 3 1   hardcover
    4 6 8 10 9 7 5 3   comb
2 4 6 8 10 9 7 5 3 1   paperback

CONTENTS

PHOTOGRAPHY CREDITS

Photographers:
Carl Doney: pp. 44, 46, 113
Donna M. Hornberger: p. 111
Mitchell T. Mandel: p. 182
Alison Miksch: pp. 43, 112, 247, 249, 250
Christie C. Tito: pp. 179, 181
Sally Shenk Ullman: pp. 45, 114, 180, 248

Photographic Stylists:
Heidi Actor: p. 179
Mary Early: pp. 112, 113, 182
Marianne G. Laubach: pp. 43, 45, 46, 114, 180, 181,
    247, 248
Kay Seng Lichthardt: pp. 44, 111, 249, 250

ACKNOWLEDGMENTS

Early in my restaurant cooking career I realized the success of a menu depended on the team behind the chef. The kitchen brigade, the dining room staff, the office workers, even the grocers and suppliers all contribute their special, vital ingredient to guarantee a satisfied customer — a happy eater. This seafood cookbook is the result of a lifetime affinity to fish cookery. The dedicated food and publishing professionals at Rodale Press, the local fishmongers, my friends and family are the people who endow this book with their energy. Their combined efforts made this book possible.

My heartfelt thanks to:

Charlie Gerras, my gifted editor and friend, who welcomed me to publishing nine years ago and continues to inspire me today.

Camille Bucci, associate editor, for her absolutely meticulous attention to detail and marvelous fascination with food. Her editing touch is the perfect garnish.

Lisa D. Andruscavage, senior copy editor, whose careful eye and valuable suggestions were vital in helping produce a better product.

Glen Burris who has a steady finger on the precise point where technique and aesthetics become one. The visual pleasure of this book is a tribute to his design skills.

Diane Drabinsky, R.D., who was my nutritional conscience. She provided sound and accurate data throughout this book.

Jean Rogers who saved my day by writing the very informative nutrition chapter.

JoAnn Brader who lived with my manuscript for over three months, testing and polishing every recipe.

Sarah Leonard for pampering every word of this manuscript with her remarkably accurate keyboarding.

Julie Moyer who focused her keen eye on every line and proofed the marathon-length manuscript.

Heidi Actor, Mary Early, Marianne G. Laubach and Kay Seng Lichthardt who styled my fish to be incredibly appealing in full-color pictures. They make beautiful food look even better.

The photographers Carl Doney, Donna M. Hornberger, Mitchell T. Mandel, Alison Miksch, Christie C. Tito and Sally Shenk Ullman, who captured every essence of taste, health and beauty in the seafood kitchen.

Nancy Zelko who assisted in testing the recipes, using a gentle touch and solid culinary talent.

Marilee Stahler, our whiz in the marketplace, for befriending the best fishmongers in the valley to secure all the fish needed for recipe testing.

Ellen Greene, marketing director, who originally conceived the idea for this book.

Anita Hirsch for sharing her solid judgment and legendary kitchen savvy over the years.

Emily Folland who, with Greta Feather, kept the kitchens sparkling clean throughout the months of testing.

Marge Kemmerer and a dedicated foodservice staff who maintained our high kitchen and dining room standards while my mind was occupied with this book.

Ken Hauser of Emmaus Seafood Center, Roger Sinclair of Peterson's Seafood, 7th Street Seafood, Heckenberger's Seafood, Laneco and Shop Rite of Allentown —my favorite fishmongers.

T. L. Gettings, a steady inspiration in photography, food and life.

John Haberern, my constant teacher, visionary and friend.

The Culinary Institute of America, my alma mater. There I learned the basics of cookery and how to convert them to instinct, which freed my mind and hands to create.

Lewis Starr, my mentor in the seafood restaurant business. He handed me the tiller, pointed the course, then went to his cabin to chart new seas.

Alice Ney, Veronica Ney and Maude Plunkett—my culinary heritage. And, taffi Ney—my culinary sensibility.

Seafood
Is Super Nutrition

~~~~~~~~~~~~~~~~~~~~~~~~~~~~~~~~~~

"Gone fishin'."

I always liked that expression. It evokes images of lazy summer afternoons at an out-of-the-way pond. No cares, no stress, not a worry in the world. Lately, it reminds me of something even better— robust good health and benefits that go far beyond much-needed rest and relaxation.

Yes, scientists have now proven what moms have been telling us all along. Fish *is* brain food. In fact, it's one of the smartest meals you can eat! Fish—that is, seafood in general—is low in fat, high in nutrition and just swimming in omega-3 fatty acids, the stuff that fish oil is made of. The power of fish oil is so impressive that some researchers believe omega-3's should be considered an essential nutrient. Scientists connect a growing list of health benefits with omega-3's, including:

- Reduced levels of blood fats (triglycerides and cholesterol), which translates into reduced risk of heart disease.
- Possible improvement of inflammatory conditions such as rheumatoid arthritis.
- Possible prevention of breast cancer.
- Prevention of blood clots.
- Possible lowering of blood pressure.
- Possible relief of migraine headaches.

But wait a minute. How can fish be both low in fat *and* high in fat? And how can any fat possibly be good for you? Isn't it true that our love of fatty foods is possibly the single worst thing about the American diet? The cause of a whole host of health problems?

1

Well, yes—and no.

You see, not all fats are bad. Some—like the omega-3's—can actually be good for your heart. It's mainly an excess of *saturated fats* that does damage. These "bad" fats usually turn up in protein-rich foods of animal origin, such as red meat, eggs and full-fat dairy products. Fish is very low in those fats. But *polyunsaturated fats* and their near relatives the *monounsaturates*—let's call them the "good" fats—don't deserve the bad rap. Usually found in fish, vegetables, vegetable oils, seeds and nuts, these good fats can displace saturated fats and, in effect,

Where's the Fat?

All fats are not created equal. Polyunsaturated and monounsaturated fats are actually good for you, helping to prevent heart attacks and lower blood pressure. The omega-3's found in fish are a type of polyunsaturated fat. It's the saturated fat in food that can clog arteries and lead to other health problems. Clearly, it's in your best interest to eat those foods highest in polyunsaturated and monounsaturated fats, while cutting back on saturated-fat foods.

This chart shows how various fish stack up against other protein-rich foods that you might eat, starting with those having the highest percentages of omega-3's. While fish like salmon and halibut contain less than 20 percent saturated fat, cheddar cheese and whole milk tip the scales in the other direction—with close to a whopping 70 percent of their fat being saturated. The choice is yours. Just remember that when you eat hearty, you can eat healthy, too.

	Polyunsaturated Fat		Monounsaturated	Saturated
	Omega-3	Other	Fat	Fat
Shrimp	40%	14%	20%	26%
Haddock	38%	11%	24%	27%
Atlantic salmon	31%	14%	37%	18%
Atlantic and Pacific halibut	24%	22%	36%	18%

neutralize their negative effects. They help prevent heart attacks by clearing the blood of cholesterol and preventing the clotting that can trigger a heart attack or stroke. They also seem to play a part in lowering blood pressure.

Here's an easy-to-remember rule: Fats from land animals tend to be saturated (that's bad). Fats from aquatic animals tend to be unsaturated (that's good).

The Power of Omega-3's

The most glamorous of the good fats—the ones that concern us most in this book—are those found in

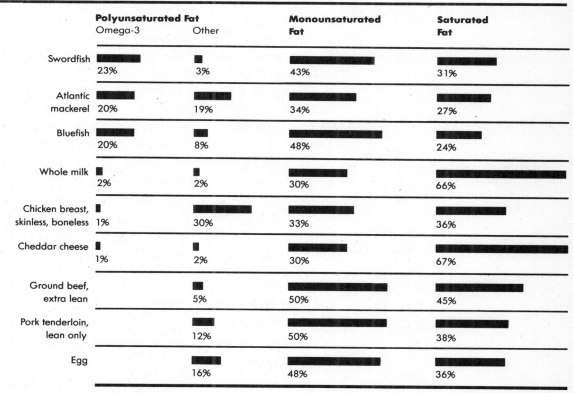

	Polyunsaturated Fat		Monounsaturated Fat	Saturated Fat
	Omega-3	Other		
Swordfish	23%	3%	43%	31%
Atlantic mackerel	20%	19%	34%	27%
Bluefish	20%	8%	48%	24%
Whole milk	2%	2%	30%	66%
Chicken breast, skinless, boneless	1%	30%	33%	36%
Cheddar cheese	1%	2%	30%	67%
Ground beef, extra lean		5%	50%	45%
Pork tenderloin, lean only		12%	50%	38%
Egg		16%	48%	36%

Source: Adapted from Agriculture Handbook Nos. 8-1, 8-5, 8-10, 8-13, 8-15 (Washington, D.C.: U.S. Department of Agriculture).

Note: Information is based on data for raw product.

fish oil. Fish, especially cold-water species, contains tremendous amounts of a class of polyunsaturated fatty acids called the omega-3 group. The secret ingredients of fish oil are eicosapentanoic acid (EPA) and docosahexanoic acid (DHA), both omega-3 fatty acids. While they're a mouthful to say, they're definitely worth swallowing.

One of the prime beneficiaries of a diet high in omega-3 is your heart. That's where the most intensive research has been done.

Scientists first became intrigued by omega-3 when they studied the diet of Greenland Eskimos. The Eskimos ate a great deal of fish, much of it very fatty. In fact, Eskimos ate more fat than any other people in the world, yet they suffered virtually no heart disease. The Eskimos' immunity to heart disease was hard to explain. Researchers reasoned that some other factor in the diet might be the key.

They were right. It was the omega-3's in fish that did the trick. Study after study now demonstrates the heart-healing properties of this important group of fatty acids. In fact, the *New England Journal of Medicine* generated national headlines when it published three major studies linking fish consumption with a decreased risk of heart disease.

"These highly unsaturated fats seem to give benefit in every study we've reviewed," says William Castelli, M.D., director of the famous Framingham Heart Study.

Adding Fish to Your Diet

You don't have to eat as much fish as Eskimos do to decrease your risk of heart disease, cancer and other illnesses. Experts think we might prevent disease by eating comparatively little: as few as two to four fish meals a week. The more you eat, obviously, the better.

"The ideal amount to eat probably varies from person to person," says William E. Connor, M.D., professor of medicine at the Oregon Health Sciences University and one of the pioneers in omega-3 research. "A couple of 6-ounce fish meals a week is probably the minimum. I certainly enjoy three to four servings of fish a week."

Of course, Dr. Connor adds, you ought to watch your weight, keep your blood pressure under control, avoid stress, eat fewer saturated fats and stop smoking. "The omega-3 theory is a tremendous advance," Dr. Connor says. "But there are other basic things to consider."

Most experts agree that fish should be *substituted* for red meat and poultry and not eaten *in addition* to what you normally consume. The meat we get from farm animals is low in omega-3.

But even among fish there is considerable variation in omega-3 content (see the box, "Your Omega-3 Scorecard," on page 6). Omega-3 fatty acids are found primarily in cold-water fish. Ocean fish has more than freshwater fish. Generally, fattier fish —sardines, salmon, herring and mackerel, for example—contain more. As a rule of thumb, the darker the fish's flesh, the higher the fat content. Shellfish, too, contains considerable amounts of omega-3.

Tuna ranks right up there with salmon and sardines in heart-healthy omega-3 fatty acids, report scientists from Massachusetts Institute of Technology's Sea Grant Program. Solid white albacore was found to be the best type of tuna, containing approximately twice as much omega-3 as other tuna varieties. Tuna packed in water proved a better source than tuna packed in oil because water-packed tuna lost only about 3 percent of its beneficial fatty acids when drained, while oil-packed tuna lost 25 percent.

Although it's true that the oil you pour off any canned fish *does* contain some beneficial omega-3 fatty acids, the flesh of the fish is still loaded with them, says William E. M. Lands, Ph.D., professor of biological chemistry at the University of Illinois and author of *Fish and Human Health*. Even if you throw away some of those fatty acids, you still come out ahead, Dr. Lands says, because fish is a "very worthy" food—low in cholesterol, fat and calories and high in protein.

"The best way to obtain the beneficial omega-3 fatty acids is to eat more seafood," he says. "All the reasons for eating polyunsaturated oil from vegetables remain, certainly. But we need to balance

Your Omega-3 Scorecard

Nutritionists recommend eating more seafood of all types, but if you'd like to get maximum benefit per mouthful, this chart listing "excellent," "very good" and "good" sources of omega-3's should help. Also shown is the total amount of fat contained in each fish. In general, those fish that are higher in total fat contain more omega-3's. The good news for seafood lovers is that most shellfish are also omega-3 treasure chests.

Seafood	Omega-3's (g)	Fat (g)	Seafood	Omega-3's (g)	Fat (g)
Excellent Sources					
Mackerel, Atlantic	2.5	13.9	Whitefish	1.4	5.9
Anchovies, canned	2.1	9.7	Salmon, chinook	1.4	10.4
Salmon, pink, canned	1.7	6.0	Salmon, sockeye	1.3	8.6
Salmon, Atlantic	1.7	6.3	Tuna, bluefin	1.2	4.9
Herring, Atlantic	1.7	9.0	Salmon, pink	1.0	3.5
Sablefish	1.5	15.3	Salmon, coho	1.0	6.0
Very Good Sources					
Shark	0.9	4.5	Bass, sea	0.6	2.0
Bass, striped	0.8	2.3	Wolffish (ocean catfish)	0.6	2.4
Swordfish	0.8	4.0	Salmon, chum	0.6	3.8
Bluefish	0.8	4.2	Drum	0.6	4.9
Trout, rainbow	0.7	3.4	Carp	0.6	5.6
Bass, freshwater	0.7	3.7	Pompano	0.6	9.5

them with omega-3 oil from fish. Omega-3 moderates the body's overutilization of chemicals called eicosanoids, formed from polyunsaturates."

One note about canned fish: It's often packed in salty oil, but you can get around this by looking for brands labeled "low sodium" or "no salt added." In actually preparing fish, the best way to preserve those heart-healing omega-3's is to broil, bake, poach or steam the fish and to add very little oil. You'll

Seafood	Omega-3's (g)	Fat (g)	Seafood	Omega-3's (g)	Fat (g)
Eel	0.6	11.6	Halibut, Atlantic and Pacific	0.4	2.3
Squid	0.5	1.4	Tilefish	0.4	2.3
Shrimp	0.5	1.7	Trout, sea	0.4	3.6
Mussels, blue	0.5	2.2	Mullet, striped	0.4	3.8
Oysters, eastern	0.5	2.5	Sturgeon	0.4	4.0
Pollack, Atlantic	0.4	1.0	Catfish, channel	0.4	4.3
Rockfish, Pacific	0.4	1.6			

Good Sources

Seafood	Omega-3's (g)	Fat (g)	Seafood	Omega-3's (g)	Fat (g)
Grouper	0.3	1.0	Scallops	0.2	0.8
Crab, blue	0.3	1.1	Tuna, yellowfin	0.2	1.0
Pike, walleye	0.3	1.2	Crawfish	0.2	1.1
Snapper, red	0.3	1.3	Flatfish (flounder and sole)	0.2	1.2
Whiting (hake)	0.3	1.3	Mahimahi (dolphinfish)	0.1	0.7
Perch, ocean, Atlantic	0.3	1.6	Pike, northern	0.1	0.7
Cod, Atlantic	0.2	0.7	Sunfish, pumpkin seed	0.1	0.7
Haddock	0.2	0.7	Clams	0.1	1.0

Source: Adapted from Agriculture Handbook No. 8–15 (Washington, D.C.: U.S. Department of Agriculture).

Note: All figures are for 3½-ounce, raw portions.

Where the Vitamins Are ...
and Aren't

When it come to fish, the vitamin story is short and sweet — as simple as A, B, D. Those are basically what you find in fish.

Vitamin A — which is essential for healthy skin, sharp vision, resistance to infection, wound healing and more — is abundant in fish oil and is found mainly in fish liver. That's why cod-liver oil, for instance, was such a popular "tonic" in days gone by. One tablespoon contains a whopping 11,560 international units (I.U.) of vitamin A, which is more than twice the Recommended Dietary Allowance (RDA) of 5,000 I.U. for adults. But don't expect to get much A from eating fish itself. Even the higher-fat varieties like herring and salmon contain very little (102 I.U. in 3½ ounces of cooked Atlantic herring and 55 I.U. in canned pink salmon). About the only exception is eel, with 3,787 I.U. in a cooked portion. Mollusks and crustaceans don't contain much vitamin A.

Keep in mind that vitamin A is fat soluble, which means it needs to be accompanied by fat to be used by the body. And because your body can store fat-soluble vitamins for future use, they can build up to toxic levels if you habitually consume large amounts.

Seafood contains significant amounts of the *B vitamins,* especially niacin and B_{12}. The B-Team — made up of thiamine, riboflavin, niacin, B_6, folacin, pantothenate, B_{12} and others — is vital to both mental and physical health. These vitamins can help chase the blues, soothe itchy skin and steady the nerves. Mollusks like clams and oysters are gold mines of B_{12}, which combats certain forms of anemia. Just 3½ ounces of cooked clams provide 99 micrograms (mcg), which is 33 times the RDA of 3 mcg. An equal serving of eastern oysters has 38 mcg. Other B vitamins are peppered throughout various fishes. Unlike fat-soluble vitamins, the water-soluble B's are not stored by the body so any excesses are readily excreted.

You may remember *vitamin D* as the "sunshine vitamin" that strengthens your bones and nourishes muscles and nerves. Well, it's another fat-soluble vitamin found in fish oil. That same tablespoon of cod-liver oil provides 1,156 I.U. of D, more than twice the RDA of 400 I.U. Unlike vitamin A, however, some vitamin D is found in the flesh of certain fatty fish, such as herring (980 I.U. in 3½ ounces), mackerel (826 I.U.), salmon (490 I.U.) and tuna (294 I.U.).

find I use these techniques almost exclusively in this book. Frying, which I've minimized, causes the greatest nutritional losses.

Fish Tackles Triglycerides

Fish oil is even more effective than polyunsaturated vegetable oil in reducing certain blood fats. In studies at the Oregon Health Sciences University, researchers found that a diet rich in polyunsaturated safflower and corn oils reduced blood-cholesterol levels by about the same margin as a diet rich in salmon and salmon oil. But the fish-oil diet reduced triglycerides (another blood fat considered almost as important as cholesterol in heart disease risk) by 33 percent below the level of a control group eating a "normal" American diet. For some of these afflicted people, the only previous dietary treatment available was to cut dietary fats to between 5 and 10 percent of their total calories. The typical American diet contains about 40 percent fat, so the treatment is radical and difficult for most people to maintain on a long-term basis.

Paradoxically, fatty fish such as salmon had usually been a strict no-no on these therapeutic diets. The researchers now suggest that instead it might be a useful—and healthy—addition.

"No other polyunsaturated oil has been able to get triglyceride levels to drop in this way," says William S. Harris, Ph.D., one of the Oregon researchers. "So the impact of the fish-oil diet is really significant. For a person with high triglyceride levels, a 33 percent reduction would be an important change toward better cardiovascular health."

Fish Oil Rebuilds the Heart

If you eat fish rich in omega-3 fatty acids, you might even be able to change your heart's structure to ward off heart disease, says a researcher at the University of Medicine and Dentistry of New Jersey.

Carl Hock, Ph.D., fed the equivalent of 4 to 5 ounces of salmon per day to rats. Their hearts changed dramatically after just four weeks on this diet. Specifically, the fish oil's polyunsaturated fatty acids meshed with heart cell membranes and protected the rats from problems associated with reduced blood flow to the heart, known as myocardial ischemia.

Such reduced blood flow occurs in hardening of the arteries and clots in the heart's blood vessels. And myocardial ischemia accounts for one-third to one-half of all deaths in the United States each year, Dr. Hock reports. He recommends two or three meals a week with fish high in omega-3 fatty acids, including salmon, albacore tuna, mackerel, herring, anchovies, sardines, shad and trout.

In a major study done in the Netherlands and published in the *New England Journal of Medicine*, researchers reported that over a 20-year period, men who ate a little more than an ounce of fish a day had approximately half the mortality from heart disease of men who did not eat fish. This was true despite the fact that some fish eaters consumed more saturated fat and more cholesterol than the nonfish eaters. This suggests that fish oil may overcome some of the bad effects caused by a high intake of saturated fat and cholesterol!

What's most interesting about this study, though, is the researchers' conclusion that "The consumption of as little as one or two fish dishes per week may be of preventive value in relation to coronary heart disease."

Still other studies corroborate omega-3's good reputation. One of them was conducted by Sanford E. Warren, M.D., of Beth Israel Hospital in Boston. He and his colleagues report that after they gave daily doses of cod-liver oil (which contains omega-3 fatty acids) to seven heart patients, the patients experienced improvement in blood-lipid chemistries. The four men and three women had increases in high-density lipoproteins, also known as HDL cholesterol (the beneficial type), favorable shifts in the ratio of total cholesterol to HDL (a predictor of heart disease) and indications that their arteries may be less likely to clog or develop blood clots.

In another study halfway around the world, an Australian researcher fed six healthy volunteers almost three egg yolks daily, along with about 2½ tablespoons of fish oil. Despite the enormous amount of dietary cholesterol consumed, the volunteers' blood-cholesterol levels remained at healthy levels.

In this study, as in others, the omega-3 fatty acids also seemed to block the body's production of low-density lipoproteins, also known as LDL cholesterol, which is the bad type of cholesterol (considered a risk factor for heart disease). Tiny globs of LDL predispose artery walls to the formation of fatty plaque deposits. Over time, plaque buildup blocks blood flow and decreases the amount of oxygen getting to the brain and heart.

One of the most intriguing results of this study was a dramatic lowering of plasma triglycerides, artery-clogging blood fats. As I've already mentioned, polyunsaturated vegetable fats also lower triglycerides, but the drop triggered by omega-3 fatty acids was "far greater," reported researcher Paul J. Nestel, M.D., of the Baker Medical Research Institute.

Elsewhere, research at the University of Chicago indicated that consumption of fish oil can *reverse* the buildup of cholesterol deposits inside blood vessels. This was the first time it had been proven that atherosclerosis (hardening of the coronary arteries) could be reversed.

In the study, 16 rhesus monkeys were fed diets high in fish oil, while another 8 monkeys were given coconut oil, a highly saturated fat. More—and more serious—arterial plaque was found in the coconut-oil group than in the fish-oil group.

The plaque that did develop in the fish-oil monkeys was found to be less likely to cause medical complications and contained fewer inflammatory cells, according to the researchers. Levels of LDL cholesterol were also lower with the fish-oil diet.

The researchers, who do not know why the fish oil has this beneficial effect on arterial walls, recommend that people replace the saturated fat in their diets at least once a day with a marine-oil source. Robert Wissler, M.D., Ph.D., professor of pathology

Good News for Shrimp Lovers

Due to its reputed high-cholesterol content, shellfish has long been taboo for people on low-cholesterol diets. Now researchers have found that the cholesterol in mollusks—like clams, oysters and scallops—is considerably lower than was once believed.

Professor William Connor, M.D., found that feeding healthy men approximately 1 pound of mixed shellfish didn't significantly raise their blood-cholesterol levels.

Crab, lobster and shrimp are higher in cholesterol than mollusks, but even a pound of these foods raised cholesterol levels only slightly in healthy men, Oregon Health Sciences University researchers found.

"It would appear that shrimp [which is higher in cholesterol than clams, oysters or crabs] can be included in the diets of high-cholesterol patients on an occasional basis," they concluded.

Here's another fact that further secures the place of seafood in a healthy diet: Shellfish contains virtually no saturated fat. When you take into consideration *both* cholesterol and saturated fat, shellfish is a better dietary choice than even the leanest red meats.

Dr. Connor and his wife, registered dietitian Sonja Connor, have done exhaustive computations on a wide variety of foods and have come up with a rating system that combines both cholesterol and saturated fat. This new Cholesterol-Saturated Fat Index, or CSI, comes closer to representing the actual artery-clogging potential of foods than any other index compiled so far.

The lower a food's CSI number, the better it is for your heart. A 3½-ounce serving of ground beef, for instance, has a CSI rating of 18, while an equal amount of many fish and shellfish rates only 4. That's a pretty striking demonstration of the difference between fish and beef, without having to wrestle with a tangle of at the University of Chicago, says he does this himself, substituting cold-water fish, such as sardines, tuna and salmon, for meat.

In a separate study conducted at Wake Forest University, test monkeys were switched from animal fat to fish oil. Following the change, some of the built-up cholesterol in the monkeys' arteries was reduced to liquid form, which is easier for the bloodstream to remove.

numbers. The Connors say that in their system the daily allowable CSI total would be 37 for a person eating 2,000 calories (35 percent of which would come from fat).

Here are some representative CSI figures for various seafood and a few other foods, plus actual cholesterol counts for comparison.

Foods	CSI	Cholesterol (mg)	Foods	CSI	Cholesterol (mg)
Halibut	4	41	Poultry, skinless	6	34
Tuna, water-packed	4	42	Crab, Alaska king	6	53
Snapper, red	4	47	Lobster	6	72
Cod	4	55	Crab, blue	6	100
Clams	4	67	Shrimp	6	195
Sole	4	68	Steak, flank	9	71
Oysters	4	109	Ice cream (1 cup)	13	45
Perch	4	115	Beef, ground	18	90
Salmon, coho	5	49	Egg (1)	15	274
Salmon, sockeye	5	87	Cheese, cheddar	26	105

Sources: Adapted from

Agriculture Handbook Nos. 8-1, 8-5, 8-13, 8-15 (Washington, D.C.: U.S. Department of Agriculture).

Connor, William, M.D., and Sonja Connor, R.D. *The New American Diet* (New York: Simon & Schuster, 1986).

Note: Unless otherwise noted, all figures are for 3½-ounce portions, cooked where applicable.

Eating Fish Thins the Blood

Perhaps the most important thing omega-3's do, at least as far as heart disease is concerned, is to keep blood platelets from grouping together, or clotting, as they do when you are cut. By inhibiting the blood's clotting ability, omega-3's can help keep stray clots from throwing a monkey wrench into your machinery. A clot that lodges in the arteries feeding your heart muscle causes a heart attack. A clot that travels to your neck or head can induce a stroke. One that settles in your lungs creates a deadly pulmonary embolism.

Clots develop when flat, disk-shaped cell fragments in the blood, called platelets, are activated. That means they are triggered to stick together (called platelet aggregation) and to stick to blood vessel walls (platelet adhesion). We are grateful this occurs after we've cut ourselves because clotting can stop bleeding in seconds. But this same process, gone awry, can be life-threatening.

Fortunately, there are things you can do to keep everything under control. Strictly speaking, you can't actually thin your blood, but you can alter its readiness to clot.

Investigation has shown that a diet rich in omega-3 fatty acids reduces the number of blood platelets and reduces platelet aggregation. Omega-3's interfere with platelets' manufacture of thromboxane, a biochemical that makes platelets clump together and causes blood-vessel constriction.

That effect in itself would probably be enough to limit clotting. But omega-3's have another effect. They also accumulate in the cells lining the artery walls. These cells make anticlotting prostacyclin, and omega-3 fatty acids are readily converted into prostacyclin. Both these actions may help prevent heart disease in its early stages, researchers speculate. The benefits of omega-3's are probably best seen when you substitute fish for high-saturated-fat foods like beef and dairy products.

Cholesterol: Winning the Numbers Game

In addition to preventing blood clots from forming, omega-3's seem to help prevent atherosclerosis as well as by influencing cholesterol.

Omega-3's may be very beneficial to people whose cholesterol levels are on the high side—between 230 and 260. According to Framingham's Dr. Castelli, people with cholesterol levels this high are particularly at risk for heart attack. Despite this, he says, many doctors don't express concern until the levels reach 300 or higher.

"Doctors are missing three-quarters of all the heart attacks in their town by overlooking all the lower numbers," Dr. Castelli says. "The bulk of all our heart attacks occur at cholesterol levels between 230 and 260. If you do not lower cholesterol, you will not have a favorable effect on heart disease."

Easier Just to Catch a Capsule?

What about supplements—those fish-oil capsules advertised in magazines and on TV? Are they a quick fix for a diet of cheeseburgers? In a word, no. At best, these supplements are a complement to a healthy diet rather than a substitute for an unhealthy one.

Look at the figures: You'd need to take *ten capsules* of concentrated marine lipids to get 1.8 grams (g) of EPA, one of the omega-3 components. A serving of cooked coho or sockeye salmon (3½ ounces) contains nearly as much (1.3 g)—and is much more enjoyable to consume.

What's more, there can be something fishy about fish-oil supplements. After testing ten major brands of fish-oil capsules, researchers from Tufts University were surprised to find only 38 percent and 85 percent of advertised levels of EPA and DHA, respectively.

They suspect that insufficient amounts of the antioxidant vitamin E had been added to the capsules to protect against EPA and DHA oxidation. So even if you take the supplements, you could be shortchanged.

Cod-liver oil, that bane of so many childhoods, also contains EPA, but the amount varies from brand to brand. The problem with cod-liver oil—besides it taste—is that it usually contains high amounts of vitamins A and D, which can be toxic in large amounts, so it's not a good alternative.

One way to lower your cholesterol, says Dr. Castelli, is simply to eat more fish.

In one recent study at Vanderbilt University School of Medicine, patients took about 3 tablespoons of an omega-3-rich fish-oil supplement every day. At the end of the four-week study, serum cholesterol was reduced by 15 percent.

Fishing for Arthritis Relief

Another intriguing area of omega-3 research involves rheumatoid arthritis.

There is no cure for this painful disease. But some researchers have found that omega-3 fatty acids might offer some relief from the pain and swelling. "We may be recommending omega-3 as an adjunct to traditional therapy in the future," says arthritis researcher Joel M. Kremer, M.D., of Albany Medical College.

A group of chemicals called leukotrienes, formed in the body, are thought to cause the characteristic pain and inflammation of rheumatoid arthritis. But omega-3 appears to change the chemical composition of the leukotrienes, making them less inflammatory.

In a study conducted by Dr. Kremer and his associates, 23 arthritis patients were each given 1.8 grams of a concentrated fish-oil supplement every day for 12 weeks. Twenty-one other patients received placebos—capsules filled with nothing but wax. As the study progressed, the pain and swelling were reduced in the patients taking supplements. The patients taking placebos showed no improvement.

"In our studies, the doses were roughly equal to a salmon dinner or a can of sardines. We also found benefits four weeks after the fish oil was discontinued. The results are very encouraging," says Dr. Kremer.

Daily doses of fish oil also led to modest but significant improvement in the symptoms of rheumatoid arthritis patients studied at Harvard Medical School.

These efforts were among the first to show definite clinical effects of fish oil on an inflammatory disease. Previous work showing favorable results had been done on mice. These latest findings have prompted the National Institutes of Health to get additional clinical studies under way.

"Our trial, although it was relatively small, shows evidence that fish oil does have promise for inflammatory disease," days Richard I. Sperling, M.D., a Harvard University instructor of medicine.

Dr. Sperling's study targeted the biochemical aspect of fish oil in the body. Earlier, he and his colleagues looked at the cells of people who did not have inflammatory disease. Fish oil was added to their diets, and their cells were later examined to see if the fish oil could inhibit what researchers call inflammatory products.

One such product thought to cause or contribute to the painful swelling of arthritis is leukotriene B_4. At the end of Dr. Sperling's initial study, the added fish oil in the patients' diets seemed to result in significantly less leukotriene B_4 production and a small increase in the generation of a less inflammatory substance, leukotriene B_5.

The second step for the Harvard team was to repeat the trial with cells from 12 patients with active arthritis. "We saw the same thing in the diseased state—a suppression of inflammatory products," Dr. Sperling explains. "And the patients definitely felt better. They had fewer tender joints and reported less pain."

Both Dr. Kremer and Dr. Sperling note that more research must back their early findings before any new recommendations on adding fish or fish-oil supplements to the diet are made with a higher degree of confidence.

In the meantime, "It's irrefutable that eating

Weight Watchers, Take Note

Whether you count them or flout them, you can't ignore calories. Eat too many and it's as plain as the double chin on your face. That's why fish is the perfect food for the calorie conscious. Seafood is low in calories, low in fat and high in protein.

Below are calorie counts for some of the most slimming seafood.

Seafood	Calories	Seafood	Calories
Oysters, eastern	69	Squid	92
Clams	74	Pike, walleye	93
Monkfish	76	Tilefish	96
Pout, ocean	79	Wolffish (ocean catfish)	96
Cod, Atlantic	82	Bass, striped	97
Mahimahi (dolphinfish)	85	Snapper, red	100
Mussels, blue	86	Trout, sea	104
Crab, blue	87	Shrimp	106
Cusk	87	Halibut, Atlantic and Pacific	110
Haddock	87	Bass, freshwater	114
Pike, northern	88	Catfish, channel	116
Scallops	88	Trout, rainbow	118
Crawfish	89	Drum	119
Sunfish, pumpkin seed	89	Swordfish	121
Lobster, northern	90	Bluefish	124
Whiting (hake)	90	Shark	130
Flatfish (flounder and sole)	91	Whitefish	134
Perch	91	Salmon, Atlantic	142
Grouper	92	Tuna, bluefin	144
Pollack, Atlantic	92		

Source: Adapted from Agriculture Handbook No. 8-15 (Washington, D.C.: U.S. Department of Agriculture).

Note: All figures are for 3½-ounce, raw portions.

more fish is a healthy step for any person, arthritis or not," says Dr. Kremer.

"If you've got arthritis now," says Dr. Sperling, "you can use traditional therapies for relief and also continue to eat more fish. It certainly won't hurt and may help your inflammation."

Help for Psoriasis

Patients with psoriasis may also benefit from omega-3, since leukotrienes are believed to trigger the characteristic inflammation of this red, scaly skin disorder. In British and U.S. studies, omega-3 fatty acids appeared to render leukotrienes less active, resulting in some improvement—but not in all cases. In any event, omega-3 may give some relief from the itching and scaling of psoriasis.

In a study at the University of Michigan Medical School, doctors supplemented the daily diets of 13 psoriasis patients with 2 to 3 ounces of fish oil. The amount of other fats in their diets was reduced accordingly. Eight of the patients showed visible improvement.

What would account for some of the improvement in this incurable condition? The EPA in fish oil does not produce the same inflammatory compounds in the skin that fats from red meat and dairy foods do, explains researcher Charles N. Ellis, M.D., associate professor of dermatology. "That may be why we had such good results in the patients whose tissues absorbed the most EPA. Even with these results, we can't say EPA would be an overall effective treatment for psoriasis. But in the future it may prove to be a good ancillary treatment for psoriasis."

In a study reported in the British medical journal *Lancet*, patients with psoriasis experienced noticeable improvement after 12 weeks of taking ten fish-oil capsules daily. The researchers involved said that the therapeutic effect could be the anti-inflammatory properties of EPA in fish oil. And they noted that approximately 5 ounces of an oily fish, such as mackerel, would provide the same dose of EPA.

Tumor Prevention

Scientists studying omega-3 also appear to have taken a hopeful step in the battle against breast cancer. Studies linking omega-3 with the prevention of breast tumors are still in a very early stage, but they seem to hold promise.

Prostaglandins are chemicals in the body that lower immunity and encourage tumor growth, says Rashida A. Karmali, Ph.D., associate professor of nutrition at Cook College, Rutgers University.

As a result of an overabundance of these chemicals, says Dr. Karmali, "tumors form faster and the body can't fight them off."

Omega-3's appear to fight off the harmful effects of these overactive chemicals. Dr. Karmali fed fish oil to laboratory rats with breast tumors. The result was a reduction in the number of tumors. "Even when we transplanted tumors from one rat into another, the growth of those established tumors was much slower when we fed them fish oil," she says.

It is one thing to prevent cancer in rats. It is quite another to prevent cancer in people, Dr. Karmali cautions. But the preliminary results of her studies offer some encouragement.

Other studies in the United States tend to support Dr. Karmali's theory. One conducted at the University of Rochester School of Medicine showed that rats fed fish oil developed fewer tumors.

Researchers at Cornell University had encouraging results, too, when they fed fish oil to laboratory rats. There were fewer tumors, and the tumors that did develop were smaller.

No one can guarantee that eating fish will definitely help prevent breast cancer. But if you want to hedge your bets, Dr. Karmali advises eating more fish or replacing dietary fat with fish-oil supplements.

Substituting salmon or mackerel for beef or pork might be your best bet, Dr. Karmali says. "That would cut back on overall fat intake while boosting dietary fish oil. We really have to look at the role of overall nutrition in breast-cancer prevention."

Another study on cancer and fish oil was conducted by researchers at Harvard Medical School. Rats with breast cancers that were known to metastasize, or spread to other parts of the body, were fed one of four diets: a high-saturated-fat diet, a high-polyunsaturated-fat diet, a low-fat diet or a diet high in omega-3 fatty acids from fish oil.

The rats fed the fish oil survived the longest. At the end of the study period, their tumors were smallest and had spread the least.

"It could be that the immune system in animals fed fish oil is better able to recognize tumor cells as foreign or better able to act against tumor cells," says Debra Szeluga, Ph.D., the study's main researcher.

"I think the evidence suggests that modifying your diet to reduce fat intake and replace red meat with fish would not be an unreasonable thing to do. I think that may help in the prevention, or perhaps even become a part of the treatment, of cancer."

Mackerel Works Miracles with Blood Pressure

Researchers have also shown that an easy-to-follow diet rich in mackerel can lower blood pressure in people with mild hypertension. Researchers from the Central Institute for Cardiovascular Research, in West Germany, gave mackerel canned in tomato sauce to men who had mild hypertension. The men didn't usually eat much fish, but during the study, that changed. For two weeks, the men ate two cans of the mackerel a day. Then they switched to eating just three cans of the fish per week and followed that regimen for eight months. After that, they went back to their normal diet for two months.

(continued on page 24)

Ol' Salts—and Other Minerals from the Sea

Almost all seafood comes from the mineral-rich oceans, so it's no surprise that fish and shellfish are high in minerals, too. Here's a rundown on the most significant nutrients. (Unless otherwise noted all figures are for 3½ ounces of cooked seafood.)

Calcium plays a pivotal role in preventing osteoporosis, the devastating bone-loss disease that strikes so many older women. Fish with edible bones, such as canned sardines and canned salmon, are an excellent source of calcium, especially for those who can't eat dairy products. They contain up to half the RDA of 800 milligrams (mg) each. (Atlantic sardines, 382 mg; Pacific sardines, 240 mg; sockeye salmon, 239 mg and pink salmon, 213 mg). And you don't have to be wary of consuming the bones because they soften considerably in the canning process.

Fish is also a great source of *phosphorus*, which works with calcium to form strong bones and teeth. Those same four fish mentioned contain nearly half the RDA of 800 mg each (Atlantic sardines, 490 mg; Pacific sardines, 366 mg; sockeye salmon, 326 mg and pink salmon, 329 mg).

Now you might expect seafood to be high in *sodium* because the ocean is so salty. Not so. In fact, almost all seafood is low in sodium. So is freshwater fish. That's good news, considering sodium's unhealthy link with high blood pressure. Only when fish is processed by such methods as canning, smoking, pickling and salting do the sodium levels rise, going well above the minimum 200 mg that we actually need per day. This chart tells the whole tale.

Fish	Sodium (mg)
Tuna, bluefin, cooked	50
Salmon, sockeye, cooked	66
Cod, Atlantic, cooked	78
Herring, Atlantic, cooked	115
Tuna, light, water-packed	356
Salmon, sockeye, canned	538
Salmon, chinook, smoked	784
Herring, Atlantic, pickled	870
Herring, Atlantic, kippered	918
Lox	2,000
Cod, Atlantic, dried and salted	7,027

Source: Adapted from Agriculture Handbook No. 8-15 (Washington, D.C.: U.S. Department of Agriculture).

Note: All figures are for 3½-ounce portions.

Potassium works to regulate blood pressure, helps nerves transmit messages and ensures the proper functioning of every muscle in the body, most notably the heart. When it comes to controlling high blood pressure, getting enough potassium may be just as important as decreasing sodium. Fortunately, most seafood is considered a very good source of this mineral. Although no minimum daily requirement for potassium has been set, a range of 2,000 to 6,000 mg a day is considered safe and adequate. Some good sources include coho salmon (534 mg), haddock (399 mg), sockeye salmon (375 mg), flounder (344 mg), Pacific sardines (341 mg) and light tuna (314 mg).

Iron is an important mineral that's needed to prevent anemia. Unfortunately, it's one mineral that is likely to be lacking in our diets. Women, in particular, need an adequate intake because of monthly losses. While all fish contribute some iron to the diet, clams, oysters and mussels are iron champs. Twenty-two small clams provide 28 mg, which is 1½ times the RDA for women (18 mg). Eastern oysters have 13.4 mg and blue mussels, 6.7. Other good sources are water-packed light tuna (3.2 mg),

shrimp (3.1 mg), Atlantic sardines (2.9 mg), rainbow trout (2.4 mg) and haddock (1.4 mg).

Zinc influences night vision, wound healing, prostate function and the senses of taste and smell. Oysters are an amazing source of zinc, with eastern oysters providing a staggering 182 mg. That's more than 10 times the RDA of 15 mg. Less impressive—but still significant—sources include Alaska king crab (7.6 mg) and blue crab (4.2 mg).

Copper, a trace mineral that helps prevent anemia by improving iron utilization, is abundant in shellfish, especially oysters (8.9 mg in eastern oysters). Alaska king crab has 1.2 mg. Although no RDA has been established, a safe and adequate daily intake of 2 to 3 mg has been set.

Iodine, which is plentiful in the ocean and in the creatures living there, is important for preventing goiter, an enlargement of the thyroid caused by an iodine deficiency. Sea animals often have ten times the amount that freshwater fish does. The RDA for adults is 150 micrograms (mcg). Good sources include haddock (397 mcg), cod (183 mcg), shrimp (163 mcg), ocean perch (93 mcg), halibut (65 mcg) and herring (65 mcg).

After the first dietary period, the men's triglyceride levels, cholesterol levels, blood pressures and blood-clotting tendencies dropped significantly. But their levels of HDL cholesterol increased. During the second dietary period, when the amount of mackerel was cut back, all of those measurements returned to their initial levels—except blood pressure. That remained significantly lower and didn't return to the initial level until the men went back to their old habits—diets low in fish and high in cold cuts.

Help for Migraines

"The Eskimos have no word in their vocabulary for headache," says Robert J. Hitzemann, Ph.D., associate professor of psychiatry and behavioral sci-

---

A Raw Deal?

Over the past several years, there's been a major trend toward the consumption of raw or uncooked seafood: sushi, sashimi, seviche, gravlax, "green" herring and "lightly done" fillets, among others. And with this trend has come an increase in parasitic diseases. The only way to become infected is by consuming raw or improperly prepared infected fish. But you can protect yourself by always making sure to cook fish to an internal temperature of 145°F.

Additionally, seafood can harbor potentially harmful bacteria and viruses. Mollusks are especially efficient at concentrating undesirable microorganisms. Again, cooking will kill them. Of course, avoiding contaminated seafood in the first place is your best bet. That's why it's so important to deal with a fishmonger that you can trust (see the chapter

"Buying the Very Best," beginning on page 26). When you get your purchases home, store them in the refrigerator at a temperature between 32° and 40°F. Freeze anything you can't use within a day or two.

If you're a sportfisherman, contact your state Department of Public Health for the location of clean fishing waters. People who fish in rivers, bays and coastlines near urban industrial areas should realize that various chemical contaminants may be present in their catch. For that reason, they should probably limit their consumption of those fish to once a week. One way to reduce any contamination is to broil the fish so that fats and juices where contaminants are stored will drip away, advises Donald Malins, Ph.D., of the National Marine Fishery Service.

ences at the State University of New York at Stony Brook. All that fish in the Eskimo diet, it seems, can go to your head, too.

One reason why migraine sufferers are predisposed to these unusually painful headaches might be a shortage of EPA. Without EPA, Dr. Hitzemann says, the body releases too much serotonin, a brain chemical that has the capability of either tightening or loosening blood vessel walls in the brain. All that excess serotonin appears to put the squeeze on blood vessels, resulting in pain.

To test the theory, Dr. Hitzemann and his colleagues gave omega-3 supplements to 15 migraine patients. For about half the test subjects, the supplements alleviated pain and resulted in fewer headaches.

It's too soon to tell whether eating fish or taking fish-oil supplements can help relieve most migraines, says Dr. Hitzemann. But, he adds, if you've already sought conventional medical advice, it might be worth a try.

And so it goes, with each new study the case for omega-3's mounts. And the case for making fish an integral part of your diet strengthens. To help you get the most from your seafood—the most nutrition, the most flavor and the most value for your dollar—the following chapters detail all the ins and outs of seafood cookery. I'll show you how to buy the very best fish; how to clean, cut and store it and how to cook your catch to perfection. Once you have an excellent grasp of "sea cuisine," you'll never have to fish for compliments again.

Buying the Very Best

~~~~~~~~~~~~~~~~~~~~~~~~~~~~~~~

Your mission: Find, cook and serve the freshest, tastiest fish you can afford. Your starting point: The neighborhood fish market.

Your local fishmonger, whom you should get to know personally, is your biggest ally in this quest. For finding, cooking and enjoying fish means you must start by buying the best of the best. And that almost always means buying fish that is as fresh as possible.

Get to know your fishmonger just as you would a new neighbor. Scout out a shop that looks clean, inviting and has a good word-of-mouth reputation. Introduce yourself there. Ask questions. Form a friendly relationship. Let the owner or manager know that you are serious about fish cookery. Specialists love to talk about their specialty, and they're flattered to be asked for information and advice.

Cultivate your fishmonger's loyalty by returning regularly to shop or just to visit. You might stop by to report on a dish you created using the fresh fish you bought there. Imagine the service the flattery will get you on your next visit!

Don't be afraid to offer suggestions—I don't mean complaints—about the fish you prefer and the way you like to have it cut. Constructive ideas offered in a pleasant way are sure to be received gratefully.

I like to see fresh fish displayed uncovered, lying directly on a bed of snowy white, shaved ice or on a drainable tray imbedded on the ice. (Fresh fish wrapped tightly in plastic, like beef or chicken, spoils quickly.) Some fishmongers lay a piece of plastic over the fish on the ice to keep the surface of the fillets from drying out. I don't like this method of display because it prevents the buyer from seeing the fish clearly. I like to be able to really *see* the fish that I pick.

When it comes to variety, fish has a big advantage over red meat and chicken. True, there are different types of steers and different types of chicken, but basically you only experience a choice of sizes or cuts. You get a choice of sizes and cuts from fish too, but the added bonus is the disparate selections that the seas, lakes, rivers and streams have to offer. From lobster tail to monkfish tail, from humble haddock to the kingly salmon, nature's wild seafood provides a seemingly unlimited choice of color, flavor and texture.

Encourage your fishmonger to get in on the adventure. Ask him or her to stock new species. Ask about tasting a fish you just read about in this book or in a magazine. If you dine on a unique type of fish in a restaurant and you want to cook it at home, ask your fishmonger to get some for you. Who knows, other fish explorers in the neighborhood might like to try it, too.

Buying in Season

Seasons, life cycles and locale often dictate availability and quality of different fish. For guaranteed top quality, stick with fish that is running in waters closest to you. For instance, if you live in Pennsylvania, fresh bluefish is at its best during its annual migration up the East Coast, when it is caught off the nearby New Jersey shore in early summer. Pacific salmon is at its succulent best when caught just offshore, before its spawning run up freshwater rivers. The struggle of the long swim to spawning grounds upriver diminishes the flavor. Yellow perch is a highly prized, commercial, freshwater fish found in great abundance throughout the Great Lakes, so midwestern fish eaters know better than anyone the fine taste of these premium fillets. Your fish-monger can alert you to the fresh fish species that are running close to your region.

Aquaculture, or fish farming, is a system that minimizes the limitations of seasons and regions by breeding certain species of fish and other sea creatures in carefully monitored, man-made ponds, pens and beds, for harvesting on demand. The advantages, such as consistency and year-round availability, are making aquaculture a major factor in the world's commercial fish industry.

The most successful aquaculture ventures have provided fish markets with top-quality fresh fish in abundant supply. Atlantic salmon from fish pens in the fjords of Norway are satisfying salmon lovers in home kitchens and restaurants across the United States. The popularity of cultured catfish has spread from the Deep South to all corners of the country. Rainbow trout from farms in Idaho has been marketed fresh and frozen year-round for some time. Top-quality striped bass is being cultivated in California. Shellfish, such as oysters and mussels, is being successfully cultured and marketed. Shrimp farms in the tropics work overtime attempting to satisfy the demand.

Beware of Fake Fish

Surimi is a seafood product made by washing and mincing fresh fish flesh, such as Alaskan pollack, and combining it with stabilizers and other additives. This mixture is pressed into various shapes resembling shellfish and marketed as imitation crab, shrimp, lobster and scallops.

Personally, I don't like the idea of fake food. Even though many surimi products have real shrimp or crab in the mixture, the ingredients list often offends me with the addition of imitation colors and monosodium glutamate (MSG). Nevertheless, these imitation shellfish products are offered at reasonable prices in every fish market from coast to coast. They have done their part to increase fish consumption in the United States and, unknown to the consumer, have also increased the eating of underutilized fish, like pollack.

I suggest that you buy it at least once and try it at home so you can recognize its taste (for me it's not hard to distinguish real crab from the imitation variety and I doubt it will be for you, either) so that you can tell when a surimi product is being passed off as the real thing in the restaurant. And protest — loudly, if you must.

The Smart-Shopper's Buying Guide

Get familiar with this guide or check it before setting out to your fish market. It's invaluable in helping you select the best of the best.

Fresh Whole Fish

Display: When a fishmonger keeps whole fish on ice and cuts it to order, you have a better chance to observe the freshness. The fish, however, should be gutted. If the innards are still in the belly by the time the fish reaches the store, it is highly suspect. Fish organs spoil quickly and affect the flavor of the adjacent flesh.

Eyes: They are clear, bright and bulging. The eyeballs of some fish deteriorate quickly after leaving the water. If the eyes are slightly milky, freshness is waning. Sunken, opaque, white or gray eyes indicate bad news. Move on.

Gills: They are bright red, almost burgundy, moist and glistening. Pink gills are okay. Gray or brown gills with slime are a sure sign of an old, unacceptable fish. Note: Have gills removed if you intend to cook the whole fish.

Skin: If scales are still attached, skin is bright and shiny, with tight, smooth scales. Loose, dried scales indicate an old or poorly handled fish.

Flesh: If you press your fingertip down on the fish, it is firm and springs back when you lift your finger. If a dent remains, the flesh of the fish is soft and old.

Odor: When you smell the gut cavity, it smells clean and looks clean. Off-odors will develop there first.

Fillets, Steaks and Other Cuts

Display: These exposed cuts of flesh are stored on ice.

Color: Freshly cut flesh is translucent or brilliant in color. If flesh is milky white or dull and muddy in color, it is low in quality. If the surface is opaque white, suspect that it has been dipped in a preservative.

Surface: The surface of the flesh glistens. It should never be slimy.

Flesh: The flesh is somewhat firm and tight. If it is separating at the seams, leaving holes in the fillets, it is beyond its prime.

Odor: It has the fresh scent of lake or ocean water. Any hint of ammonia or iodine means the fish should be rejected.

Finding the Freshest of the Fresh

Picking the freshest fish from the numbers in the display cases is something you'll learn to do through trial and error. If you're a novice fish shopper, you'll have to rely on the honesty and integrity of your fishmonger at first. There are, however, some

Picking the Right Cut

By the time a fish gets from the water to the retail counter it usually undergoes some type of transformation. It gets sliced in specific cuts (much like the beef you find at the market). It can even be dressed in various ways. If you find the styles of fish presentation a bit confusing, this guide will help you find the right cut.

Whole-dressed: Gutted and scaled; can be boned.

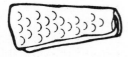

Pan-dressed: Gutted and scaled; head, fins and tail removed; can be boned.

Rib steak: A cross section, 1 inch thick or more, sliced from the front half of a fish, starting at the head; bone and skin intact.

Tail steak: A cross section, 1 inch thick or more, sliced from the rear half of a fish, ending at the tail; bone and skin intact.

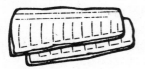

Fillet: The fleshy, full side of a fish, from head to tail, removed from the bone structure, offered with or without skin. Some fillets are boneless; others have a row of pin bones running from the head end to approximately halfway down the fillet. The row of pin bones can be easily removed for a completely boneless fillet.

Loin fillet: A cross section, 1 inch thick or more, sliced from a skinless fillet.

Loin cutlet: A cross section, no more than ¾ inch thick, sliced from a skinless fillet.

Tail fillet: The rear half of a full fillet; offered with or without skin; boneless.

Quarter fillet: Half of a vertically halved flatfish; offered with or without skin; boneless.

basic facts about fish shopping you should know before setting foot in the shop.

The most important thing to remember—I call it the golden rule of seafood buying—is this: Always ask to sniff the fish before it is wrapped for the trip home. And don't be too bashful to ask. If the fishmonger refuses, consider it a clue that you need a new fishmonger. Your nose knows best. Any off-odor will alert you quickly that the fish is beyond its prime. Fresh fish should have the scent of ocean, lake or river water. If it smells of ammonia or iodine, cooking won't improve it.

Don't be afraid to reject stale fish. Your fishmonger knows better than you when fish is beyond its prime. If he tries to sell it to you, just presume it's a mistake and tell him so. It is better that you throw up a red flag at the store than to be disappointed at home and never return.

Portions per Person

In each chapter, I offer advice on the amount of raw fish to purchase for each person. But only you know how it will be used—as appetizer or main dish. Also, appetites vary. Take my recommendations as a guide you can apply to the appetites of your family and friends.

I like to serve 1½ to 3 ounces of edible flesh per person as appetizers and 4 to 6 ounces per person as main dishes. Personally, I see nothing wrong with serving larger portions if you like. Just try to be sure that the fatty ingredients in the recipe do not increase with the portion size. For example, doubling a recipe that calls for 1 pound of fish to be sautéed in 1 tablespoon of butter doesn't mean you'll need 2 tablespoons of fat to double the fish size. Try it with 1 tablespoon and add a little bit as needed.

It is easy to calculate the portion sizes of skinless fillets just by appearance: What you see is what you get. For steaks, I usually add 2 ounces to cover the weight of bones and skin. For pan-dressed fish, I add 2 ounces per person just as with steaks. You must consider the head and tail weight when calculating a portion weight for whole-dressed fish. I multiply by 2, since the edible yield is approximately 50 percent on most fish.

Facts on Freezing

At one time or another, for one reason or another, you'll want to buy frozen fish. Lobster tail, of course, is a good example that comes to mind.

Whatever your reason, remember these tips. Look for fish that is rock solid, with no signs of freezer burn or refreezing. If the fish is not pack-

Portions per Person

Market Form	Appetizer	Main Dish
Finfish		
Skinless fillet	1½–3 oz.	4–6 oz.
Pan-dresed and steaks	3½–5 oz.	6–8 oz.
Whole-dressed	3–6 oz.	8–12 oz.
Bivalves		
Clams, oysters, mussels (small)	4–10	12–20
Clams, oysters, mussels (medium)	3–8	9–16
Clams, oysters, mussels (large)	2–6	9–16
Scallops	1½–3 oz.	4–6 oz.
Crabs		
Blue (whole)	1–3	4–8
Blue (meat only)	1½–3 oz.	4–6 oz.
Blue (claws)	4–8 oz.	8–12 oz.
Dungeness (whole)	6–10 oz.	12–16 oz.
King and snow (clusters, legs, claws)	4–8 oz.	8–12 oz.

aged tightly in a moisture-proof covering, it is likely that freezer burn has occurred. (Freezer burn looks like light-colored tan spots. The flesh may also look stringy.) If the fish or fillet is frozen into a contorted shape, it may have thawed and been refrozen.

Once a frozen fish is thawed, it must be used quickly. Previously frozen fish should be just as fresh looking as fresh fish. However, it won't last long in that condition before it starts to deteriorate.

I cook frozen fish before it is completely thawed. It is best to remove it from the freezer to room temperature for 30 minutes before cooking. It should be "frosted" or still somewhat solid when it is exposed to the cooking heat. Do not overcook; it will dry out easily.

Market Form	Appetizer	Main Dish
Soft-shell (whole)	1	2-3
Stone (claws)	4-8 oz.	8-12 oz.
Crawfish		
Whole	3-5	6-10
Lobster		
Meat only	1½-3 oz.	4-6 oz.
Tail	3-5 oz.	6-8 oz.
Whole	½-¾ lb.	1-1½ lbs.
Shrimp		
45-50 per lb. (medium)	5-10	12-20
26-30 per lb. (large)	3-6	8-12
16-20 per lb. (extra jumbo)	2-4	5-8
Squid		
Whole	3½-5 oz.	6-8 oz.
Cleaned tubes and rings	1½-3 oz.	4-6 oz.

Cleaning, Cutting and Storing Fish: The Do's and Don'ts

~~~~~~~~~~~~~~~~~~~~~~~~~~~~

Regardless of whether you catch your own fish or buy it at the store, there's no reason why you shouldn't end up with the cut, size and style you and your family like best.

Of course, the easiest way to have clean or properly cut fish it to let an expert do it. But it's up to you to tell the expert exactly what you want done with the fish. If purchasing in a store, it shouldn't cost extra to have a whole fish cleaned or filleted by the fishmonger. Just understand that you will be paying for the weight of the whole fish as it was before the head, tail and bones were removed.

If you catch your own fish or are lucky enough to have a fisherman friend who shares the catch, you can make good use of the following instructions. Fish cleaning and cutting can be fun, so you might want to bring a whole fish home from the market and do it yourself.

Tools of the Trade

Let's begin with the basic tools you will need to clean and cut fish.

For finfish you will need the following:

Scaler—Do not spend a lot of money on this tool. You can pick up a cheap metal or plastic scaler at a sportfishing bait shop. In fact, if you don't have a scaler, you can use the dull back edge of a fillet knife.

Cutting board—I like the large, white, plastic cutting boards (at least ½ inch thick), usually available where kitchenware is sold. I keep it ready in my kitchen at all times for small jobs. To prevent the board from slipping on the countertop, dampen a paper towel and lay it flat under the board.

I also have made my own 12-inch pine board, which is nice and sturdy because it is 1 inch thick and heavy. I use it only when a large catch of fresh bluefish or trout require quick but messy cleaning. I've designed it to fit snugly on my deep sink so it won't slide when I run water over it.

Fillet knife—This tool is indispensable if you want to do the job right. I suggest you invest in a good knife that you can sharpen easily. I did and I have been using the same one for the past 16 years!

It is most important that your fillet knife be razor sharp so it can glide across the bone structure of fish, separating the flesh easily as it goes. I sharpen my knife on a sharpening stone (if you don't have one, get one) before each fillet job because the bones tend to dull even a razor-sharp edge.

Fillet knives have flexible blades and commonly come in 6-inch and 9-inch lengths. The longer knife is best for larger fish.

Chef's knife—This straight-edge knife is essential for skinning fillets. I also use it to cut steaks and cutlets.

Although it is most important that a chef's knife be super sharp for slicing, chopping and dicing, I keep a semi-dull chef's knife on hand to skin fillets. It sounds odd, but it works best for this job. A razor-sharp edge has a tendency to slip through the skin, making the skinning process difficult.

For shellfish you will need the following:

Clam knife—Keep two kinds of clam knives handy. A flexible blade (thin) is perfect for opening small, hard-shell clams for serving on the half shell. A rigid blade (thick) is necessary to open stubborn, large chowder clams. Neither blade should be sharp.

Oyster knife—This is pointed with a semi-dull edge on both sides of the blade. The point is used to penetrate the tightly clamped oyster shell. This is not an essential purchase, since oysters are generally sold already shucked. Also, shucking oysters is very difficult and is best left to the professionals. Amateurs have been known to injure themselves attempting this task.

Lobster pliers — These sturdy culinary pliers come in handy for cracking through lobster and crab claws and the hard shells of crab legs.

Kitchen shears — I use these heavy shears to cut lobster tail shells and crab leg shells. They are also quite handy for snipping fins when pan-dressing fish.

Be a Knowledgeable Consumer

If you can identify all parts of a fish, you are in a position to talk intelligently with your fishmonger. A knowledgeable consumer commands respect in

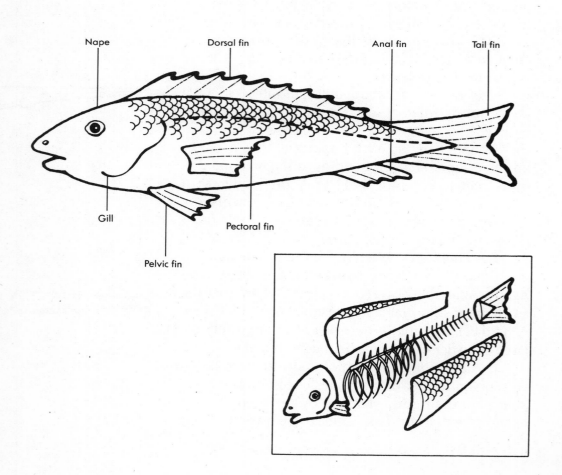

the marketplace. With the illustration on the previous page, you can learn every part of a fish.

Boning Is Basic

Boning your own fish needn't be intimidating. If you've ever attempted to bone a chicken breast, you'll find boning a fish no problem at all. In fact, I think that fish is even easier to bone than chicken is.

As you can see by the illustration on the previous page, fillets are two slabs of meat attached to both sides of a central bone structure. You will find a bone structure similar to this in most finfish.

Getting rid of the pin bones is the key to achieving a completely boneless fillet. The pin bones are the small row of bones remaining after the fillet has been removed from the central bone structure. Contrary to popular belief, pin bones are not scattered throughout the flesh; they are lined up in a nice row down the center of the fillet about halfway back from the head.

To locate the pin bones, lay the fillet flat with the skin side down. Run your fingertip down the lateral line of the fillet. You will feel the tips of the pin bones peeking through the flesh in a row.

To remove pin bones, either pull them out one at a time, or cut the whole row out along with a thin strip of flesh. The method you use depends on how you plan to make the fish.

For example, if I am poaching a salmon fillet for a buffet display, I use clean pliers to pull each pin bone out, one at a time. This leaves the fillet intact and beautiful. If I am just broiling the fillet for dinner, I might cut out the whole row of pin bones before broiling. Either way, it is important to be sure that the fish is free of any bones before you serve it.

The Guts of the Job

If a fish is your own catch, however, there are a few steps you'll have to take before worrying about boning fillets. It starts with gutting your catch.

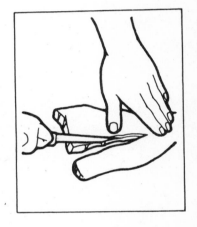

Don't worry, though. This isn't as bad as it sounds. With a sharp knife, just slit the belly from gills to anal fin. Let your fingers do the work: Pull all the organs out of the gut cavity and wash the cavity with cold running water. Scrape the dark blood from the backbone area.

Note: It is essential that a fish be gutted immediately after it is caught. Never buy a fish at the market that has the gut intact. The organs spoil quickly and the meat is affected. Besides, who wants to pay a premium price per pound for organs that are to be discarded.

Hopping onto the Scales

The next step is scaling the fish. Here is the best tip I can give you about cleaning fish: When scaling, hold the fish underwater. If you scale a fish on a cutting board, the scales tend to fly everywhere and stick to everything. But when you submerge the fish in cold water as you scale it, the scales stay in the water and can easily be scooped out of the basket strainer after the water is drained.

To scale, scrape the scales forward from tail to head for removal. It is more difficult to remove dried scales, so keep them moist. If you don't have a scaler, use the dull back edge of a fillet knife. It is just as effective as a scaler.

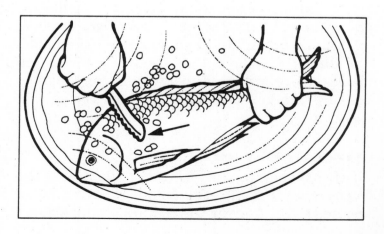

Getting All Dressed Up

Next you've got to dress the fish. Beheading may seem like a strange way to dress something up, but that's the way we talk about it in the fish world!

With a large chef's knife, cut off the head on an angle behind the gill opening and pectoral fin. Cut off the tail fin. Remove all fins with kitchen shears or a chef's knife. Presto! You have a fish all dressed up.

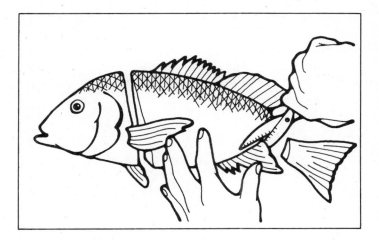

Bare Bones Filleting

There are two methods for filleting a fish. The sport-fishermen's method is quick but has little regard for wasted meat since their pocket cash doesn't depend on their catch.

I learned to fillet by the fishmonger's method. The fishmonger's livelihood depends on the ability to remove all the flesh from the bone structure without any waste. Also, this method offers a cleaner-looking fillet. Here's how it's done:

1. Make a slanted cut from the nape to the belly on both sides of the fish behind the gill openings and pectoral fins. Or, the head can be cut off. There is no need to scale the fish if you are after skinless fillets.

2. With the fish on its side, make a ½-inch-deep cut from nape to tail along the back next to the dorsal fin. Flip the fish over and make an iden-

tical cut along the back on the other side of the dorsal fin.

3. Following the plane of the backbone, continue to slide the blade from nape to tail, separating the flesh from the bone structure. Peel back the flesh as you go until you have separated one whole fillet from the backbone and rib cage.

4. Turn the fish over and repeat the filleting procedure described in step 3.

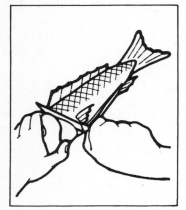
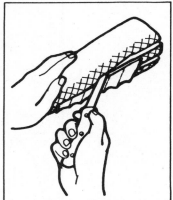
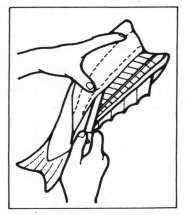

As I said, this is the method I prefer and I suggest you at least give it a try. You'll have a better-looking fish and an even better feeling of accomplishment. But in case you're interested, the sport-fisherman's method is relatively simple.

Starting at the tail end, strip off the fillet with a sawing motion from tail to head. Turn and do the same on the other side. It is quick, all right, but leaves a lot of fish flesh on the bone structure. And, to me, the method leaves a lot to be desired.

Quarter-Cutting a Flatfish

You can remove a whole fillet from a flatfish in the same manner as above, but some people prefer to quarter-cut flatfish. Here's how:

1. With your fillet knife, make a cut down the middle of each side for the entire length of the center bone.

2. Slide the blade between the flesh and bone structure and cut the fillets from the center bone out toward the edges of the fish.

Using this method, you will get four separate boneless fillets from each fish.

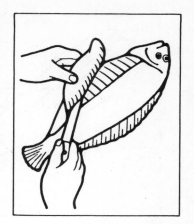

Getting Skinned

Skinning a fish takes a little bit of practice since some fish tends to be stubborn and doesn't want to give up its skin easily. As I've already mentioned, the secret is in the knife: Use a chef's knife that is slightly dull. Then proceed as follows:

1. Place the fillet, skin side down, on a cutting board with the tail end closest to you.

2. Grasp the tail tip tightly with your thumb and forefinger. Cut through the flesh to the skin ½ inch from the tip.

3. Flatten the knife, keeping the edge on the skin and board. With a sawing motion, continue cutting forward, separating the flesh from the skin.

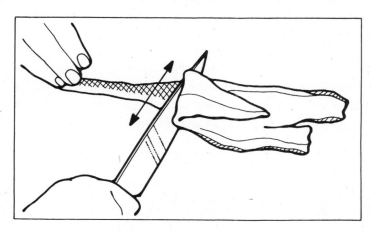

Calling It Splits

Splitting is a step that's purely optional but one I like to take advantage of when working with small fish for the barbecue. Here's how it's done:

1. Cut the head off a whole-dressed fish.

2. Using a fillet knife inside the gut cavity, cut through the rib cage along the center bone. Split

the fish from head to tail leaving the two halves attached at the back.

Steaking a Fish

Steaking is easy and a good method for you to perfect. Cut properly, a steak will cook evenly. Here's how it's done:

1. Pan-dress the fish.

2. Using a large, sharp chef's knife, crosscut the fish to the center bone, marking 1-inch intervals for the steaks.

3. Using a firm downward motion, cut through the center bone and slice off each steak. If the fish is large, you might want to help the blade through the center bone with a mallet or dowel.

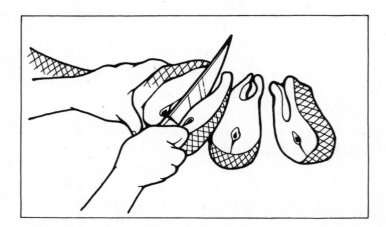

***Spicy Chilled Flounder
with Dill and Dijon Mustard***

page 69

43

Poached Cod from Lewis Street
page 78

Sautéed Portuguese Bluefish
page 90

Buffet-Poached Side of Salmon
page 97

Filing Down Fillets

Large fish make for large fillets, often too large for easy cooking or for individual or small servings. You can elegantly portion a large fillet by following this method:

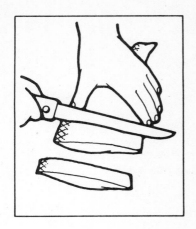

1. Lay the fillet flat, skin side down, on a cutting board. Remove the pin bones with pliers.

2. Crosscut 1- to 2-inch slices with a chef's knife for fillet steaks. Cut ½-inch slices for thin cutlets.

What's in Store for Fish

Fresh fish is the most perishable food in the marketplace. That's why it's always displayed on ice. Fish requires cold, fresh storage at temperatures below the normal refrigerator setting. When you put fish on ice in the refrigerator, the ice brings the temperature of the fish down close to freezing — but doesn't freeze it. During warm weather and when you can't proceed directly home from the store, ask your fishmonger to throw a small bag of ice in with your fish. A conscientious dealer will be glad to accommodate you.

When you get home, cook the fish immediately, or refrigerate it for 2 to 3 hours, or ice it in the refrigerator for no more than 24 hours.

I don't recommend freezing fish that you purchase in the marketplace. You don't know how long the fish has been out of the water. Furthermore, home freezers don't freeze fish quickly enough.

If you catch fish yourself or know when it came from the water, by all means feel free to freeze it. Make sure you put it in a very cold storage freezer (the upright or chest type) that is set below 0°F. Wrap each fillet tightly with freezer wrap and freeze separately. Do not pile fillets together. If space in the freezer is a concern, do not freeze whole fish, particularly the larger types. The useless heads and bones take up too much room. If you're preserving the heads and bones for stock, fillet the fish, make the stock right away and freeze both.

I like to be conservative when recommending

freezer shelf life for fresh fish. For example, I would not keep fish flesh in a home freezer for more than six months. Some fatty fish, like bluefish, don't make it past the first month in a freezer without deteriorating.

Freezer Life for Fish and Shellfish

Seafood	Maximum (months)	Seafood	Maximum (months)
Bass, freshwater	3	Pollack	3
Bass, striped	2	Pout, ocean	3
Bluefish	1	Sablefish	1
Catfish, freshwater	2	Salmon	1
Clams	3	Scallops	3
Cod	3	Shad	1
Crab	3	Shark	3
Crawfish	3	Shrimp	3
Cusk	3	Skate	3
Drum	3	Smelts	2
Eel	1	Snapper, red	3
Flounder	3	Sole	3
Grouper	3	Squid	3
Haddock	3	Sunfish	3
Halibut	2	Swordfish	2
Lobster	3	Tilefish	3
Mackerel	1	Trout, freshwater	2
Mahimahi (dolphinfish)	3	Trout, sea	3
		Tuna	2
Monkfish	3	Walleye	3
Mussels	3	Whitefish	1
Orange roughy	3	Whiting (hake)	2
Oysters	3	Wolffish (ocean catfish)	2
Perch, yellow	3		
Pike, northern	3		

Note: Length of time applies when freezer is set at 0°F or colder.

Cooking Fish
to Perfection

~~~~~~~~~~~~~~~~~~~~~~~~~~~~~

Fish is the ideal meal for any cook to serve. But more important, it is the ideal meal for the *busy* cook to serve.

I'm a firm believer that fish is at its best served simply. It enables the diner to truly savor the delicate, natural flavor that makes fish unique.

Most simple fish dishes can be completely cooked and ready for the table in 15 minutes. That's because the secret to cooking perfect fish is not to overcook it.

I'm not suggesting that you undercook fish as some pop-chefs do. They like to leave it with a rare, warmed center. But I don't recommend it. You never know what unwholesome organism might survive in an undercooked piece of fish.

Fish flesh is a soft, delicate protein that needs quick and gentle cooking to firm the flesh and make it easily digestible. As with cooking any fresh meat or vegetable, preserving moisture is most important to the success of the dish. If you cook and cook fish, it becomes dry, hard or mushy and the odor becomes stronger.

But cooked to perfection, fish will always be moist, have a nice firm, flaky texture and entice you with it's delicate aroma. Ummmmh! I get hungry just thinking about it!

But when I think delicious fish I also think healthy fish. I can't think of any food that can stand on its own natural goodness better than fish can. There is just no need to laden such a nutritiously and naturally delicious piece of eating with unnecessary calories.

Cooking fish healthfully means keeping fat to a minimum. Forget the deep-frying, globs of butter

49

and heavy cream. When cooked right, you can also forget the salt. There are many ways to prepare delicious fish entrées for your family and friends that will neither skyrocket their cholesterol levels nor raise their blood pressures. The recipes in this book are all the proof you'll need.

Butter is something you'll find little of in my recipes. I use olive oil as the preferred fat. Olive oil is one of the good fats I discussed in the first chapter. It's a monounsaturated fat, a type that scientists now believe to be a more healthful choice than polyunsaturated oils like corn oil and safflower oil.

I don't use salt in any recipe, either. You'll discover, as I have, that matching the right herbs and spices to the right ingredients does more for flavor than salt could ever do.

Perfect Timing

Of course, all the herbs in the world won't do a bit of good if you keep the fish on the stove or under the broiler too long. The universal rule of thumb for perfect fish is this: 10 minutes total cooking time for every inch of thickness at the fish's thickest point. But it's only a rule of thumb. Don't expect it to work for every manner of cooking or with every type or piece of fish.

My rule of thumb is a little looser. I use 10 minutes per inch only as the average. If I use a direct intense heating method, such as broiling, I usually reduce the total cooking time to 6 or 7 minutes per inch. If the piece of fish is particularly thick, like a 2-inch-thick cod loin, I will use a less intense cooking method, such as baking, and increase the time to 15 minutes per inch.

In other words, the true measure of perfection includes the method of cooking and the thickness of the fish as well as the timing. Also, the amount of fish you're cooking and what you're cooking it with can also play a part. And, fish coming directly from the refrigerator takes a bit longer to cook through than fish that has been on the counter 10 minutes. There are many factors to consider when timing fish.

What this all boils down to is this: You've got to get a feeling for fish cookery. But don't fear. The more you cook fish, the easier it gets to second-guess the dish. And better yet, there is a tried-and-true way to make sure you score perfect every time.

Cooking Times for Fish

Cooking Method	½"-Thick Fillet	1"-Thick Fillet, Steak	2"-Thick Fillet, Steak, Pan-Dressed	3"-Thick Fillet, Steak, Pan-Dressed, Whole-Dressed
Baking				
400°F	8–12 min.	10–15 min.	12–17 min.	18–25 min.
350°F	10–15 min.	12–17 min.	15–20 min.	20–30 min.
Broiling				
4" from high heat	4–6 min.	6–8 min.	*	*
5"–6" from high heat	6–8 min.	8–10 min.	10–12 min.	*
Grilling (high heat)				
on grill	*	2–4 min. each side	3–6 min. each side	4–8 min. each side
on tile	4–8 min.	5–10 min.	10–15 min.	*
on plank	*	*	10–15 min.	15–20 min.
Poaching (simmer)	8–12 min.	10–15 min.	12–17 min.	18–25 min.
Steaming	6–10 min.	8–12 min.	10–15 min.	15–20 min.
Sautéing (medium-high heat)	3–4 min. each side	3–5 min. each side	4–6 min. each side	*
Pan-frying (medium heat)	4–5 min. each side	4–6 min. each side	5–7 min. each side	*
Braising	8–12 min.	10–15 min.	12–17 min.	18–25 min.
Smoking (additional standing time)	8–12 min. (10 min.)	10–15 min. (10 min.)	12–17 min. (10 min.)	15–20 min. (10 min.)
Microwaving (1 lb. on high — 100%) (additional standing time)	3½–5½ min. (2 min.)	4–6 min. (3 min.)	4½–6½ min. (3 min.)	5–7 min. (4 min.)

*Cooking method not recommended for this cut.

Testing for Doneness

No matter what temperature or timing I choose for a dish, I always set a minimum point in the process where I will test the fish to determine doneness.

I've come to be fairly confident that after 8 minutes at 4 inches under a broiler, a 1-inch-thick salmon steak will be fully cooked by the time it reaches the dining table. I've also found that after 8 minutes in a 400°F oven, a ½-inch-thick flounder fillet will be fully cooked. But I've also found that there's no good reason not to check for doneness a minute or two beforehand—just in case.

Doneness is measured with your fingertips and your eyes. All flesh becomes firmer as it cooks. Press gently with a fingertip on the thickest part of the fish before you cook it. Then repeat the gentle press when you think it is fully cooked. Experience will help you with this test.

Raw fish flesh is translucent and darker than cooked fish flesh. When fish cooks, it lightens in color and turns opaque white or light gray. When you think the fish is cooked, use the tip of a paring knife blade to probe the center of the thickest flesh. Do this carefully and gently. You only need to sneak a peek at the color. Don't cut the fish open or dig a hole. Just slide the knife tip between the layers of flake until you reach the center. Gently separate the flake and observe the color.

If the center flesh is still dark and translucent, return the fish for a few more minutes of cooking. If the center flesh is solid white, the fish is done. Serve it immediately.

The Basic Methods of Cooking

One of the most wonderful challenges of fish cookery is the variety of cooking methods that can be used. Most people, unfortunately, think fish cookery is limited to frying. That's simply not the case. In this book you'll find a variety of recipes incorporating the following cooking methods.

Baking—I like baking fish in a hot oven—400°F.

It cooks the fish quickly and gives it just a touch of crust. This dry-heat method will suck all the moisture from the delicate flesh of fish if you cook it too long, so beware. I recommend that you bake on the top shelf of the oven. The heat seems to be more even there.

Broiling—This is a direct, overhead heat that will cook fish quickly. It can dry out the delicate flesh of fish so I advise that you always baste it. A small amount of vegetable oil will help, but it is not absolutely necessary. Usually the only variable you can control in broiling, besides timing, is the distance at which you place the fish from the heat.

Delicate fish like sole and crabmeat are best broiled 4 to 6 inches from the heat. Fatty fish like bluefish and salmon should be no more than 4 inches from the heat. The ideal vicinity of the heat, how-

Hardy Fish
for Hearty Cooking

Some fish will hold up better than others for cooking methods that require a little tumbling and poking in the process. You should only use fish that has a firm flesh that holds its form under less than delicate situations. Chowders, stir-fries, grilling and even making fish for salads all require this type of fish. The fish listed below are those that qualify in this category.

Catfish	Ocean pout
Clams	Oysters
Crawfish	Salmon
Drum	Scallops
Eel	Shark
Grouper	Shrimp
Lobster	Red snapper
Mahimahi	Striped bass
Marlin	Swordfish
Monkfish	Tilefish
Mussels	Tuna

ever, really depends on the type of fish. Generally speaking, never place a fish less than 3 inches from the heat or farther than 6 inches.

Grilling—Good grilling requires a quick touch. Fish cooks faster than you can say, "Dish out the coleslaw."

By grilling I mean placing the fish directly on the grill. Wrapping fish in foil and laying it on a barbecue grill is not my idea of grilling. You don't get grilled fish; you get steamed fish. To keep fish moist, you can marinate it beforehand and baste throughout cooking.

Some fish can fall apart if it quickly overcooks on the grill. I avoid that by protecting the fish with a quarry tile or a soaked oak plank.

Rectangular quarry tiles (available in various sizes from any tile store) are great for cooking fillets. Coat the tiles with vegetable cooking spray and place on the grill. Lay the fish right on them. The tiles can take the intense direct heat from the coals and they allow the fish to cook more gently while the aromas of hardwood or charcoal permeate the fillets. Trout fillets or flounder fillets, in particular, cook beautifully and stay in one piece on quarry tiles.

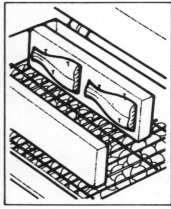

I soak 2-inch-thick oak planks for 30 minutes and tack or lightly wire split, whole- or pan-dressed fish to the planks. Prop the planks on their sides on the grill. Turn the planks midway in the grilling process to cook the other side of the fish. It takes a little longer to cook fish this way but you can cover the grill with a lid to speed the process. To remove planked trout or other small sportfish from the board, pull off the tacks or snip the wire and slide a knife under the fish. Or, make a great presentation by serving it right on the plank as many restaurants do.

You can also use a fish-grilling basket. It allows you to turn the fish easily without it falling apart.

Poaching—Poaching is the most gentle and delicate method for cooking fish and is perfect for fillets, steaks and whole- or pan-dressed fish.

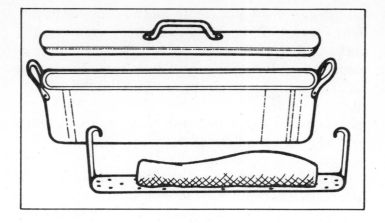

You can poach on top of the stove in a fish poacher (an elongated pot with a lowering platform and lid), soup pot or deep roasting pan. You can also poach in the oven.

The idea of poaching is to gently simmer (never boil) in an aromatic liquid in a tightly covered container. Fish should be poached until just done, approximately 10 minutes per inch of thickness.

A skimmer or cheesecloth can be used to lower the fish into the bouillon and for lifting it when it is cooked.

Poaching Bouillon

I prefer an aromatic bouillon for poaching fish. The bouillon imparts a hint of citrus or herbal flavor to the cooked fish. Here is a simple poaching bouillon:

    2 quarts water
    ¼ cup wine vinegar
    3 bay leaves
    12 sprigs of parsley
    12 peppercorns
    1 teaspoon mustard seeds
    6 slices of lemon

Combine all ingredients in a 4-quart pot. Bring to a boil. Cover, reduce heat and simmer for 15 minutes. Remove from heat and let stand for 15 minutes. Strain and reserve bouillon for poaching fish. This will be enough liquid to poach about four 8-ounce fish.

Steaming—My favorite method for steaming fish is a wok. Pour a cup of water with aromatic herbs and spices in the bottom of the wok over medium-high heat. Place the fish on a metal steaming rack or a bamboo steaming section. Put the rack or steamer in the wok above, not touching, the liquid, and cover. Steam is hot and cooks quickly, so be sure to check the fish often.

Steaming is a moist method for cooking delicate, lean fish such as sole or flounder. But almost any fish responds beautifully to wok steaming.

Sautéing—I recommend a nonstick skillet for sautéing fish. It allows you to keep the fat to a minimum. I use olive oil most often and sometimes add citrus juice or a small amount of stock to the oil. I prefer to sauté over medium heat, but I do use medium-high heat at times.

Be careful when turning the fish to cook the other side. To avoid breaking the cooked fish, cook it only one-third of the time on the first side, then turn it over and cook it for the final two-thirds of the time. Fish will usually hold together if you don't wait too long to turn it.

Stir-frying—Stir-frying fish is most successful when using firm-fleshed fish or seafood like monkfish, tilefish, shark, swordfish, tuna, catfish, shrimp and scallops. You simply cut the fish into ½-inch strips or bite-size pieces and cook quickly for a few minutes, stirring all the while.

Occasionally, I like to dredge the pieces of raw fish in cornstarch and add it to hot peanut oil in the wok. Stir-fry fish on its own and remove it before adding any accompanying vegetables. Cook the vegetables for a few minutes and return the fish to the wok. Stir once, cover and heat for 1 to 2 minutes.

Pan-frying—This is not the healthiest way to cook fish, but sometimes your family may insist upon pan-fried fish.

To pan-fry, dredge the fish in seasoned flour to

coat. Heat fresh peanut oil or other vegetable oil (no more than 1 tablespoon) in a nonstick skillet over medium-high heat for 1 to 2 minutes. Cook fish quickly in hot oil. A crust will form on both sides, sealing the fish. Drain the fish on paper towels before serving.

Braising—This is a moist method of cooking in which you smother the fish in chopped vegetables and stock and simmer it in a covered casserole or roasting pan in the oven or on top of the stove. Figure about 10 minutes per ½-inch thickness of fillet for this slow-cooking method. For a whole-dressed fish, cook about 25 to 30 minutes.

Stewing or chowder—The most important tip I can give you for stewing fish or cooking fish chowder is this: Add the fish at the very end of the cooking time so the fish does not overcook. Cook all other ingredients in the liquid until they are tender. Then add the raw, boneless fish pieces to the simmering chowder, stir and remove from the heat. Allow the soup to steep for 5 to 10 minutes and serve. The fish will remain in bite-size chunks and will not disintegrate in the broth.

Smoking—Smoking fish for preserving shelf life is too complicated for home kitchens. If you have a well-ventilated kitchen, however, you can hot-smoke fish to give it that smoky taste.

I use a wok with a metal steaming rack. Spread 2 to 4 tablespoons of hardwood sawdust or chips (mesquite, hickory, maple, apple, etc.), dried herbs (rosemary leaves, bay leaves, pickling spice, etc.) or a combination of both in the bottom of the wok. Lay the fish on the steaming rack and place it in the wok. Cover the wok with a dome lid. Heat over medium heat for 1 minute, reduce heat to medium and smoke for 10 to 20 minutes. *Do not lift the lid.* Turn off the heat and let the wok stand for 10 minutes to allow the smoke to subside.

If you don't have a well-ventilated kitchen you

can try this on an outside grill. Be patient. It might take some experimenting to get it right; a grill doesn't provide the same control as a stove.

You can serve hot-smoked fish hot, warm or chilled with a savory sauce.

Microwaving—Microwaving is a simple method that can turn out healthful and perfectly cooked fish without any added fat.

To microwave, arrange the fish in a single layer around the edge of a dish; brush with stock, water or juice and cover with a lid, loose plastic or paper towel. Remember to rotate the dish often during the cooking process. This will help the fish to cook evenly.

It doesn't take long to microwave fish so pay close attention to the timing and check for doneness often. I usually cook finfish on high (100%) for 3½ to 7 minutes depending on the thickness of the cut. Scallops and shrimp have flesh that turns rubbery if overcooked, so I cook them on medium (70%) for 4 to 6 minutes per pound.

Be sure to let the fish stand, covered, for 2 to 5 minutes after cooking. This allows the heat to be distributed evenly and the fish to finish cooking.

Notes on Marinating

Marinating raw fish before you cook it can enhance the flavor of fish. But unlike beef or chicken, it should never be marinated overnight. Fish flesh is too delicate and long marinating will only make it mushy.

I limit marinating time for fish to 1 hour in the refrigerator. It can handle a bit more than that, but 1 hour is a good benchmark. Make sure you always refrigerate fish while marinating.

Fish that takes well to marinating includes striped bass, bluefish, catfish, eel, mackerel, mahi-mahi, marlin, monkfish, salmon, scallops, sea trout, shark, shrimp, skate, snapper, swordfish and tuna. Market cuts that marinate well are fillets and steaks.

Cooking Frozen Fish

When fish is frozen, the cells in the flesh burst from the crystallization of the liquids inside. As long as the fish remains frozen, the juice stays in the fish. When the frozen fish thaws completely, however, all the essential juices drop out of the fish onto the thawing plate or paper. These juices are what keeps fish moist as it cooks. If you completely thaw frozen fish, most likely it will be dry when it is finished cooking.

To successfully cook frozen fish, do not allow it to thaw completely before cooking. Remove frozen fish from the freezer and allow it to thaw at room temperature for 30 to 40 minutes, or until it is frosted but still firm. Cook it gently from this state over low heat for 1½ to 2 times longer than you would fresh fish.

If you follow this procedure and do not over-cook the fish, you will have a moist and flavorful finished fish.

Notes on Fish Stock

Many recipes call for fish stock and any chef worth his toque blanche will tell you that there is no real substitute.

Ask your fishmonger for clean (no guts or gills) fish heads and fish carcasses. He should give them to you free of charge.

Lean fish offers the best base for fish stock. Avoid fatty fish like bluefish, mackerel and shad. Heads and carcasses should be fresh that day and not frozen or left over from yesterday.

Place the heads and carcasses in a large soup pot and cover with cold water. Add lemon slices, parsley sprigs, a bay leaf, celery leaves, a dozen peppercorns and ¼ teaspoon of dried thyme leaves.

Bring the water to a boil. Reduce the heat to low and simmer for 30 minutes. *Do not cook the fish broth longer than 30 minutes.*

Strain the broth through a fine sieve or double layer of cheesecloth. Discard the fish, herbs and spices.

If you desire a stronger flavor to your stock, return the strained broth to a clean pot, bring it to a boil and reduce the volume by a third. Otherwise, let the strained broth stand for 30 minutes and refrigerate or freeze it in small containers or ice cube trays. This way you'll always have a little on hand when a recipe calls for it.

Flounder
and Other Flatfish

~~~~~~~~~~~~~~~~~~~~~~~~~~~~~~

Flatfish is the favorite of the marketplace. Although a few varieties command higher prices because of quality or demand, Americans seem to love them all. It's easy to see why. Every fillet cooks to a snow white color, and the flesh is always delicate of flake and mild in flavor.

Flounder, fluke and sole are small flatfish with two flat, football-shaped fillets. These fillets are among the most versatile in fish cuisine, making them the one type of fish that can appeal to anyone's taste. That's why they're such favorites.

As evidenced by its extensive use in classical French cuisine, sole adapts well to many different sauces, vegetables and culinary herbs. You can cook it using just about any method you please. The same goes for flounder.

Halibut is a large flatfish found in both the Atlantic and Pacific oceans. It has white, lean flesh that is usually marketed as steaks or sometimes cut fillets.

I find these low-calorie flatfish to be quite popular on any menu—home or restaurant.

Talking to Your Fishmonger

Flatfish fillets are available at your market year-round and are always easy to find. Although I prefer small fillets, even large fillets of flounder, fluke and sole are tasty and tender. If I can get whole-dressed fish filleted to order, I like that best.

When purchasing fillets, look for translucent white or bluish gray flesh that is glistening and plump. If the surface is milky white, it means it has

61

School of Nutrients

Flounder, fluke, sole
3½ oz. raw

		Low	Moderate	High
Calories	91	~~~~		
Protein	19 g	~~~~~~~~~~		
Fat	1.2 g	~		
Omega-3	0.2 g	~~		
Saturated fat	0.3 g	~		
Sodium	81 mg	~~~		
Cholesterol	48 mg	~~~~~		

Halibut
3½ oz. raw

		Low	Moderate	High
Calories	110	~~~~		
Protein	21 g	~~~~~~~~~~~		
Fat	2.3 g	~		
Omega-3	0.4 g	~~~		
Saturated fat	0.3 g	~		
Sodium	54 mg	~~		
Cholesterol	32 mg	~~~~		

Source: Adapted from Agriculture Handbook No. 8–15 (Washington, D.C.: U.S. Department of Agriculture).

been dipped in a preserving solution or has been soaking in melted ice and its own juices. Neither is desirable. As usual, I let my nose perform the true test.

One of the major attractions of flounder and sole fillets is that they are virtually boneless. They don't even have pin bones. Now and then, a sloppy filleting job will miss a few rib bones near the belly or fin bones around the perimeter of the fillet. But you can see or feel those and remove them easily before cooking.

Of course, if I am buying whole-dressed flounder or sole for stuffing and baking or for grilling, I go for the small fish.

The much larger halibut is usually offered in the form of 1-inch-thick steaks. Look for freshly sliced, glistening skin and flesh that is translucent and pinkish white. I reach for the solid tail steaks with the flesh all around the backbone. This choice is only personal preference. Others prefer the large flake of a loin steak.

One more opinion on flatfish. Fillets from the white (or under) side are considered premium by some people—and are priced accordingly. I prefer the fillet from the dark (or upper) side and usually pay a discount price. The point is, if two fillets come from the same fresh fish, why not buy the least expensive, especially when they cook and taste the same?

If you are willing to pay a premium price, you might as well choose gray sole on the East Coast or petrale sole on the West Coast. These are prime-quality fish, and pricey due to great demand.

The Fillet Board

Small portions are easy to cut from flatfish fillets. Just cut along the center line down the length of each fillet. This sample cut creates two smaller, natural-looking fillets from the larger one. These single pieces are easier to handle when cooking and serving.

You can fillet a whole-dressed flatfish just as you do a round fish. However, I prefer to quarter-cut when filleting a whole-dressed flounder or sole. A flatfish fillet is so broad that it makes sense to cut one half at a time off each side. The narrow fillets are also easier to skin.

Flatfish is ideal for stock, so remember to save and make use of the remaining carcass.

You can remove the bone from raw halibut steak very easily: Take off the skin and cut the two loins of flesh away from the backbone and other bones. Remember, however, that fish cooked on the bone retains its moisture best.

Flounder, Fluke, Sole

Market form	Amount per person (lb.)
Fillets	¼–⅓
Whole-dressed	¾–1

Halibut

Market form	Amount per person (lb.)
Fillets	¼–⅓
Steaks	⅓–½

Cooking the Catch

The best part about cooking the thin fillets of flatfish is that they don't take long to cook. If you've cooked a sole or flounder fillet more than 10 or 15 minutes, you've cooked it too long. Of course, I recommend a simple cooking procedure. Then you can add the flourish at the end, in the form of sauce or garnish.

I particularly recommend poaching these tender fillets in a light bouillon. That way the lean flesh is sure to stay moist. Don't get me wrong, baked or broiled sole can be delicious. Just watch the timing and don't overcook.

The classic sautéing method is in butter, but I like to substitute safflower oil and a splash of chicken stock for the butter. A dusting of flour on the fillet helps it to crisp quickly. I've been known to season the flour first with paprika, white pepper, ground mustard, garlic powder (very little) or a ground spice blend. This also works for broiling with a top crust.

When broiling or baking, it is best to avoid a lot of fat. You can brush on a mixture of vegetable oil and citrus juice or be creative with other juices and stocks. Sometimes I make a topping with chopped fresh herbs, minced scallions or onions, bread crumbs and a few drops of olive oil. This protects the fillet from hot, dry heat and gives a crusty topping.

Whole-dressed flounder and sole can be rubbed with oil and grilled. However, if you want to barbecue a fillet, use the quarry tile method (page 54). It keeps the fish in one place without wrapping it in foil—a practice I don't like.

Halibut steaks are just as versatile. They cook evenly and are very good even when slightly overcooked. They need a brushing of moisture like juice, stock or vegetable oil when baked or broiled.

These hearty fish steaks take well to the delicate methods of steaming and poaching.

Halibut fillets can be cooked by every method used for steaks.

~~~~~
~~~~~
Galley Tips
Flounder, fluke, sole (1 lb.)

Technique Market form	Directions	Time (min.)	Temp.
Bake Fillet, whole-dressed	Use a flat nonstick pan; brush fillet lightly with vegetable oil or butter; sprinkle with citrus juice; rub dressed fish with vegetable oil.	Fillet: 10–15 dressed: 12–18	400°F
Broil Fillet	Use a flat nonstick pan; brush lightly with vegetable oil; dust with seasoned flour or bread crumbs and paprika; broil 4 inches or less from heat.	8–12	High
Grill Fillet, whole-dressed	Use a quarry tile coated with vegetable cooking spray to protect fillet; baste fillet often with vegetable oil/ juice mixture; rub dressed fish with vegetable oil.	Fillet: 6–12 dressed: 8–15	High
Poach Fillet, whole-dressed	Use a fish poacher or deep baking pan; combine citrus juice or wine vinegar with herbs and spices in stock or water.	Fillet: 8–12 dressed: 10–15	Simmer
Sauté Fillet	Use a nonstick skillet; mix vegetable oil with stock to moisten while sautéing; turn once; sprinkle with citrus juice in pan.	8–12	Med. to med.-high
Microwave Fillet	Brush with stock, water or juice; arrange fish in 1 layer around edge of dish; cover with lid, loose plastic or paper towel; rotate often; let stand for 2 minutes after cooking.	4–6	High (100%)

~~~~~~
~~~~~~

Galley Tips
Halibut (1 lb.)

Technique Market form	Directions	Time (min.)	Temp.
Bake Fillet, steak	Use a flat nonstick pan; brush lightly with vegetable oil or butter; sprinkle with citrus juice.	10-15	400°F
Broil Fillet, steak	Use a flat nonstick pan; brush lightly with vegetable oil; dust with seasoned flour or bread crumbs and paprika; broil 4 inches or less from heat.	10-12	High
Grill Fillet, steak	Cook directly on grill; baste often with vegetable oil/juice mixture; turn once.	8-12	High
Poach Fillet, steak	Use a fish poacher or deep baking pan; combine citrus juice or wine vinegar with herbs and spices in stock or water.	10-12	Simmer
Microwave Fillet, steak	Brush with stock, water or juice; arrange fish in 1 layer around edge of dish; cover with lid, loose plastic or paper towel; rotate often; let stand for 2 minutes after cooking.	4-6	High (100%)

Milk-Poached Flounder Fillets with Warm Mustard Sauce

OPTIONS: Sole, Fluke, Turbot

¼ cup chopped scallions
1 tablespoon white wine Worcestershire sauce
2-2¼ cups skim milk
1½ pounds flounder fillets
8 whole wheat toast triangles, crusts removed
¾ cup Warm Mustard Sauce (recipe follows)

In a large skillet, combine scallions, Worcestershire sauce and milk. Blend thoroughly.

Over medium heat, bring 2 cups milk to a gentle simmer and then drop in fish fillets. If needed, add more milk to cover fillets. Return milk to a gentle simmer and poach for 10 to 12 minutes.

Lift fillets from milk (reserve ¾ cup of poaching liquid for making sauce) and drain fish well. Serve on toast and drizzle with Warm Mustard Sauce.

4 servings
343 calories per serving

~~~~~~~~~~~~~~~~~

Warm Mustard Sauce

¼ cup minced scallions, white part only
2 teaspoons vegetable oil
1 tablespoon flour
¾ cup hot poaching milk from Milk-Poached Flounder Fillets (recipe precedes)
1 tablespoon brown mustard

In a heavy saucepan, sauté scallions in oil over medium heat for 1 to 2 minutes. Do not brown.

Add flour and stir quickly with a whisk. Cook for 1 minute, stirring constantly. Add hot milk all at once while whisking. Bring to a boil, reduce heat to low and cook for 2 minutes, whisking continuously. Remove from heat.

Add mustard, whisk to blend, and serve.

Makes ¾ cup

Surf and Slaw Sandwich

OPTIONS: Sole, Fluke, Turbot

1 egg white
¼ cup skim milk
½ cup finely ground blanched almonds
¼ cup bread crumbs
½ teaspoon paprika
1¼ pounds flounder fillets, cut into 4 equal pieces
4 7-inch Italian rolls
1 cup coleslaw (page 260)

In a shallow bowl, whisk together egg white and milk.

In a baking dish, combine almonds, bread crumbs and paprika.

Dip fillets in egg white mixture to coat evenly, then coat with almond mixture. Place on a nonstick baking sheet and bake in a 400°F oven for 15 to 18 minutes, or until crumb coating is golden brown.

Slice rolls in half lengthwise without slicing all the way through. Place fillets on bottom of rolls, top with equal amounts of coleslaw and serve.

4 servings
251 calories per serving

Mediterranean Flounder Sticks with Tomato and Watercress

OPTIONS: Sole, Fluke, Turbot

1½ pounds flounder fillets, cut into strips
½ cup plain low-fat yogurt
⅔ cup cracker crumbs
⅛ teaspoon garlic powder
⅛ teaspoon ground white pepper
½ teaspoon paprika
¼ teaspoon rubbed sage
¼ teaspoon dried thyme leaves
1 tablespoon safflower oil
1 small clove garlic, minced
2 tablespoons sliced black olives
2 teaspoons olive oil
1 cup coarsely chopped canned plum tomatoes, drained
1 tablespoon minced watercress

In a small bowl, toss fish with yogurt to coat evenly.

In a shallow baking dish, combine cracker crumbs, garlic powder, pepper, paprika, sage and thyme. Dredge fish strips in seasoned crumbs and coat evenly.

In a large nonstick skillet, heat half of the safflower oil over medium-high heat. Add half of the fish strips and sauté for 5 to 7 minutes, browning on both sides. Remove fish from skillet and keep warm in a 200°F oven. Heat remaining safflower oil and sauté remaining fish strips.

In the same skillet, sauté garlic and olives in olive oil over medium heat for 1 minute. Add tomatoes and watercress and cook for 3 to 4 minutes.

Remove fish to a serving plate, spoon hot tomato sauce around fish, and serve immediately.

4 servings
321 calories per serving

Baked Sole Romano

OPTIONS: Flounder, Fluke

⅓ cup flour
⅛ teaspoon ground white pepper
⅛ teaspoon freshly ground nutmeg dash of cayenne pepper
1½ pounds sole fillets
1 tablespoon plus 1 teaspoon olive oil
1 small clove garlic, smashed
1 large can (28 ounces) tomato puree
4 ounces part-skim mozzarella cheese, shredded
1 teaspoon minced fresh oregano or ¼ teaspoon dried oregano
2 teaspoons minced fresh parsley
2 tablespoons freshly grated Romano cheese

In a shallow bowl, combine flour, pepper, nutmeg and cayenne. Dredge fillets in seasoned flour, coating both sides.

In a large nonstick skillet, heat 1 tablespoon oil. Add fillets and quickly brown over medium-high heat for 1 minute on each side. Pat fillets dry with paper towels.

Rub garlic clove and remaining oil on the surface of a large baking dish. (Discard garlic clove.) Spread 1 cup tomato puree evenly over bottom of dish. Arrange fillets on puree in one layer and sprinkle with mozzarella. Spoon remaining puree over mozzarella and sprinkle with oregano, parsley and Romano. Bake in a 400°F oven for 15 minutes, or until sauce bubbles. Serve hot.

4 servings
397 calories per serving

Spicy Chilled Flounder with Dill and Dijon Mustard

OPTIONS: Sole, Fluke, Turbot

2-2¼ cups chicken stock
1 teaspoon red-hot pepper sauce
1 teaspoon Mrs. Dash seasoning
   (lemon and herb)
2 teaspoons lemon juice
2 bay leaves
2 teaspoons white wine
   Worcestershire sauce
1¼ pounds flounder fillets
¼ cup reduced-calorie mayonnaise
¼ cup plain low-fat yogurt, drained
   overnight
2 teaspoons snipped dill or
   1 teaspoon dried dill
2 teaspoons Dijon mustard
1 tablespoon minced scallions
   dash of ground white pepper
¼ pound fresh spinach leaves

In a large skillet, combine 2 cups chicken stock, hot pepper sauce, Mrs. Dash seasoning, lemon juice, bay leaves and 1 teaspoon Worcestershire sauce. Bring to a boil, cover, lower heat and simmer for 10 minutes.

Add fish fillets to poaching bouillon. If needed, add more stock to cover fillets. Return to simmer and poach for 8 to 10 minutes. Remove from heat and let stand for 30 minutes. Refrigerate for at least 2 hours in poaching bouillon.

In a small bowl, blend together mayonnaise, yogurt, dill, mustard, 1 teaspoon Worcestershire sauce, scallions and pepper. Let stand for 15 minutes and then refrigerate.

Remove fillets from poaching bouillon and arrange on a bed of spinach leaves. Serve with mustard sauce.

4 servings
200 calories per serving

Zesty Sole Soup with Orzo

OPTIONS: Flounder, Fluke, Turbot

3 cups chicken stock
1 cup clam juice
1 tablespoon lemon juice
1 teaspoon grated lemon peel
¼ teaspoon dried thyme leaves
2 tablespoons sliced scallions
1 tablespoon minced fresh parsley
1 tablespoon diced pimientos
¼ cup orzo pasta
1 tablespoon flour
1 teaspoon paprika
½ teaspoon ground coriander
¼ teaspoon dry mustard
⅛ teaspoon ground white pepper
¾ pound sole fillets

In a 4-quart pot, combine chicken stock, clam juice, lemon juice, lemon peel and thyme. Bring to a boil, reduce heat, cover and simmer for 10 minutes.

Strain stock and return to pot. Add scallions, parsley, pimientos and pasta. Return to a simmer and cook for 8 minutes.

In a cup, combine flour, paprika, coriander, mustard and pepper and spread mixture on one side of fillets. Cut into small pieces.

Heat a well-seasoned cast-iron skillet over medium-high heat for 3 to 4 minutes, or until very hot. Quickly add fillets to the skillet, spice side down, and blacken fish on one side for 1 to 2 minutes.

Slowly and gently pour stock into skillet until sizzling stops and fish is covered, about 1 minute. Carefully return stock with fish pieces to the pot. Remove from heat and let stand for 5 minutes. Serve soup in shallow bowls.

4 servings
158 calories per serving

Broiled Flounder Rio Grande

OPTIONS: Sole, Fluke, Turbot

1 tablespoon olive oil
1 tablespoon lime juice
1 tablespoon minced fresh cilantro
    or 1 teaspoon dried parsley
    flakes
1 small clove garlic, minced
½ teaspoon minced fresh chili
    peppers
⅛ teaspoon ground cumin
¼ teaspoon paprika
1½ pounds flounder fillets
½ cup chunky salsa
2 tablespoons sour cream

In a small saucepan, combine oil, lime juice, cilantro or parsley, garlic, peppers, cumin and paprika and cook over medium heat for 2 to 3 minutes.

Coat a broiling pan with vegetable cooking spray. Place fillets on the pan, spoon oil/lime juice mixture over fish and broil at least 4 inches from the heat for 6 to 8 minutes, or until surface of fillets begin to brown.

Remove fish from broiler and let stand for 1 minute. Serve with salsa and sour cream and garnish with lime wedges.

4 servings
213 calories per serving

Curry Halibut Steak

OPTIONS: Flounder or Fluke Fillets

2 tablespoons safflower oil
1 tablespoon curry powder
1½ pounds boneless halibut steak,
    cut into 4 equal pieces
½ cup cracker meal

In a small saucepan, combine oil and curry powder and cook over medium heat for 4 to 5 minutes. Let stand for 5 minutes.

Dredge fish steaks in cracker meal, coating all sides evenly.

Pour oil off curry powder into a nonstick skillet and discard curry powder. Add fish and sauté over medium-high heat for 4 to 5 minutes on each side.

Peach chutney makes a nice accompaniment.

4 servings
284 calories per serving

Sautéed Flounder Veronique

OPTIONS: Sole, Haddock, Orange roughy

My 90-year-old grandmother, Veronica Ney, loves a Friday flounder meal. Keeping in mind that the classical French dish is graced with white grapes and is known by the French version of her name, I created this recipe for Grammy.

1¼ pounds flounder fillets, cut in
    half lengthwise
⅓ cup flour
3 teaspoons olive oil
1 cup white seedless grapes, sliced
    in halves
½ cup chopped scallions
1 teaspoon minced gingerroot or
    ½ teaspoon ground ginger
¼ cup orange juice

Dredge fillets in flour.

Heat 2 teaspoons oil in a nonstick skillet over medium heat for 2 minutes. Add fillets and sauté for 3 to 4 minutes on each side. Remove fish from skillet and keep warm in a 200°F oven.

Add remaining oil to skillet. Stir in grapes, scallions and ginger and sauté over medium-high heat for 3 to 4 minutes. Add orange juice and bring to a boil. Remove from heat.

Remove fish to serving plates. Spoon sauce over fish, garnish with small bunches of white seedless grapes and serve.

4 servings
236 calories per serving

Fragrant Flounder Fingers

---

1 tablespoon minced gingerroot or 1 teaspoon ground ginger
1 tablespoon rice wine vinegar
¼ cup orange marmalade
2 tablespoons low-sodium soy sauce
½ cup cornstarch
¼ teaspoon garlic powder
½ teaspoon ground mustard
1¼ pounds flounder fillets, cut into 1-inch strips
2 teaspoons peanut oil
1 teaspoon sesame oil

In a cup, combine ginger and vinegar. Let stand for 30 minutes. Discard ginger.

In a small saucepan, combine vinegar, marmalade and soy sauce. Stir to blend, bring to a boil over medium-high heat and remove from heat immediately. Pour into a small bowl and cool in the refrigerator for 15 minutes.

In a small, shallow bowl, combine cornstarch, garlic powder and mustard. Stir with a fork to blend. Dredge flounder strips in seasoned cornstarch.

In a large nonstick skillet, heat the oils together over medium-high heat. Add flounder and sauté for 5 to 8 minutes, turning once. Serve with chilled dipping sauce.

4 servings
281 calories per serving

Sautéed Flounder with Vegetables and Dill
OPTION: Sole

---

2 tablespoons minced shallots
3 teaspoons olive oil
2 cups sliced fresh mushroom caps
1 cup sliced fresh zucchini
1 cup chopped plum tomatoes
1¼ pounds flounder fillets
1 tablespoon snipped dill or ½ teaspoon dried dill

In a large nonstick skillet, sauté shallots in 2 teaspoons oil over medium heat for 1 to 2 minutes. Add mushrooms, zucchini and tomatoes. Stir-fry over medium-high heat for 2 to 3 minutes. Remove and reserve vegetables.

Sauté fillets in remaining oil over medium heat for 3 to 4 minutes. Turn fillets over and spoon on vegetables. Sprinkle with dill, cover and cook for 4 to 6 minutes, or until fish is fully cooked and white throughout. Gently arrange fillets and vegetables on a platter and serve.

4 servings
184 calories per serving

Oven-Poached Flounder Roll-Ups

OPTION: Sole

1¼ pounds flounder fillets, cut in half lengthwise
1 cup julienne of carrots
1 cup julienne of snow peas
1 cup julienne of celery
2 cups chicken stock
¼ cup sliced scallions
1 clove garlic, minced
2 or 3 sprigs of parsley, chopped
¼ teaspoon dried thyme
dash of ground white pepper
¼ cup julienne of scallions

Form small bundles of carrots, peas and celery.

Coat a baking dish with vegetable cooking spray. Wrap fillets around vegetable bundles and place upright in the dish.

In a saucepan, combine stock, sliced scallions, garlic, parsley, thyme and pepper. Bring to a boil over high heat. Reduce heat to low, cover and simmer for 15 minutes.

Strain hot stock over fish rolls, cover with foil and bake in a 400°F oven for 15 to 20 minutes. Serve with julienne of scallions.

4 servings
170 calories per serving

Mexican Fish Bake

OPTION: Sole

1 cup crushed unsalted tortilla chips
2 cups cooked rice
1 cup canned kidney beans, drained
1¼ pounds flounder fillets, cut into 1-inch strips
1 cup chunky salsa
½ cup shredded Monterey Jack cheese
¼ cup finely sliced scallions
3 ounces unsalted tortilla chips, for serving

Coat a 2-quart casserole with vegetable cooking spray. Using half the ingredients at a time, make alternate layers of crushed tortilla chips, rice, beans, fish strips, salsa, Monterey Jack and scallions.

Bake in a 400°F oven for 25 to 30 minutes. Serve with tortilla chips.

4 servings
562 calories per serving

The Cod Clan

~~~~~~~~~~~~~~~~~~~~~~~~~~~~

My first job as a head chef at a restaurant was at the Boathouse Restaurant in Beach Haven, New Jersey. Along with the promotion, I inherited the responsibility of filleting all the fresh codfish used on the restaurant menu. That first month I filleted 4,000 pounds of whole cod. No wonder! We served cod in fish-and-chips, broiled cod, poached cod and as a major ingredient in a bouillabaisse and steamed shellfish combo.

It's not unusual for a restaurant to make such widespread use of cod. It is undoubtedly the most versatile fish from the sea and has earned a reputation as the "workhorse" of the seafood menu. And there is good reason for it. For one thing, codfish and its cousins haddock and pollack are the leanest fish in the sea, making them popular among the calorie conscious. For another, their tender, white, light-flavored flesh makes them just plain good eating.

Talking to Your Fishmonger

It is easy to find cod, haddock and pollack fillets anytime, both fresh and frozen. When buying fresh, check for the row of pin bones that remains in many fillets and ask your monger to remove them. I prefer small, whole fillets or pieces cut off the thick loin meat of a large fillet.

Steaks are less expensive and easier to cook properly. The bone and skin of a steak keep the flesh moist and the uniform thickness allows it to cook evenly. I prefer tail steaks in cod because they have less bone and are firmer than the rib steaks.

Look for translucent flesh that smells like fresh

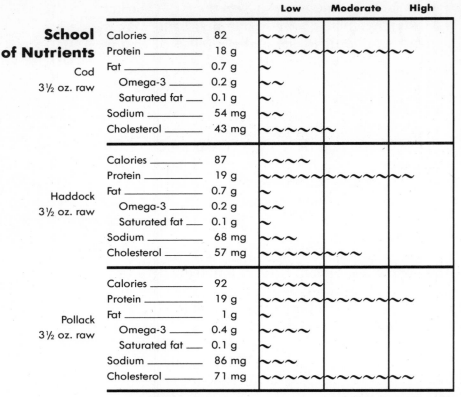

		Low	Moderate	High
Cod 3½ oz. raw	Calories	82		
	Protein	18 g		
	Fat	0.7 g		
	Omega-3	0.2 g		
	Saturated fat	0.1 g		
	Sodium	54 mg		
	Cholesterol	43 mg		
Haddock 3½ oz. raw	Calories	87		
	Protein	19 g		
	Fat	0.7 g		
	Omega-3	0.2 g		
	Saturated fat	0.1 g		
	Sodium	68 mg		
	Cholesterol	57 mg		
Pollack 3½ oz. raw	Calories	92		
	Protein	19 g		
	Fat	1 g		
	Omega-3	0.4 g		
	Saturated fat	0.1 g		
	Sodium	86 mg		
	Cholesterol	71 mg		

Source: Adapted from Agriculture Handbook No. 8–15 (Washington, D.C.: U.S. Department of Agriculture).

seawater. An opaque white surface on a fillet means that it has been dipped in a preservative.

Small cod or haddock, I mean small—2 to 3 pounds for the whole fish—is called scrod. Its youth makes for a more delicate-textured cod. The fillets should weigh no more than 1 pound.

For a real treat, ask your fishmonger to get you cod cheeks—those tender nuggets of meat that nestle just behind the mouth of a large fish and can be scooped out with a knife before or after cooking. I used to cut them out as I dressed whole fish in the kitchen at my former restaurant, the Lewis Street Chowderhouse, in Greenwich, Connecticut. Like most fish lovers, my business partner at that restaurant, Tom Brody, savored the delicacy baked or pan-fried.

Pollack is sometimes sold on the fresh market as Boston bluefish. The more familiar name makes it more salable. It's tasty and firm-fleshed (many people prefer it to bluefish) but *it is not* bluefish. Don't be fooled by the name if you see Boston bluefish in the case—it's pollack.

Pollack also turns up in the fish case reincarnated as "crab deluxe," "nearly shrimp" or some such market name. The natural properties of the pollack flesh make it ideal for mixing with a small amount of genuine crab or shrimp for flavor, and processing into a product named surimi by its Japanese inventors. It is then formed into the familiar shapes of crab legs and shrimp and frankly labeled as an imitation of the real thing. Surimi is intended to offer relief from high-priced shellfish. Personally, I prefer to buy real crab or shrimp when I can afford it and to enjoy pollack for itself as a pure fillet or a hearty steak.

The Fillet Board

These market fish are usually filleted or steaked before they are displayed on ice at the fish market. Look out for pin bones. Because they are so obvious, it is easy to remove skin and bones from the steaks.

Cooking the Catch

These fish are at their best baked or broiled. Most people like their fish tender and moist on the inside, crispy on the outside. To achieve that effect, first brush the fillets with a vegetable oil/juice mixture and dust the top with seasoned flour or bread crumbs and paprika. Then bake or broil at high temperatures for a short time.

For a truly low-calorie dish, steam or poach these fish. Add flavor with herbs, spices and sours such as vinegars or citrus juices in the poaching stock or the steaming liquid.

In my mind there is no better fish for chowder than cod, haddock or pollack. (My secret chowder

Cod	
Market form	**Amount per person (lb.)**
Fillets	¼–⅓
Steaks	⅓–½

Haddock	
Market form	**Amount per person (lb.)**
Fillets	¼–⅓
Steaks	⅓–½

Pollack	
Market form	**Amount per person (lb.)**
Fillets	¼–⅓
Steaks	⅓–½

ingredient is prepared mustard—just enough to spark the flavor.) Add the boneless fish chunks just after the vegetables have cooked, then stir and remove the pot from the heat immediately and allow the chowder to steep for 5 to 10 minutes before serving.

If you like the super speed and nutrient-saving characteristics of microwave cooking, these tender white fish are perfect for that process.

~~~~~~
~~~~~~

Galley Tips
Cod, haddock, pollack (1 lb.)

Technique Market form	Directions	Time (min.)	Temp.
Bake Fillet, steak	Use a flat nonstick pan; brush lightly with vegetable oil or butter; sprinkle with citrus juice.	10–15	400°F
Broil Fillet, steak	Use a flat nonstick pan; brush lightly with vegetable oil; dust with seasoned flour or bread crumbs and paprika; broil 4 inches or less from heat.	8–12	High
Poach Fillet, steak	Use a fish poacher or deep baking pan; combine citrus juice or wine vinegar with herbs and spices in stock or water.	10–12	Simmer
Steam Fillet, steak	Use a steamer rack in a wok; add herbs and spices to water for an aromatic bouillon; cover tightly.	12–15	Med.-high
Chowder Fillet	Cook vegetables, herbs and spices in fish stock or chicken stock; add fish chunks (boneless) last, stir and remove from heat.	5	Steep
Microwave Fillet, steak	Brush with stock, water or juice; arrange fish in 1 layer around edge of dish; cover with lid, loose plastic or paper towel; rotate often; let stand for 2 minutes after cooking.	4–6	High (100%)

Aromatic Steamed Cod with Shrimp

OPTIONS: Haddock, Pollack

---

1 cup water
1 tablespoon Mrs. Dash seasoning
   (lemon and herb)
4 cod steaks (about 1½ pounds)
2 tablespoons julienne of roasted
   sweet red peppers or pimientos
2 tablespoons minced shallots
1 tablespoon lemon juice
6 medium shrimp, peeled,
   deveined and sliced

In a wok or large pot, combine the water and seasoning. Place steaks on a metal steaming rack coated with vegetable cooking spray in wok or pot and cover. Steam over high heat for 10 minutes. Remove and discard skin and bones and place fish on a platter.

Combine peppers, shallots, lemon juice and shrimp in a small saucepan. Strain steaming bouillon into saucepan and sauté shrimp over medium-high heat for 1 minute.

Pour shrimp mixture over fish and serve immediately.

4 servings
141 calories per serving

North Atlantic Fish Chowder

OPTIONS: Cod, Pollack

½ cup diced onions
½ cup diced leeks
1 cup thinly sliced celery
1 tablespoon olive oil
1 small clove garlic, minced
2 cups diced potatoes, covered
   with 1½ cups water
2 cups chicken stock
1 cup clam juice
1 teaspoon Dijon mustard
1 tablespoon minced fresh parsley
½ teaspoon dried thyme leaves
⅛ teaspoon ground white pepper
¼ teaspoon red-hot pepper sauce
2 bay leaves
1 teaspoon Worcestershire sauce
2 cups milk
¾ pound haddock fillet, cut into
   1-inch cubes

In a large, heavy pot, sauté onions, leeks and celery in oil over medium heat until soft. Do not brown. Add garlic and potatoes with water. Bring to a boil.

Add chicken stock, clam juice, mustard, parsley, thyme, pepper, hot pepper sauce, bay leaves and Worcestershire sauce and bring to a boil. Lower heat and simmer until potatoes are tender, 15 to 20 minutes.

Warm milk in a separate pot or in the microwave. Do not boil.

Add fish cubes to stock and vegetables. Remove from heat and let steep for 5 to 6 minutes.

Stir in milk, remove bay leaves, and serve.

4 servings
281 calories per serving

Oven-Crisped Pollack and Potatoes (fish-and-chips)

OPTIONS: Cod, Tilefish, Haddock

½ teaspoon paprika
dash of ground white pepper
dash of garlic powder
½ cup bread crumbs
1 egg white
¼ cup skim milk
1¼ pounds pollack fillet, cut into 8 equal pieces
2 tablespoons flour
2 large potatoes, cut lengthwise into 8 wedges

Mix ¼ teaspoon paprika, pepper, garlic powder and bread crumbs together in a shallow bowl.

With a fork, lightly whip egg white in another small bowl. Add milk and blend thoroughly.

Coat a baking pan with vegetable cooking spray. Dip each piece of fish into egg white mixture and coat evenly. Then coat each piece with bread crumb mixture and place in the baking pan. Set aside.

Coat another baking pan with vegetable cooking spray. Mix remaining ¼ teaspoon paprika with flour in a paper (or plastic) bag. Add potato wedges and toss to coat. Place potatoes in the prepared baking pan and bake in a 450°F oven for 10 minutes. Add fish to the oven and continue baking for another 10 to 15 minutes, or until fish and potatoes are golden brown.

4 servings
257 calories per serving

Poached Cod from Lewis Street

OPTIONS: Haddock, Cusk, Whiting

Although the British favorite, fish-and-chips, was a big seller at my former restaurant, the Lewis Street Chowderhouse in Greenwich, Connecticut, the only customer we ever had from merry old England ordered his cod in this delicate version several times a week. He said he preferred the fish free of the fryer's fat. He was ahead of his time—but right on.

¼ cup sliced leeks
1 small clove garlic, minced
1 teaspoon olive oil
2 tablespoons white wine vinegar
2½ cups water
⅛ teaspoon ground white pepper
¼ teaspoon dried thyme leaves
2 bay leaves
1¼ pounds cod fillet, cut into 4 equal pieces
1 tablespoon minced fresh parsley

In a 4-quart saucepan, sauté leeks and garlic in oil for 2 to 3 minutes. Add vinegar and water and bring to a rolling boil for 2 minutes. Add pepper, thyme and bay leaves. Bring to a boil, reduce heat, cover and simmer for 10 minutes. Remove bay leaves.

Immerse fish pieces in simmering bouillon, return to a simmer and poach for 10 minutes.

Lift out fish and place onto four individual shallow soup plates. Bring bouillon to a rolling boil for 2 minutes and then pour over each serving. Sprinkle with parsley.

4 servings
133 calories per serving

Haddock, Egg and Cheese Casserole

OPTIONS: Cod, Pollack

---

1 cup skim milk
½ cup low-fat cottage cheese
¼ cup water
2 tablespoons cornstarch
dash of ground white pepper
⅛ teaspoon red-hot pepper sauce
¼ teaspoon Worcestershire sauce
1¼ pounds haddock fillet, cut into 4 equal pieces
2 hard-cooked eggs, coarsely chopped
2 tablespoons minced fresh parsley

In a blender, puree milk and cottage cheese together. Pour into a saucepan and bring to a simmer, stirring constantly.

Combine water and cornstarch and add slowly to simmering milk/cheese mixture, stirring constantly. Continue to cook, while stirring, until sauce thickens and coats the spoon. Add pepper, hot pepper sauce and Worcestershire sauce and stir thoroughly.

Place fish pieces in one large or four individual casseroles. Pour sauce over fish, top with eggs and parsley and bake in a 400°F oven for 10 to 15 minutes.

4 servings
220 calories per serving

Crispy Cod Cakes

OPTIONS: Haddock, Pollack

¾ pound cod fillet
1 teaspoon olive oil
2 tablespoons minced onions
1 tablespoon minced green peppers
1 tablespoon minced pimientos
½ cup plus 1 tablespoon bread crumbs
½ teaspoon ground mustard
½ teaspoon Worcestershire sauce
3 tablespoons reduced-calorie mayonnaise
¼ teaspoon paprika

Place fillet in a baking dish and bake in a 375°F oven for 10 to 15 minutes, or until it flakes easily. Remove from the oven and let cool. Flake into small pieces.

In a skillet, heat oil. Add onions, peppers and pimientos and sauté until soft.

In a medium bowl, mix together flaked fish, sautéed vegetables, 1 tablespoon bread crumbs, mustard, Worcestershire sauce and mayonnaise. Form mixture into 4 round, flat cakes.

In a shallow bowl, mix ½ cup bread crumbs with paprika. Gently coat cakes on all sides with bread crumb mixture.

Spray a baking pan with vegetable cooking spray. Place fish cakes on the pan and bake in a 450°F oven for 10 to 15 minutes, or until cakes are golden brown.

4 servings
169 calories per serving

Roast Cod Loin
with Diced Vegetables

OPTIONS: Pollack, Tilefish

2 tablespoons minced fresh
 parsley
1 tablespoon plus 1 teaspoon olive
 oil
1 tablespoon minced onions
1 can (6 ounces) tomato paste
¾ cup diced carrots
¾ cup diced celery
½ cup diced onions
1½ pounds cod loin

In a small bowl, mix together parsley, 1 teaspoon oil, onions and tomato paste.

In another small bowl, toss carrots, celery and onions with remaining oil.

Place fish in a shallow baking dish. Coat all sides evenly with tomato paste mixture. Surround fish with diced vegetables, cover and roast in a 400°F oven for 15 minutes. Remove cover and roast for another 10 to 15 minutes, or until carrots are tender and fish is cooked through. Slice fish into thick slices and serve with diced vegetables.

4 servings
236 calories per serving

Baja Baked Haddock

OPTIONS: Cod, Pollack

1 teaspoon olive oil
1¼ pounds haddock fillet
½ cup orange juice
1 cup chunky salsa
4 pimiento-stuffed green olives,
 sliced
12 strips sweet red, green and
 yellow peppers

Coat the bottom of a flat casserole dish with oil. Place fillet in the dish and pour orange juice over it. Spread salsa over all, top with olives and arrange peppers in colorful cross-stripes along fillet. Bake, uncovered, in a 400°F oven for 15 to 20 minutes. Serve immediately.

4 servings
175 calories per serving

Braised Haddock
on Herbed Pilaf

OPTIONS: Cod, Pollack

¼ cup finely chopped onions
1 small clove garlic, minced
2 teaspoons olive oil
1 cup rice
¼ cup lentils
½ teaspoon mustard seeds
½ teaspoon dried marjoram
1 teaspoon minced fresh parsley
2½ cups chicken stock
1¼ pounds haddock fillet
 freshly ground black pepper

In a deep skillet, sauté onions and garlic in oil for 1 minute. Stir in rice, lentils, mustard seeds, marjoram and parsley. Add chicken stock and bring to a boil.

Gently place fillet on top of rice mixture. Sprinkle with pepper to taste, cover, reduce heat and cook for 20 minutes.

Remove lid and serve from skillet immediately.

4 servings
369 calories per serving

Chilled Cod
with Parsley Relish

OPTIONS: Haddock, Tilefish

---

 2 cups chicken stock
 1 cup clam juice
 1 teaspoon minced chili peppers
   or ¼ teaspoon cayenne pepper
 1 teaspoon crushed coriander
   seeds
 ¼ cup lemon juice
 2 bay leaves
 1¼ pounds cod fillet
 ½ cup minced fresh parsley
 ½ cup minced, seeded cucumbers
 1 tablespoon minced scallions
 1 tablespoon minced capers
 1 tablespoon white wine vinegar
 1 cup pickled sweet pepper strips

In a saucepan, combine chicken stock, clam juice, chili peppers or cayenne, coriander, lemon juice and bay leaves and bring to a boil.

Place fillets in a 9- × 5-inch loaf pan, pour hot stock over fillet to cover and bake in a 400°F oven for 15 to 20 minutes. Remove from oven and let stand for 30 minutes. Place pan in refrigerator and chill for at least 2 hours.

In a small bowl, mix together parsley, cucumbers, scallions, capers and vinegar and let stand at room temperature for 2 hours.

Remove fish fillets from chilled poaching stock and arrange on a bed of sweet pepper strips. Serve with parsley relish.

4 servings
195 calories per serving

Wally's Own
Baked Haddock

OPTIONS: Cod, Pollack, Tilefish

My good friend Wally has a fastidious palate that isn't won over easily. But I did it with this creation that bastes the haddock with a tomato-cheese sauce providing the authentic Italian flavor that Wally loves.

 1 clove garlic, minced
 1 tablespoon olive oil
 3 tablespoons tomato paste
 ¼ cup water
 ¼ teaspoon dried oregano
 1 tablespoon grated Parmesan
   cheese
 1¼ pounds haddock fillet
 1 tablespoon bread crumbs
 1 tablespoon minced fresh parsley

In a saucepan, sauté garlic in oil over medium heat for 1 to 2 minutes. Do not brown. Add tomato paste, water, oregano and Parmesan. Stir to blend thoroughly and remove from heat.

Coat a baking sheet with vegetable cooking spray. Place fish on the baking sheet and spoon tomato sauce evenly over top of fillet.

In a cup, combine bread crumbs and parsley. Sprinkle crumbs over fillet and let stand for 5 minutes. Bake in a 400°F oven for 10 to 12 minutes, or until topping browns. Remove from oven and let stand for 2 minutes. Serve hot.

4 servings
178 calories per serving

Harvey's Sautéed Haddock Cutlets with Basil and Pepper Strips

I zip up these cutlets with red pepper strips and fresh basil leaves in a dish I created for my hometown friend Harvey, and I cook it whenever he comes east from his adopted home in Hollywood.

½ cup flour
½ teaspoon paprika
½ teaspoon ground mustard
⅛ teaspoon ground white pepper
1¼ pounds haddock fillet, crosscut into ¾-inch cutlets
3 teaspoons olive oil
1 sweet red pepper, sliced into ¼-inch strips
¼ cup fresh basil or 1 tablespoon dried basil
¼ cup chopped fresh parsley
¼ cup lemon juice

In a shallow bowl, mix together flour, paprika, mustard and white pepper. Dredge cutlets in seasoned flour and coat evenly.

In a nonstick skillet, heat 2 teaspoons oil over medium-high heat. Add fish and sauté for 3 minutes. Turn over and sauté for another 3 to 5 minutes. Remove fish from skillet and keep warm in a 200°F oven.

Add remaining oil to the skillet and heat for 30 seconds. Add pepper strips, basil and parsley and stir-fry for 2 minutes. Add lemon juice and stir-fry for 1 minute. Remove fish to a serving platter, spoon red pepper mixture over cutlets and serve.

4 servings
223 calories per serving

Broiled Haddock Romano

1¼ pounds haddock fillet
1 tablespoon lemon juice
1 tablespoon orange juice
1 clove garlic, minced
1 tablespoon olive oil
1 teaspoon fresh oregano or ¼ teaspoon dried oregano
1 tablespoon minced fresh parsley
2 tablespoons finely shredded Romano cheese

Spray a broiling pan with vegetable cooking spray. Place fillet on the broiling pan and sprinkle with lemon juice and orange juice. Let stand for 5 minutes.

In a small skillet, sauté garlic in oil over medium heat for 2 to 3 minutes. Do not brown. Discard garlic.

With a spoon, pour oil evenly over fillet and sprinkle with oregano and parsley. Broil 4 to 6 inches from the heat for 6 to 8 minutes. Top with Romano and broil for 1 to 2 minutes more. Serve with lemon and orange wedges, if desired.

4 servings
180 calories per serving

Bluefish

~~~~~~~~~~~~~~~~~~~~~~~~~~~~~~~

As a restaurant chef, I used to buy bluefish along the docks from the first mates of charter boats hired by sportfisherman for a day of angling. The day-trippers usually caught more fish than they wanted, which provided extra income for the mates, a bonanza of cheap fresh fish for me and a happy eating experience that always brought my customers back for more.

And there's good reason for the popularity of bluefish. For one thing, it ranks high among the bargain fish on the market. And for a bargain price you get a lot of versatility. It is simple to bake or broil. I also like to use it in fish salads and chowders. And it tastes really great quickly hot-smoked.

Best of all, bluefish is kind to the cook. Because it is so fatty, you can almost be sure of producing a dish that is nice and moist.

Talking to Your Fishmonger

Bluefish is usually available in the market, but it's most abundant during the summer. The Atlantic Ocean off Florida keeps bluefish coming lightly during the deep winter. Then they start their annual spawning migration up the East Coast. By May, you'll know that summer has arrived when "blues" start hitting sportfishing lines off the New Jersey shore. The small, young and delectable "snappers" are the fruit of spawning off New England in late summer.

Freshness is crucial when it comes to bluefish, so ask to see and smell the whole-dressed fish before any filleting is begun.

In the seafood display, look for bluish gray, translucent fillets with a reddish tinge. If the fillets

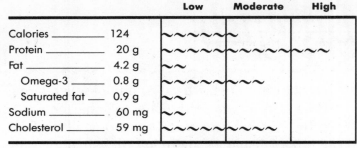

		Low	Moderate	High
Calories	124			
Protein	20 g			
Fat	4.2 g			
Omega-3	0.8 g			
Saturated fat	0.9 g			
Sodium	60 mg			
Cholesterol	59 mg			

Source: Adapted from Agriculture Handbook No. 8–15 (Washington, D.C.: U.S. Department of Agriculture).

are milky gray with a green tinge, I suggest you opt for another fish. I like to see the fillets glistening, moist and, in this case, with the skin on. Bluefish should smell like fresh seawater. If it doesn't, don't buy it.

The Fillet Board

You are in luck if a neighborly fisherman presents you with a whole bluefish caught that morning off the coast. It's the perfect opportunity to enjoy a fresh, whole fish.

Gut the fish immediately if that hasn't been done already. After it's scaled, trim all the fins and head to better fit a roasting pan and the oven. If you prefer, fillet both sides of the fish, leaving the skin on.

One whole fillet (about 2 pounds) is enough for a dinner for four, plus leftovers. Wrap the other fillet for freezing.

You might want to skin a store-bought fillet and remove the row of pin bones. Skin the fish carefully to keep the loose flesh intact.

Cooking the Catch

You won't believe how delicious bluefish is when cooked on the bone! If you get a whole-dressed fresh fish, wash it, rub it with safflower oil and fill the body cavity with your favorite stuffing.

Bake the fish, uncovered, in a moderate oven, basting often. Or roast it in a covered barbecue grill

Bluefish	
Market form	**Amount per person (lb.)**
Fillets	¼–⅓
Whole-dressed	¾–1

with a scattering of fragrant hardwood chips, basting occasionally.

Baking and broiling fillets works best. If you pan-fry or bread and deep-fry, the fillets tend to fall apart. As with all fatty fish, bluefish tends to stay tender and moist under the dry heat of the oven or broiler, with only a touch of added oil or citrus juice.

To use the fish in a salad, bake, steam or poach the fillet before chilling it.

I poach this flavorful fish in savory and spicy bouillon and serve it with a tangy sauce.

Fillets of bluefish cook perfectly in a microwave. Add some citrus slices or juice to enhance the flavor. These fish tend to remain moist, but be careful not to overcook.

One more thing. When serving bluefish, discourage your guests from eating the dark line of meat down the center of a large fillet near the skin side. The dark meat is strong flavored, oily and could contain concentrated levels of toxic substances.

~~~~~~ **Galley Tips**

~~~~~~ Bluefish (1 lb.)

Technique Market form	Directions	Time (min.)	Temp.
Bake Fillet, pan-dressed, whole-dressed	Use a flat nonstick pan; brush fillet lightly with vegetable oil or butter; sprinkle with citrus juice; rub dressed fish with vegetable oil.	Fillet: 10–15 dressed: 15–20	425°F
Broil Fillet	Use a flat nonstick pan; brush lightly with vegetable oil; dust with seasoned flour or bread crumbs and paprika; broil 4 inches or less from heat.	8–12	High
Grill Fillet, pan-dressed, whole-dressed	Use a quarry tile to protect fillet; baste fillet often with vegetable oil/juice mixture; do not turn fillets; rub dressed fish with vegetable oil; turn dressed fish once.	Fillet: 6–12 dressed: 8–15	High
Poach Fillet, pan-dressed, whole-dressed	Use a fish poacher or deep baking pan; combine citrus juice or wine vinegar with herbs and spices in stock or water.	Fillet: 10–12 dressed: 12–15	Simmer
Steam Fillet	Use a steamer rack in a wok; add herbs and spices to water for an aromatic bouillon; cover tightly.	12–15	Med.-high
Chowder Fillet	Cook vegetables, herbs and spices in fish stock or chicken stock; add fish chunks (boneless) last, stir and remove from heat.	5	Steep
Microwave Fillet, pan-dressed	Brush with stock, water or juice; arrange fish in 1 layer around edge of dish; cover with lid, loose plastic or paper towel; rotate often; let stand for 2 minutes after cooking.	Fillet: 4–6 dressed: 4–8	High (100%)

Rosemary-Smoked Bluefish with Creamy Horseradish Sauce

OPTIONS: Sea trout, Salmon

---

    2 tablespoons dried rosemary
    1 pound bluefish fillet, skin on, cut
        into 4 equal pieces
    1 teaspoon olive oil
    ½ cup Creamy Horseradish Sauce
        (recipe follows)

Spoon rosemary onto the bottom of a wok. Place fish pieces on a metal steaming rack in wok, then cover with a dome lid. Smoke fish for 5 to 6 minutes over medium-high heat. *Do Not Lift Lid.*

Turn off the heat. Allow wok to stand for 1 to 2 minutes before removing lid. Vent range area well.

Spread oil evenly on a flat baking dish. Arrange smoked fish on dish and bake in a 450°F oven for 7 to 10 minutes. Serve hot or chilled with Creamy Horseradish Sauce.

    4 servings
    168 calories per serving

~~~~~~~~~~~~~~~~~~~~

Creamy Horseradish Sauce

    ⅓ cup plain low-fat yogurt, drained
        for 1 hour
    2 tablespoons reduced-calorie
        mayonnaise
    2 tablespoons prepared
        horseradish
    1 teaspoon Dijon mustard
        dash of ground white pepper

In a small bowl, combine yogurt and mayonnaise. Fold with a spatula to blend thoroughly. Fold in horseradish, mustard and pepper and blend thoroughly. Cover and refrigerate for at least 1 hour.

    Makes ½ cup

Fillet of Bluefish en Casserole

OPTIONS: Sea trout, Haddock, Tilefish

    ½ cup skim milk
    ¼ cup low-fat cottage cheese
    1 tablespoon cornstarch
        dash of ground white pepper
        dash of ground nutmeg
    2 large potatoes, cooked and sliced
    1 pound bluefish fillet
    ¼ cup sliced scallions
    1 tablespoon minced fresh parsley
    1 hard-cooked egg, coarsely
        chopped
    1 tablespoon bread crumbs
    1 teaspoon olive oil

In a blender or processor, puree milk, cottage cheese, cornstarch, pepper and nutmeg. Pour mixture into a heavy saucepan and cook over medium heat, stirring constantly with a whisk, until sauce comes to a boil and thickens.

Arrange potato slices in one layer in a large, shallow casserole, overlapping slices. Pour sauce evenly over potatoes. Place fillet on potatoes in the middle of the casserole. Spoon scallions, parsley and eggs over exposed potatoes. Toss bread crumbs with olive oil and coat the top of fillet. Bake in a 400°F oven for 15 to 20 minutes. Serve immediately.

    4 servings
    265 calories per serving

Broiled Bluefish Fillet with Lemon and Black Pepper

OPTIONS: Sea trout, Flounder, Red snapper

1	tablespoon olive oil
1	tablespoon lemon juice
½	teaspoon freshly ground black pepper
¼	teaspoon paprika
1¼	pounds bluefish fillet, skin on

In a small saucepan, combine oil, lemon juice, pepper and paprika and stir to blend. Cook over medium heat for 2 minutes, stirring until mixture thickens slightly.

Coat a broiling pan with vegetable cooking spray. Place fillet on the pan and spread pepper mixture evenly over fish. Broil at least 4 inches from the heat for 7 to 10 minutes. Serve immediately.

4 servings
171 calories per serving

Crunchy Bluefish with Apricots

½	cup finely chopped dried apricots
¼	cup finely chopped scallions
¼	cup orange juice
1	tablespoon rice wine vinegar
1¼	pounds bluefish fillet, skin on
1	teaspoon peanut oil
½	cup finely ground unsalted peanuts

In a small bowl, combine apricots, scallions, orange juice and vinegar. Stir with a fork to blend. Let stand for 15 minutes.

Rub flesh side of fillet with oil. Coat a flat broiling pan with vegetable cooking spray. Place fillet, skin side down, on the pan and spread evenly with peanuts. Broil 4 to 6 inches from the heat for 6 to 9 minutes, or until peanuts are crispy brown. Spoon apricot mixture over all and serve.

4 servings
331 calories per serving

Bluefish Smothered with Onions and Horseradish

OPTIONS: Sea trout, Red snapper

1	cup sliced Spanish onions
1	tablespoon butter
2	tablespoons freshly grated horseradish
1	teaspoon cider vinegar
1¼	pounds bluefish fillet, skin on

In a small skillet, sauté onions in butter for 3 to 5 minutes. Do not brown. Stir in horseradish and vinegar.

Place fillet diagonally on a large sheet of aluminum foil. Spread onion mixture evenly on fillet. Fold foil into a tight package and bake in a 450°F oven for 10 to 15 minutes. Remove from oven, carefully unwrap foil and serve.

4 servings
208 calories per serving

Bluefish
Baked on a Bed of Cabbage and Onions

OPTIONS: Sea trout, Mackerel

---

1 tablespoon butter
1 tablespoon safflower oil
3 cups sliced cabbage
1 cup sliced onions
½ teaspoon caraway seeds
1 tablespoon Chinese mustard
2 tablespoons cracker crumbs
⅛ teaspoon paprika
1 pound bluefish fillet, skin on

Melt butter with oil in a large skillet. Add cabbage, onions and caraway seeds and sauté for 5 minutes. Stir, cover and cook for 10 to 15 minutes over medium heat.

In a small bowl, combine mustard, cracker crumbs and paprika.

Spoon cabbage and onion mixture into a large, shallow casserole dish. Place fillet, skin side down, on cabbage, spread evenly with mustard/crumb mixture and bake in a 400°F oven for 15 to 20 minutes, or until crumbs are golden brown.

4 servings
310 calories per serving

Bluefish
Poached in Salsa Broth

OPTIONS: Sea trout, Mackerel

---

1 cup chunky salsa
1 cup chicken stock
1¼ pounds bluefish fillet, skin on
¾ cup julienne of celery
¾ cup julienne of carrots
½ cup julienne of green peppers

In a large, deep nonstick skillet, combine salsa and chicken stock. Place fish flat in salsa mixture and arrange celery, carrots and peppers around fillet. Bring to a simmer over medium-high heat. Reduce heat to low, cover and poach for 10 minutes. Remove fillet to serving plate and top with vegetables and salsa. Serve immediately.

4 servings
206 calories per serving

Baked Bluefish
with Green Peppers
and Tomatoes

OPTIONS: Sea trout, Red snapper

---

1 teaspoon olive oil
½ cup diced green peppers
1 can (15-ounces) stewed tomatoes
1 teaspoon red wine vinegar
¼ teaspoon coarsely ground
  coriander seeds
1 teaspoon Dijon mustard
  dash of ground white pepper
1¼ pounds bluefish fillet, skin on

Heat oil in a small skillet. Add peppers and sauté for 3 to 5 minutes.

In a medium bowl, combine sautéed peppers, tomatoes, vinegar, coriander seeds, mustard and white pepper. Blend thoroughly.

Place fillet, skin side down, in a large baking dish. Pour tomato mixture over fillet and bake in a 400°F oven for 15 to 20 minutes. Serve immediately.

4 servings
209 calories per serving

Sautéed Portuguese Bluefish

OPTIONS: Sea trout, Mackerel

¼ cup flour
1 teaspoon paprika
⅛ teaspoon cayenne pepper
⅛ teaspoon ground white pepper
1¼ pounds bluefish fillet, skin on, cut into 4 equal pieces
1 tablespoon plus 2 teaspoons olive oil
1 cup sliced fresh spinach or kale leaves
8 black olives, sliced
1 tablespoon julienne of pimientos
1 small clove garlic, minced
1 tablespoon minced fresh parsley

In a shallow bowl, combine flour, paprika, cayenne and white pepper. Dip each piece of fish in seasoned flour, coating all sides evenly.

In a large nonstick skillet, heat 1 tablespoon oil, Add fish and sauté for 4 to 5 minutes on each side. Remove fish from skillet and keep warm in a 200°F oven.

In the hot skillet, quickly sauté spinach or kale, olives, pimientos, garlic and parsley in remaining oil for 3 to 4 minutes. Serve fish topped with spinach or kale mixture.

4 servings
260 calories per serving

Citrus–Bluefish Salad

OPTIONS: Sea trout, Salmon, Red snapper

1 pound bluefish fillet, skin on
1 teaspoon safflower oil
1 teaspoon lemon juice
1 teaspoon lime juice
1 teaspoon orange juice
dash of ground white pepper
¼ cup reduced-calorie mayonnaise
4 Boston or Bibb lettuce leaves
4 wedges ripe avocado
4 slices fresh pineapple, ½ inch thick
8 whole, unsalted roasted cashews

Coat both sides of fillet with oil and place in a shallow baking dish. Bake in a 350°F oven for 15 to 20 minutes, or until flesh flakes easily. Discard skin and dark meat. Chill light meat in refrigerator for 1 hour.

In a medium bowl, combine lemon juice, lime juice, orange juice, pepper and mayonnaise. Add fish to dressing and toss lightly. Serve on lettuce leaves with avocados, pineapple and cashews on the side.

4 servings
277 calories per serving

Red, White and Bluefish

OPTIONS: Sea trout, Pollack

---

 1 cup diced tomatoes
 ¼ cup diced pimientos or roasted
    sweet red peppers
 ¼ cup sliced scallions, white part
    only
 ⅛ teaspoon ground white pepper
 1 tablespoon white wine vinegar
 1 teaspoon olive oil
 1 tablespoon chopped fresh basil
    or ½ teaspoon dried basil
 2 teaspoons chopped fresh
    oregano or ¼ teaspoon dried
    oregano
 1¼ pounds bluefish fillet, skin on
 1 tablespoon cracker meal

In a medium bowl, combine tomatoes, pimientos or red peppers, scallions, pepper, vinegar, oil, basil and oregano. Toss to blend and set aside for 15 minutes.

Coat a large baking dish with vegetable cooking spray. Place fish fillet flat in dish. Spoon vegetable/herb mixture over fillet, sprinkle with cracker meal and bake in a 400°F oven for 15 to 20 minutes. Serve immediately.

    4 servings
    190 calories per serving

Bluefish and Green Sauté

 1¼ pounds bluefish fillet, skin on,
    cut into 4 equal pieces
 1 tablespoon catsup
 3 teaspoons olive oil
 ½ pound fresh spinach leaves
 ½ pound escarole, torn into
    bite-size pieces
 ¾ cup scallion pieces
 ¼ teaspoon freshly ground black
    pepper
 ⅛ teaspoon crushed fennel seeds
 ⅛ teaspoon crushed coriander
    seeds

Rub flesh side of fish pieces with catsup. Let stand, skin side down, for 10 minutes on a plate.

Heat 2 teaspoons oil in a large nonstick skillet and sauté fish, skin side up, over medium-high heat for 4 minutes. Turn fillets over, cover and cook for 4 to 6 minutes.

Meanwhile, in a bowl, combine spinach, escarole, scallions, pepper, fennel seeds and coriander seeds and toss to mix.

Remove fish from skillet and arrange on a serving plate. Add remaining oil to skillet and heat for 30 seconds. Add greens and stir-fry for 1 to 2 minutes. Serve sautéed greens with bluefish.

    4 servings
    224 calories per serving

Salmon

~~~~~~~~~~~~~~~~~~~~~~~~~~~~~~

Salmon is the filet mignon of seafood.

One thing that sets salmon apart from other fish is its elegant appearance. A cooked whole-dressed salmon is simply beautiful. That's why it is often poached and displayed in its entirety as a centerpiece for stately buffets. And salmon steaks bring one of the most graceful, symmetrical designs in nature right to your plate.

Chefs often attribute the culinary success of salmon to its color — subtle, pastel when cooked; brilliant and fiery red when smoked and cured. Either way, it's a work of art when complemented by the rich colors of fresh green vegetables and herbs.

Of course, the other thing that sets salmon apart from other fish is its taste. Few can argue that it's a standout when it comes to flavor. Its sweetness, moist texture and attractive color make it the fish of choice among restaurant diners and a perfect showcase for special dinners at home.

Salmon has been in the spotlight for years and its popularity is still rising. So it's no wonder that prime, fresh salmon is readily available. For example, a steady supply of quality Norwegian-farmed salmon is reaching U.S. markets today, just 48 hours after leaving the ice-cold water of the fjords. And our own Pacific salmon fisheries are enjoying large catches of five or six salmon varieties — all top quality — after years of strict conservation.

Aquaculture, an industry in which fish are farmed, is a welcome resource for increased supply, but it will never give us the choice provided by wild harvests.

	Low	Moderate	High
Calories ———— 142	~~~~~ ~	~	
Protein ————— 20 g	~~~~~ ~~~~~	~~~~	
Fat ——————— 6.3 g	~~~		
Omega-3 ——— 1.7 g	~~~~~ ~~~~	~~~	
Saturated fat — 1 g	~~		
Sodium ————— 44 mg	~~		
Cholesterol ——— 55 mg	~~~~~ ~~~		

School of Nutrients

Salmon
3½ oz. raw

93
~~~~~
Salmon

Source: Adapted from Agriculture Handbook No. 8-15 (Washington, D.C.: U.S. Department of Agriculture).

Ask your fishmonger to stock the different types of fresh, wild salmon that are available in seasons throughout the year, so you can get to know the difference in color, texture and flavor.

Talking to Your Fishmonger

At the iced display case, I usually find fresh salmon fillets with skin. If you want the skin removed, ask your fishmonger to do it, or you can do it easily at home.

It can be argued that the thick, front loin of a salmon fillet is the best-tasting meat. And, I have to agree. However, I often ask specifically for the tail end of the fillet. For one thing, there are no pin bones on the tail end, so I start with a fillet that is completely boneless. Also, it allows me to serve guests whole fillets or natural-looking portions by slicing a piece that really looks as though it came from the side of a fish. Serving square blocks of fish cut from a large fillet doesn't appeal to me.

If you do choose that wonderful-tasting loin meat on the head end of a fillet, remember to remove the row of pin bones before you cook and serve it.

Salmon steaks are ready-made portions for every size appetite and they hold up well in the cooking process. Steaks usually cost less per pound than a fillet, but, of course, you do pay for the bone weight.

I consider the bone a plus. Any protein flesh cooked on the bone with the skin intact stays moist longer during the cooking process than the boneless,

Salmon	
Market form	**Amount per person (lb.)**
Fillets	¼–⅓
Pan-dressed	⅓–½
Steaks	⅓–½
Whole-dressed	¾–1

skinless version. (A chicken breast is a good example of my point.) The bones in a salmon steak allow you more flexibility in cooking time and are removed quite easily after cooking.

I look for fillets and steaks that have firm flesh and are brilliant in color. If any slime or off-odor is noticeable, I move on to the next fish of preference.

Whole-dressed salmon is my favorite. There is no more impressive sight than a salmon in full-length glory, head and tail intact, as the focal point for an hors d'oeuvres table or a dinner buffet.

The Fillet Board

Here's what you need to know about preparing salmon:

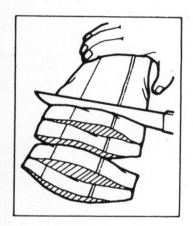

- Salmon should always be skinned before you use it in a casserole or soup.
- Unless you have a large, flat spatula that will hold large fillets, cut them into more manageable portions before grilling, broiling or sautéing. I like to crosscut salmon fillets into thin scallops or thicker loin steaks. You can also butterfly a thick loin steak.
- If you need to remove skin and bones from a raw salmon steak use a short-bladed, sharp knife.

Cooking the Catch

Salmon responds well to most any cooking method. However, I would never embarrass a salmon fillet by deep-frying it.

Because it is a slightly fatty fish, salmon fillets need little, if any, added fat when broiling or baking. Any combination of citrus juice, broth or vegetable oil will do. Ordinarily I avoid overpowering salmon with spicy ingredients. Fillets can be baked, broiled, grilled, poached, steamed, sautéed, steeped in chowder, microwaved or hot-smoked.

No matter what method you use, be careful not to overcook. I start checking doneness after 8 to 10 minutes, depending on the cooking method. If the salmon is a light, opaque pastel in the center, then I know it is fully cooked. If the flesh is still a dark orange or red in the center, I continue cooking for a few more minutes.

After some experience, you won't have to probe the inside of the fish to tell if it is done. The timing will become second nature.

Steaks cook evenly because they are of an equal thickness all around. Both tail steaks and rib steaks are easy to cook. Sometimes I fill the cavity of the rib steak with a mound of vegetables and fresh herbs to protect the thin rib fingers from overcooking.

Steaks can be cooked using any of the methods mentioned for fillets. Once again, I check doneness after 8 to 10 minutes by probing carefully into the center just around the backbone. Steaks usually need 10 to 15 minutes cooking, depending on thickness.

To poach a whole-dressed salmon, use a large fish poacher or a deep baking pan. Fashion a sling of double layer cheesecloth under the fish and gently lower it into a simmering bouillon to cover. Cook, at a low simmer on top of the range, 10 minutes for every inch of thickness. Any fish that requires longer than 30 minutes probably won't fit into your pan.

Gently raise the salmon from the hot bouillon using the cheesecloth sling. Let salmon rest on a sheet pan at room temperature for 30 minutes. Carefully remove the cheesecloth, cover with plastic wrap and refrigerate for at least 3 hours.

To serve, peel the skin from the exposed upper side and carefully remove the gray fatty tissue. Coat with aspic, garnish and serve with a tangy white dill or horseradish sauce.

When the top fillet has been completely removed and the bone structure is exposed, cut the backbone through with a sharp knife at the head and tail ends. Lift the bone structure from the fish and continue serving the bottom fillet. This is really a lot easier than it sounds.

Technique Market form	Directions	Time (min.)	Temp.
Bake Fillet, steak, pan-dressed	Use a flat nonstick pan; brush lightly with vegetable oil or butter; sprinkle with citrus juice; rub dressed fish with vegetable oil.	Fillet and steak: 10–15 dressed: 15–20	400°F
Broil Fillet, steak	Use a flat nonstick pan; sprinkle with citrus juice; brush with vegetable oil; broil 4 inches or less from heat.	8–12	High
Grill Fillet, steak	Cook directly on grill, skin side down; baste often with vegetable oil/juice mixture; do not turn fillet; turn steak once.	6–12	High
Poach Fillet, steak, whole-dressed	Use a fish poacher or deep baking pan; combine citrus juice or wine vinegar with herbs and spices in stock or water.	Fillet and steak: 10–15 dressed: 15–20	Simmer
Steam Fillet, steak, pan-dressed	Use a steamer rack in a wok; add herbs and spices to water for an aromatic bouillon; cover tightly.	Fillet and steak: 12–15 dressed: 15–20	Med.-high
Sauté Fillet, steak	Use a nonstick skillet; mix vegetable oil with stock to moisten while sautéing; turn once; sprinkle with citrus juice in pan.	8–12	Med. to med.-high
Chowder Fillet	Cook vegetables, herbs and spices in fish stock or chicken stock; add fish chunks (boneless) last, stir and remove from heat.	5	Steep
Microwave Fillet, steak	Brush with stock, water or juice; arrange fish in 1 layer around edge of dish; cover with lid, loose plastic or paper towel; rotate often; let stand for 2 minutes after cooking.	4–6	High (100%)

Buffet-Poached
Side of Salmon

OPTION: Whole freshwater trout

---

  2 quarts water
  ½ cup white wine vinegar
  ¼ cup sprigs of parsley, packed
  1 teaspoon mustard seeds
  1 teaspoon black peppercorns
  6 bay leaves
  2- to 3-pound side of salmon
  1 tablespoon unflavored gelatin
  ¼ cup cold water
  1 tablespoon pimiento slivers
  2 scallion greens, slivered into
     long, pointed leaves
  3 small radishes, thinly sliced

In a fish poaching pan, deep roasting pan or large skillet, combine water, vinegar, parsley, mustard seeds, peppercorns and bay leaves. Bring to a boil, lower heat and simmer for 10 minutes.

Place whole fillet on a large piece of double layer cheesecloth, skin side down, and fold the cheesecloth over fish. (Tie each end with a 1-foot piece of twine, making a handle for lowering and raising fish.) Lower fish into simmering bouillon to cover, return to a gentle simmer and cook for 20 minutes. Remove pan from heat and let stand for 30 minutes. Then place pan, with fish and bouillon, in the refrigerator to chill for at least 2 hours.

Carefully raise fillet from bouillon and place on a sheet pan. Keep fillet flat to avoid breaking flesh. Set aside.

Strain bouillon. Ladle 1 cup strained bouillon into a small pan. Combine gelatin with cold water, then add to bouillon. Heat over low heat until gelatin dissolves. Pour into a medium bowl and chill bouillon gelatin in a larger bowl of ice until slightly thickened, but pourable.

Arrange pimientos, scallions and radishes in an artful design on fillet. Spoon slightly thickened gelatin over all and return to the refrigerator to set glaze.

Serve fish chilled. If desired, surround fish with half slices of lemons and oranges.

    8 servings
    157 calories per serving

Baked Salmon
with Island Jewels

OPTIONS: Mako shark, Tuna

  ¼ cup chopped red onions
  ¼ cup scallion pieces
  ½ cup diced fresh mangoes
  ½ cup diced fresh pineapple
  1 tablespoon chopped pimientos
  ½ cup cooked black beans
  1 cup chopped fresh pineapple
  1 tablespoon lime juice
  1 tablespoon olive oil
  4 salmon steaks (about 1¼ pounds)

In a bowl, combine onions, scallions, mangoes, diced pineapple, pimientos and black beans.

In a blender, combine chopped pineapple, lime juice and oil and puree for 1 minute.

Coat a shallow baking dish with vegetable cooking spray. Arrange steaks in the baking dish and spoon vegetable/fruit mixture over fish. Then pour pineapple/lime juice mixture over all and bake in a 350°F oven for 15 to 17 minutes.

    4 servings
    302 calories per serving

Salmon and Fettuccine with Snow Peas

OPTIONS: Red snapper, Ocean perch, Tilefish

½ pound spinach fettuccine
4 teaspoons olive oil
1¼ pounds salmon fillet, skinless, cut into bite-size pieces
½ pound fresh snow peas
1 tablespoon minced shallots or scallions
¼ teaspoon crushed black peppercorns
1 tablespoon minced fresh tarragon or 1 teaspoon dried tarragon
1 tablespoon freshly grated Romano cheese

In a 3- or 4-quart pot of simmering water, cook fettuccine for 8 to 10 minutes.

While pasta is cooking, heat 2 teaspoons olive oil in a non-stick skillet over medium heat. Add fish pieces and sauté for 5 to 6 minutes. Remove fish and reserve.

Add remaining oil to the skillet. Add peas, shallots or scallions, peppercorns and tarragon and quickly sauté over medium-high heat for 1 minute. Return fish to the skillet and toss lightly.

Strain pasta and place in a large serving bowl. Spoon snow pea mixture over pasta, add Romano, toss lightly and serve.

4 servings
486 calories per serving

Salmon Starr with Roquefort and Parsley

My all-out effort to honor Lewis Starr, my mentor in the seafood restaurant business, fittingly features Roquefort cheese. Lew, a seasoned sailor and veteran seafood cook, always demanded the real thing (no blue cheese, please) and was ever on the search for ways to use it.

1 ounce Roquefort cheese
2-3 tablespoons skim milk
⅓ cup low-fat cottage cheese
1½ teaspoons lemon juice
¼ cup finely chopped fresh parsley
1¼ pounds salmon fillet, skinless, crosscut into 12 cutlets
1 cup water

In a blender, combine Roquefort, milk, cottage cheese, lemon juice and parsley and blend on low for 30 seconds. Then puree on high for 1 minute, or until smooth. Add more milk if too thick to blend. Pour into a bowl and set aside.

Arrange salmon cutlets on their sides in a pinwheel formation on a 12-inch round plate.

Pour water into a 14-inch wok. Place plate on a metal steaming rack in wok and bring water to a simmer over high heat. Cover wok with a dome lid, reduce heat to medium-high and steam salmon for 10 minutes.

Remove plate from wok and carefully pour off condensation, keeping salmon intact. Pour Roquefort-parsley sauce around cutlets, garnish with lemon slices and parsley sprigs and serve.

4 servings
248 calories per serving

Purin Simple Poached Salmon with Pine Nut–Pineapple Relish

OPTIONS: Flounder, Haddock

The Purins, my aunt and cousins, are the travelers in my family, and their stories of stupendous dining inspired me to bid for their attention with this easy-to-do pineapple relish to adorn that international favorite, salmon.

½ cup pine nuts
2 tablespoons white wine vinegar
1 tablespoon plus 1 sprig of rosemary or 1¼ teaspoons dried rosemary
1 cup finely chopped fresh pineapple
1 tablespoon minced scallions
3 cups water
4 lemon slices
10 black peppercorns
1¼ pounds salmon fillet

Spread pine nuts on a baking sheet and roast in a 300°F oven for 6 to 8 minutes, or until lightly browned, stirring at least once. Set aside.

Bring vinegar to a boil in a small saucepan over medium-high heat. Remove from heat. Add 1 tablespoon fresh or 1 teaspoon dried rosemary and let steep for 5 minutes. Strain and reserve 1 tablespoon vinegar. Discard rosemary.

In a bowl, combine pine nuts, reserved vinegar, pineapple and scallions. Stir to blend.

In a large, deep skillet, combine water, 1 sprig or ¼ teaspoon dried rosemary, lemon slices and peppercorns. Bring to a boil. Cover, reduce heat to low and simmer for 10 minutes.

Add fish fillet, bring to a simmer over medium heat and poach for 10 to 12 minutes. Remove fish from skillet and drain.

Garnish with rosemary sprigs and serve hot or chilled with pine nut-pineapple relish.

4 servings
314 calories per serving

Salmon Steaks with Honey–Mustard Glaze

OPTIONS: Tuna, Mako shark, Swordfish

1 tablespoon orange juice
1 teaspoon dry mustard
1 teaspoon safflower oil
2 tablespoons honey (preferably orange blossom)
4 salmon steaks (about 1½ pounds)

In a small saucepan, combine orange juice and mustard, stirring to dissolve mustard. Stir in oil and honey and heat over low heat until glaze is well combined.

Brush both sides of steaks with honey-mustard glaze, place on a large, shallow baking pan or dish and bake in a 400°F oven for 10 to 15 minutes. Serve piping hot.

4 servings
255 calories per serving

Big Bob's Broiled Salmon Fillets with Brown Mustard Glaze

OPTIONS: Trout, Red snapper, Whitefish

Though mustard is a magical addition to many types of seafood, none matches it better than salmon. This dressing was born of a conversation with my friend Bob, who serves this combination at every opportunity.

    1 tablespoon rice wine vinegar
    ¼ cup chicken stock
    1 tablespoon brown mustard
    ¼ cup thinly sliced scallions
    1 tablespoon peanut oil
    1¼ pounds loin-cut salmon fillet, skinless
    16 rice crackers

In a small saucepan, combine vinegar, chicken stock, mustard, scallions and oil. Stir to blend thoroughly. Bring to a boil over medium heat and simmer for 1 minute, stirring constantly. Remove from heat and let stand for 15 minutes.

Place fillet on a broiling pan that has been coated with vegetable cooking spray and broil 4 to 6 inches from the heat for 4 to 5 minutes. Remove from broiler and brush brown mustard glaze over top of fillet. Return to broiler and broil for 5 to 6 minutes, basting with any remaining glaze. Serve hot or chilled.

    4 servings
    233 calories per serving

Salmon Fillet in Parchment Paper

OPTIONS: Cod, Flounder, Red snapper

    1¼ pounds salmon fillet, skinless, cut into 4 equal pieces
    2 hard-cooked eggs, coarsely chopped
    2 tablespoons thinly sliced scallions
    1 tablespoon snipped dill or 1 teaspoon dried dill
    ⅛ teaspoon ground white pepper
    1 tablespoon lime juice

Place each piece of fish in the middle of a sheet of parchment paper or foil. Spoon equal amounts of egg, scallions and dill over them.

Combine pepper with lime juice and spoon over fillets. Fold sheets into tightly closed pouches, place on a baking pan and bake in a 450°F oven for 10 to 15 minutes. Serve steaming hot in the pouch or on a plate.

    4 servings
    223 calories per serving

Salmon Stuffed with Wild Rice and Mushrooms

OPTIONS: Red snapper, Ocean perch, Flounder

½ cup finely chopped onions
1 tablespoon plus 1 teaspoon olive oil
¼ cup brown rice
¼ cup wild rice
1 cup chicken stock
¼ teaspoon mustard seeds
¼ teaspoon rubbed sage
¼ teaspoon dried thyme leaves
1 cup sliced small, fresh mushrooms
¼ cup bread crumbs
1 small clove garlic, minced
2 tablespoons minced fresh parsley
1 tablespoon minced scallions
1¼ pounds salmon fillet, skinless, cut into 4 equal pieces

In a saucepan, sauté onions in 1 teaspoon oil for 2 minutes. Add brown rice, wild rice, chicken stock, mustard seeds, sage and thyme. Bring to a boil, cover, reduce heat and simmer for 40 to 50 minutes. Add mushrooms and cook 5 more minutes.

In a small bowl, mix together bread crumbs, garlic, parsley, scallions and remaining oil. Toss until uniformly moist.

Coat a large, shallow casserole with vegetable cooking spray. Place 4 mounds of rice and mushroom stuffing into the casserole. Arrange a fillet on each mound and spoon topping evenly over fillets. Bake in a 400°F oven for 10 to 15 minutes, or until topping is golden brown.

4 servings
361 calories per serving

Skillet-Blackened Salmon with Salsa and Carrot Relish

OPTIONS: Red snapper, Tilefish, Ocean perch

---

1 cup minced carrots
2 tablespoons white wine vinegar
1 tablespoon honey
1 tablespoon minced scallions
1 tablespoon minced fresh parsley
1 tablespoon minced pimientos
¼ teaspoon dry mustard
⅛ teaspoon celery seeds
1 tablespoon brown mustard
2 teaspoons olive oil
1½ pounds salmon fillet, skinless, cut into 4 equal pieces
½ cup chunky salsa

In a small saucepan, combine carrots, vinegar and honey. Cook over medium heat for 4 to 5 minutes. Stir in scallions, parsley, pimientos, dry mustard and celery seeds. Spoon into a small bowl and refrigerate for at least 1 hour.

In a small bowl, blend together brown mustard and oil and rub on both sides of fish.

Heat a cast-iron skillet over medium-high heat. Add fish and sear for 1 minute on each side. Cover, reduce heat to medium-low and cook for 5 to 7 minutes, or just until fish is fully cooked. Serve with salsa and carrot relish.

4 servings
307 calories per serving

Canned Pink Salmon with Lemon Oil and Marinated Red Onions

OPTION: Albacore tuna

1 teaspoon finely shredded lemon peel
1 tablespoon safflower oil
1 can (15 ounces) pink salmon
1 teaspoon lemon juice
1 tablespoon orange juice
1 cup thinly sliced red onions
1 tablespoon white wine vinegar
1 teaspoon olive oil

In a small bowl, combine lemon peel and safflower oil. Let stand at room temperature for 1 hour.

Arrange fish on a platter. Strain lemon/oil mixture and discard peel. Mix lemon oil with lemon juice and orange juice. Spoon mixture over fish and refrigerate for 20 minutes.

Toss onions with vinegar and olive oil.

When ready, serve chilled fish with marinated red onions.

4 servings
204 calories per serving

Salmon and Spinach Terrine

OPTIONS: Red snapper, Flounder, Sole

2 cups fresh spinach leaves
1 tablespoon olive oil
¼ cup sliced black olives
½ cup chopped fresh spinach
1 tablespoon minced shallots or 2 tablespoons thinly sliced scallions
1½ pounds salmon fillet, skinless
1 egg, slightly beaten
⅓ cup skim milk
   dash of ground nutmeg
2 teaspoons sesame seeds

In simmering water, lightly blanch spinach leaves for 1 minute. Drain and pat dry. Lightly coat a small, square baking dish with vegetable cooking spray and line the bottom and sides with half of the blanched spinach leaves.

Heat oil over medium heat. Quickly sauté olives, chopped spinach and shallots or scallions in a small skillet for 2 minutes.

With a sharp slicing knife, slice fish in half horizontally, keeping the blade parallel with the cutting board. Place the bottom half of the fillet on spinach leaves. Spoon sautéed olive/spinach mixture on top and cover with the upper half of the fillet.

In a small bowl, combine beaten egg, milk and nutmeg and pour over fish. Cover with remaining spinach leaves and sprinkle sesame seeds over the top. Bake in a 350°F oven for 20 to 25 minutes.

When ready to serve, cut into four equal pieces with a sharp knife.

4 servings
228 calories per serving

Wok-Smoked Salmon with Horseradish Mayonnaise

OPTIONS: Freshwater trout, Whitefish

---

3 bay leaves
1¼ pounds salmon fillet, cut into 4 equal pieces
½ cup Horseradish Mayonnaise (recipe follows)

Sprinkle 2 tablespoons hardwood sawdust or chips (hickory, mesquite, maple, applewood) around the bottom of a wok (if no hardwood is available, use 6 additional bay leaves). Add bay leaves.

Place fillet, skin side down, on a metal steaming rack that has been coated with vegetable cooking spray in wok. Cover with a dome lid and smoke fish over medium-high heat for 20 minutes in a well-ventilated kitchen. *Do Not Lift Lid.*

Turn off heat. Let stand for 10 minutes.

Serve hot or chilled with Horseradish Mayonnaise.

4 servings
250 calories per serving

~~~~~~~~~~~~~~~~~~

Horseradish Mayonnaise

⅓ cup reduced-calorie mayonnaise
3 tablespoons prepared horseradish
1 teaspoon Dijon mustard
½ teaspoon white wine Worcestershire sauce
dash of ground white pepper

In a small bowl, combine all ingredients and stir to blend thoroughly. Let stand overnight in a covered container in the refrigerator.

Makes ½ cup

Salmon Stir-Fry with Peanuts

OPTIONS: Red snapper, Yellow perch, Freshwater trout

---

1 tablespoon safflower oil
1 cup diagonally sliced carrots
1 cup diagonally sliced celery
1 cup cooked sliced bok choy
½ cup fresh bean sprouts
¼ cup unsalted peanuts
1 teaspoon sesame oil
1 teaspoon low-sodium soy sauce
¾ cup chicken stock or water
1¼ pounds salmon fillet, skinless, cut into 8 equal pieces

In a wok, heat safflower oil for 1 minute over medium-high heat. Add carrots, celery and bok choy and stir-fry for 2 to 3 minutes. Add bean sprouts, peanuts and sesame oil and stir-fry for another minute. Add soy sauce and toss. Remove vegetables from the wok and keep warm.

Add stock or water to the wok. Arrange fish pieces on a steaming rack in the wok, cover and steam over medium-high heat for 10 to 12 minutes.

Remove fish to serving dishes and remove rack from wok. Return vegetables to the hot wok and toss for 1 minute. Serve vegetables and stock over steamed fish.

4 servings
330 calories per serving

Trout

~~~~~~~~~~~~~~~~~~~~~~~~~~~~~~~~~~~~

My first memories of fishing take me back to the Pocono mountains of my childhood. There among the Pennsylvania woodlands I discovered the joys of truly fresh fish. I can remember as a pre-schooler standing with Mom and Dad in the early morning rain, my line dangling in a dammed-up "crick," waiting patiently for a bite. When the family caught enough fish for breakfast, we all rushed back to the house for a delicious meal of pan-fried trout. What a delicious learning experience it was!

Today, trout is still the popular symbol of the true sportsfisherman. In fact, it is the most widely recognized freshwater eating fish throughout the world because it swims in the streams and lakes on every continent. But nowadays, for the most part, you've got to be a sportsfisherman or a friend of a sportsfisherman to get a taste of a fish plucked fresh from the local waters. Due to the pollution of so many waterways, fish markets must depend on cultured rainbow trout, raised in Idaho, for sale to private consumers and to restaurants.

But it really doesn't matter where they're grown —trout is really good eating. And cooking trout is something I truly enjoy.

In fact, every year on a Saturday in May, I prepare 150 to 200 of these cultured trout for the local Wildlands Conservancy's annual outdoor trout roast held on the banks of the Little Lehigh Creek near Allentown, Pennsylvania. I fill a trench 30 feet long, 3 feet wide and 6 inches deep with charcoal and line up pavement bricks down the middle to

	Low	Moderate	High
Calories ——————— 118	~~~~~ ~		
Protein ——————— 21 g	~ ~~~ ~	~~~~~~ ~~~~	
Fat ——————— 3.4 g	~~		
Omega-3 ——————— 0.7 g	~ ~~~~ ~~		
Saturated fat —— 0.6 g	~		
Sodium ——————— 27 mg	~		
Cholesterol ——————— 57 mg	~~~~~ ~~~	~~~	

**School
of Nutrients**

Trout
3½ oz. raw

105
~~~~~
Trout

Source: Adapted from Agriculture Handbook No. 8-15 (Washington, D.C.: U.S.
Department of Agriculture).

hold the roasting potatoes. I tack split trout to 2" ×
12" × 18" oak planks, baste them, then prop them
up around the perimeter of the hot coals. It takes
about 30 minutes to roast the trout in this fashion
but the tasty result is sure worth the wait. Little
Lehigh Trout Chowder, baked potatoes and tossed
salad round out the menu. (The recipes for planked
trout and the chowder follow in this chapter.)

Talking to Your Fishmonger

Rainbow trout is available virtually everywhere both
fresh and frozen. A special effort has been made to
ship freshly harvested trout throughout the United
States so that it arrives at your market the day after
it leaves the water.

The primary market form of rainbow trout is
whole-dressed, sometimes boned. I'm confident that
you will soon see more fresh trout fillets on the ice
at your local fish counter. Fish-loving consumers
are willing to pay the price for the convenience of
fillets.

Another development gaining acceptance is
the coloring of trout meat. Color has nothing to do
with quality; it only reflects the diet of the trout,
and it can vary from white to the bright red of
salmon. Trout that consumes small crustaceans,
such as crawfish or tiny crabs, has flesh tinted
orange to red. Trout farmers can feed their stock

Trout	
Market form	**Amount per person (lb.)**
Fillets	¼–⅓
Whole-dressed, boned	½–¾
Whole-dressed	¾–1

safe, natural formulas that tint the flesh toward the more salable salmon color.

Before you buy a fresh trout, open the belly cavity and sniff. A stale off-odor is a signal to look elsewhere. And don't be afraid to return (quickly) a freshly thawed, frozen trout that gives off an unpleasant odor. Your interest in truly fresh fish will alert your monger that you are a serious fish lover and a good customer to cultivate.

The Fillet Board

There is a myth that trout is a bony fish. Nonsense! It is no bonier than most fish and it is quite easy to separate a raw trout fillet from the bone structure. It's even easier once the trout is cooked. Don't be afraid to try cooking a whole-dressed trout. You are almost guaranteed a moist, tender piece of flesh. If a whole-dressed trout weighs under ¾ pound, it doesn't make sense to fillet it. Cook it whole.

A fresh, raw trout can be filleted and skinned just like any other roundfish. You can remove the fillets of a cooked whole-dressed trout simply with a table fork and knife, if you know the basic anatomy of a fish (page 36).

When plank-roasting, broiling or barbecuing trout, I prepare the whole-dressed fish by splitting it. Starting at the head end, cut through the rib cage inside the gut cavity and through the back skin.

Split the fish from head end to tail end, leaving both halves attached at the center or back.

Cooking the Catch

I like to cook trout by barbecuing, poaching or hot-smoking it, but it can be baked, broiled, pan-fried and made into chowder as well. Once again, the simplest cooking methods are the best for the delicate flesh of this fish.

Of course, the smaller trout must be whole-dressed when cooked. Even larger fish, a foot long and bigger, can be whole-dressed when cooked, but you can also fillet these. When baking large trout, I like to stuff them with rice, herbs or vegetables. Sometimes I combine all three. A slice of pimiento-stuffed olive or red radish is perfect for covering the eye of a whole-dressed fish.

When you poach trout, a classical cooking method, you can serve it hot from the bouillon or chill it for a buffet hors d'oeuvre. Hot-smoking a whole-dressed trout outdoors in a smoker or indoors in a wok provides you with a fish dish that can also be served either way—hot or chilled.

Barbecuing trout is a great reminder of stream-side feasts. To expose the trout to the heat of a flame, I tack it to a water-soaked, hardwood plank or baste a fillet on a quarry tile that can tolerate the intense heat of a barbecue. These two methods give a true outdoor flavor to the cooked trout.

Except for a freshly caught large brown or lake trout, I wouldn't cook a trout for more than 15 minutes. Most small (½-pound) to normal (¾-pound) fish don't need any more than 10 minutes, half of the time each side.

Galley Tips

Trout (1 lb.)

Technique Market form	Directions	Time (min.)	Temp.
Bake Fillet, whole-dressed	Use a flat nonstick pan; brush fillet lightly with vegetable oil/juice mixture; rub dressed fish with vegetable oil.	Fillet: 8-10 dressed: 10-15	400°F
Broil Fillet	Use a flat nonstick pan; brush lightly with vegetable oil; dust with seasoned flour or bread crumbs and paprika; broil 4 inches or less from heat.	6-10	High
Grill Fillet, whole-dressed	Use a quarry tile coated with vegetable cooking spray to protect fillet; baste fillet often with vegetable oil/ juice mixture; rub dressed fish with vegetable oil; turn dressed fish once.	Fillet: 6-12 dressed: 8-15	High
Poach Fillet, whole-dressed	Use a fish poacher or deep baking pan; combine citrus juice or wine vinegar with herbs and spices in stock or water.	Fillet: 8-12 dressed: 10-15	Simmer
Pan-fry Fillet, whole-dressed	Use a nonstick skillet and no more than 1 tablespoon peanut oil; dredge in milk and egg whites, then in flour, crumbs or cornmeal.	Fillet: 8-12 dressed: 10-15	Med. to med.-high
Chowder Fillet	Cook vegetables, herbs and spices in fish stock or chicken stock; add fish chunks (boneless) last, stir and remove from heat.	5	Steep
Microwave Fillet, whole-dressed	Brush with stock, water or juice; arrange fish in 1 layer around edge of dish; cover with lid, loose plastic or paper towel; rotate often; let stand for 2 minutes after cooking.	Fillet: 4-6 dressed: 4-8	High (100%)

Pan-Fried Trout Fillets

OPTIONS: Flounder, Catfish,
Red snapper

½ cup flour
1 teaspoon paprika
1 teaspoon turmeric
¼ teaspoon ground white pepper
½ cup milk
1 pound trout fillets
2 tablespoons olive oil

In a shallow bowl, combine flour, paprika, turmeric and pepper.

Pour milk into another shallow bowl. Dip fillets in milk, then dredge in seasoned flour, coating evenly.

In a large nonstick skillet, heat oil over medium-high heat for 1 minute. Add fillets and sauté until crispy on both sides, about 6 minutes. Remove to a paper towel-lined platter and keep warm in a 200°F oven until all fillets are cooked.

4 servings
266 calories per serving

Trout Amandine

OPTIONS: Flounder, Sole, Scrod

½ cup buttermilk
¼ cup bread crumbs
¼ cup ground almonds
1 pound trout fillets
2 tablespoons peanut oil
¼ cup sliced almonds
2 tablespoons minced shallots
¼ cup milk

Pour buttermilk into a shallow bowl.

In another shallow bowl, combine bread crumbs and ground almonds.

Dip fillets into buttermilk, then dredge in the crumb/nut mixture, coating evenly.

In a large, nonstick skillet, heat 1 tablespoon oil over medium heat for 1 minute. Add fillets and sauté on both sides for a total of 6 to 8 minutes, or until lightly browned. Remove fish from skillet and keep warm in a 200°F oven.

In the same skillet, sauté sliced almonds and shallots in remaining oil for 2 minutes, or until almonds are golden and shallots soft. Add milk, stir and cook quickly for 2 minutes.

Remove fish to a serving platter, pour sauce with almonds over fillets and serve.

4 servings
326 calories per serving

Herb-Stuffed Rainbow Trout

OPTIONS: Catfish, Black sea bass,
Salmon

---

2 tablespoons olive oil
½ teaspoon red-hot pepper sauce
4 whole-dressed trout, boneless
2 cloves garlic, minced
1 cup fresh herbs, any combination
   of thyme, rosemary, basil and
   parsley

Combine oil and hot pepper sauce and rub mixture over outside and inside surfaces of fish, then place on a sheet of aluminum foil.

Divide garlic and herbs equally among fish, filling each cavity. Wrap tightly in the foil and bake in a 425°F oven for 12 to 15 minutes. Serve with lemon wedges, if desired.

4 servings
307 calories per serving

Poached Trout Fillets with Yogurt–Chive Sauce

OPTIONS: Sole, Salmon tail

1½ cups chicken stock
⅛ teaspoon grated nutmeg
1 tablespoon honey
1 pound trout fillets
1 cup Yogurt-Chive Sauce (recipe follows)

In a large skillet, combine chicken stock, nutmeg and honey. Bring to a boil over medium-high heat.

Place fillets flat in bouillon, return to a simmer and poach for 6 to 8 minutes.

Carefully remove fillets to a serving platter and serve with Yogurt-Chive Sauce on the side.

4 servings
171 calories per serving

~~~~~~~~~~~~~~~

Yogurt–Chive Sauce

1 cup plain low-fat yogurt, drained for 2 hours
1½ teaspoons honey
½ teaspoon minced gingerroot or ¼ teaspoon ground ginger
1½ teaspoons snipped chives

In a bowl, combine all ingredients and blend thoroughly. Refrigerate for at least 1 hour to blend flavors. Serve chilled or at room temperature.

Makes 1 cup

Joe's "Pickin' " Trout with Hot-Time Marinade

OPTIONS: Catfish, Salmon

Spice is nice, says my good friend Joe, so it's no wonder that this recipe won his heart when he enjoyed it at our house.

½ cup red-hot pepper sauce
¼ cup red wine vinegar
2 tablespoons olive oil
1 tablespoon Worcestershire sauce
¼ teaspoon garlic powder
2 tablespoons smoke-flavored barbecue sauce
4 whole-dressed trout
¼ cup reduced-calorie mayonnaise
1 tablespoon Dijon mustard

In a small bowl, combine hot pepper sauce, vinegar, oil, Worcestershire sauce, garlic powder and barbecue sauce and blend thoroughly. Spoon 1 tablespoon marinade into a small bowl and set aside.

Brush remaining marinade on outside and inside surfaces of fish. Then place fish and marinade in a plastic bag, seal and marinate in the refrigerator overnight.

Add mayonnaise and mustard to the set-aside marinade and stir to blend. Cover sauce and store in the refrigerator overnight to blend flavors.

Place marinated fish on a nonstick baking sheet and bake in a 450°F oven for 10 to 12 minutes. Remove from oven, let cool for 10 minutes, and then peel off skin. Serve fish with sauce. Cocktail forks may be used to pick meat off fish.

4 servings
311 calories per serving

Baked Stuffed Red Snapper
page 121

Tuna Steak Antipasto
page 133

Greek-Style Catfish
page 143

Salad of Swordfish Ribbons
page 150

Buffet-Poached Trout with Dill Sauce

OPTION: Salmon

4 cups water
½ cup white wine vinegar
4 bay leaves
12 black peppercorns
1 teaspoon dried thyme leaves
4 sprigs of parsley
4 whole-dressed trout
1 cup Dill Sauce (recipe follows)

In a 10- to 12-inch, deep skillet, combine water, vinegar, bay leaves, peppercorns, thyme and parsley. Bring to a boil over medium-high heat. Cover, reduce heat to low and simmer for 15 minutes.

Carefully place fish in bouillon and poach over medium heat for 12 to 15 minutes. Transfer fish to a serving platter to cool.

Cut skin behind heads and in front of tails and peel off. Garnish fish with sprigs of fresh dill. If desired, surround each with half-slices of lemon. Serve with Dill Sauce.

4 servings
357 calories per serving

~~~~~~~~~~~~~~~~~~~

Dill Sauce

⅓ cup reduced-calorie mayonnaise
⅓ cup sour cream
½ cup plain low-fat yogurt, drained
  for 1 hour
1 tablespoon lemon juice
  dash of ground white pepper
1 tablespoon snipped dill or
  1 teaspoon dried dill

In a bowl, combine all ingredients and stir to blend thoroughly.
  Makes 1 cup

Trout Fillets Florentine

OPTIONS: Sole, Flounder, Catfish

1 clove garlic, cut in half
3 teaspoons olive oil
½ cup flour
1 teaspoon paprika
¼ teaspoon ground white pepper
1 pound trout fillets
½ pound fresh spinach leaves
1 cup Marinara Sauce (page 269)

In a large nonstick skillet, sauté garlic in 2 teaspoons oil over low heat for 5 minutes. Squeeze garlic with a fork, remove and discard.

In a shallow bowl, combine flour, paprika and pepper. Dredge fillets in seasoned flour, add to the skillet and sauté over medium-high heat for a total of 6 to 8 minutes, turning once to brown on both sides. Transfer to a warm platter.

Heat remaining oil. Add spinach and quickly sauté for 1 to 2 minutes, or until spinach begins to wilt.

Spoon equal portions of Marinara Sauce onto four serving plates, top with a bed of spinach and lay fish on spinach. Garnish with lemon slices and serve.

4 servings
262 calories per serving

Wok-Smoked Rainbow Trout with Creamy Orange Horseradish

OPTIONS: Catfish, Salmon, Bluefish

¼ cup orange marmalade
1 tablespoon rice vinegar
1 tablespoon prepared horseradish
½ cup plain low-fat yogurt, drained for 4 hours
4 whole-dressed rainbow trout

In a small bowl, mix together marmalade, vinegar and horseradish until well blended. Fold in yogurt until smooth. Set aside.

Spread ¼ cup mesquite wood dust or chips onto the bottom of a wok. Spray the steaming rack with vegetable cooking spray. Arrange trout on the rack and then place in wok. Cover the wok with a dome lid and hot-smoke trout over medium-high heat in a well-vented kitchen for 15 to 20 minutes. *Do not lift the lid.*

Turn off heat and let stand for 10 minutes. Remove lid and transfer trout to a plate and serve hot, warm or chilled with horseradish sauce. Garnish with lemon wedges.

4 servings
315 calories per serving

Tile-Barbecued Trout Fillets

OPTIONS: Flounder, Sole

1 tablespoon olive oil
1 tablespoon white wine Worcestershire sauce
1 tablespoon lime juice
¼ teaspoon paprika
   dash of ground white pepper
4 trout fillets (about 1¼ pounds)

In a shallow bowl, combine oil, Worcestershire sauce, lime juice, paprika and pepper. Add fillets, turning to coat on all sides. Lay fillets flat on quarry tiles coated with vegetable cooking spray, then place the tiles on a hot grill. Cover and barbecue for 6 to 8 minutes.

Remove tiles from grill. Serve fish directly from the tiles or from serving plates. Garnish with lime wedges.

4 servings
197 calories per serving

Pan-Browned Trout with Shiitake Mushrooms and Scallions

OPTIONS: Catfish, Salmon, Sole

¼ cup low-sodium soy sauce
1 clove garlic, minced
1 teaspoon sesame oil
1 pound trout fillets
1 tablespoon peanut oil
1 cup sliced fresh shiitake mushrooms
1 cup scallion pieces

In a baking dish, combine soy sauce, garlic and sesame oil. Add fillets, turn to coat on both sides, cover and marinate in refrigerator for 30 minutes.

Heat peanut oil in a nonstick skillet over high heat for 2 minutes. Lay fillets flat in the skillet and sauté for 3 minutes on each side. Transfer to a warm platter.

Add mushrooms and scallions to the skillet and stir-fry over medium-high heat for 2 minutes. Spoon mushrooms and scallions over fillets and serve.

4 servings
192 calories per serving

Little Lehigh Trout Chowder

OPTIONS: Catfish, Salmon

Every year I serve two huge kettles of this hearty soup—a meal in itself —at the Wildlands Conservancy's annual meeting and trout roast on the banks of the Little Lehigh Creek near Allentown, Pennsylvania.

  1 tablespoon olive oil
½ cup diced onions
½ cup sliced celery
½ cup sliced leeks
½ cup diced green peppers
  1 clove garlic, minced
  1 tablespoon diced pimientos
  1 cup diced potatoes
  4 cups fish stock or chicken stock
  1 tablespoon chopped fresh
      parsley
  1 teaspoon fresh thyme leaves or
      ¼ teaspoon dried thyme leaves
      dash of ground white pepper
  1 bay leaf
  1 teaspoon Worcestershire sauce
  1 teaspoon Dijon mustard
  2 cups canned crushed tomatoes
      (including juice)
¾ pound trout fillets, cut into
      1-inch pieces

In a large pot, heat oil. Add onions, celery, leeks and green peppers and sauté over medium heat for 4 to 5 minutes. Add garlic and pimientos and sauté for 2 minutes. Stir in potatoes, fish stock or chicken stock, parsley, thyme, white pepper, bay leaf, Worcestershire sauce, mustard and tomatoes (with juice) and bring to a boil. Reduce heat to medium-low and then simmer for 15 to 20 minutes, or until potatoes are tender. Remove bay leaf.

Stir in fish, then remove from heat and steep for 5 to 6 minutes. Serve hot in shallow bowls, garnished with parsley.

  4 servings
  217 calories per serving

Planked Trout

OPTIONS: Catfish, Yellow perch, Black bass

---

  4 whole-dressed trout, split
  2 tablespoons olive oil
¼ cup lemon juice
  1 clove garlic, minced
½ teaspoon mustard seeds, crushed
      or ground
¼ teaspoon paprika
¼ teaspoon freshly ground black
      pepper

Soak 2 hardwood planks (2" × 6" × 18") in water for 30 minutes. Wash 12 nails and nail 2 fish, skin side down, to each plank using 3 nails each. Use a nail at the tail fin and each pectoral fin.

In a small bowl, combine oil, lemon juice, garlic, mustard seeds, paprika and pepper and brush over fish.

Stand planks on their sides at opposite edges of a grill, fish facing in. Cover with lid and barbecue for 5 to 6 minutes over high heat. Turn the planks, fish still facing in, so that the other side will cook. Baste with oil/lemon juice mixture, cover grill and barbecue for another 5 to 6 minutes, or until fish is cooked through. Gently test the thickest part of flesh with the tip of a paring knife. The flesh should be solid white throughout. Remove nails with pliers and serve with lemon wedges, if desired.

  4 servings
  255 calories per serving

Red Snapper

~~~~~~~~~~~~~~~~~~~~~~~~~~~~~~

Red snapper is one of those "designer" names among fish. People in the industry are tempted to label all kinds of fish "red snapper" in order to capitalize on its high-profile commercial value. Other snapper species—gray snapper, mutton snapper and yellowtail snapper—are sometimes mistaken for red snapper. So look for, and insist on, the real thing.

The key is to look for the telltale red eyes and red-tinted flesh of the fish. (All red snapper fillets should be sold with the skin on, to make identification easier.) If it's not obvious, you're looking at a red snapper imposter. In California, it is legal to name some rockfish species "Pacific red snapper." However, this is not the real thing and cannot be sold by this name outside of California. Another sign of the real thing is price. You'll pay a premium price for red snapper.

Home waters for red snapper extend from the Atlantic off North Carolina, around the Florida Coast, and into the Gulf of Mexico, but most red snapper in the U.S. market comes from the Florida fisheries.

Talking to Your Fishmonger

Red snapper is usually offered whole-dressed at the premium weight of 2 to 4 pounds, or as fillets at ⅔ to 1 pound. Smaller snappers are usually marketed as pan-dressed fish. If you see a snapper for sale with the skin removed, it's most likely another species of snapper.

		Low	Moderate	High
Calories	100	~~~~		
Protein	21 g	~~~~	~~~~~~~	
Fat	1.3 g	~		
Omega-3	0.3 g	~~		
Saturated fat	0.3 g	~		
Sodium	64 mg	~~		
Cholesterol	37 mg	~~~		

School of Nutrients

Red snapper
3½ oz. raw

Source: Adapted from Agriculture Handbook No. 8-15 (Washington, D.C.: U.S. Department of Agriculture).

You can find snapper on ice year-round at the market. However, prices are best in summer and early fall.

The Fillet Board

Whole snapper is a real bonanza of flavor. I recommend you take a dressed snapper home and fillet it yourself, because the head and bone structure make a fabulous fish stock you'd be a fool to pass up. But don't forget to remove the gills before you toss the head into the soup pot!

Make sure you scale the fish before you fillet it, but don't bother removing the skin unless your recipe calls for it. Some people like to eat the skin if it is crispy.

Cooking the Catch

Snapper is truly versatile in the kitchen. It can be baked, broiled, poached, steamed, sautéed and more. Red snapper skin stays flat when cooked. The skin of other types of snapper tends to curl when cooked.

Red Snapper	
Market form	**Amount per person (lb.)**
Fillets	¼–⅓
Pan-dressed	⅓–½
Whole-dressed	¾–1

~~~~~~
~~~~~~

Galley Tips

Red snapper (1 lb.)

Technique Market form	Directions	Time (min.)	Temp.
Bake Fillet, pan-dressed, whole-dressed	Use a flat nonstick pan; brush fillet with vegetable oil/juice mixture; rub dressed fish with vegetable oil.	Fillet: 10–15 dressed: 15–20	400°F
Broil Fillet	Use a flat nonstick pan; brush lightly with vegetable oil; dust with seasoned flour or bread crumbs and paprika; broil 4 inches or less from heat.	8–12	High
Grill Fillet, pan-dressed, whole-dressed	Cook directly on grill; baste fillet with vegetable oil/juice mixture; do not turn fillets; rub dressed fish with vegetable oil; turn dressed fish once.	Fillet: 6–10 dressed: 10–15	High
Poach Fillet, pan-dressed, whole-dressed	Use a fish poacher or a deep baking pan; combine citrus juice or wine vinegar with herbs and spices in stock or water.	Fillet: 10–12 dressed: 12–15	Simmer
Steam Fillet, pan-dressed	Use a steamer rack in a wok; add herbs and spices to water for an aromatic bouillon, cover tightly.	Fillet: 12–15 dressed: 15–20	Med.-high
Sauté Fillet	Use a nonstick skillet; mix vegetable oil with stock to moisten while sautéing; turn once; sprinkle with citrus juice in pan.	8–12	Med. to med.-high
Microwave Fillet	Brush with stock, water or juice; arrange fish in 1 layer around edge of dish; cover with lid, loose plastic or paper towel; rotate often; let stand for 2 minutes after cooking.	4–6	High (100%)

Red Snapper Soup

OPTIONS: Ocean perch, Black sea bass, Rockfish

---

1 small whole-dressed red snapper (about 2½ pounds), filleted, skin removed and head and carcass reserved
7 cups water
½ lemon, sliced
2 cups sliced onions
¼ cup flour
2 teaspoons safflower oil
1 teaspoon olive oil
½ cup sliced celery
1 clove garlic, minced
1 cup tomato juice
¼ cup rice
1 tablespoon Dijon mustard
¼ teaspoon red-hot pepper sauce
1 cup fresh sorrel or spinach leaves

Cut fillets into 1-inch cubes and refrigerate. Clean head and carcass with running water. Remove gills and entrails.

In a 6- to 8-quart pot, cover head and carcass with water. Add lemon and bring to a boil. Reduce heat, cover and simmer for 30 minutes. Strain and reserve 5 cups stock. Clean pot.

Toss onions with flour in a paper bag. In a large nonstick skillet, brown onions in safflower oil over medium-high heat for 5 to 7 minutes. Remove onions and set aside.

In the pot, heat olive oil. Add celery and garlic and sauté for 2 minutes. Add reserved stock, tomato juice, rice, mustard, hot pepper sauce and browned onions and bring to a boil.

Reduce heat, cover and simmer for 20 minutes.

Add fish and sorrel or spinach leaves. Stir, remove from heat and allow to steep for 5 minutes.

4 servings
307 calories per serving

Baked Stuffed Red Snapper

OPTIONS: Porgy, Ocean perch, Rockfish

---

1 teaspoon olive oil
1 cup thinly wedged, seeded plum tomatoes
¼ cup sliced scallions
1 cup diced, seeded orange sections
¼ cup diced, seeded lemon sections
¼ cup bread crumbs
1 teaspoon snipped dill or ½ teaspoon dried dill
2 red snapper fillets (about 1½ pounds)

In a nonstick skillet, heat oil. Add tomatoes and scallions and sauté over medium-high heat for 1 minute. Remove vegetables to a medium bowl. Add oranges, lemons, bread crumbs and dill and toss to blend thoroughly.

Arrange 2 mounds of citrus stuffing in the shape of long triangles on a nonstick baking sheet. Place fillets on top of stuffing mounds, skin side up, and bake in a 425°F oven for 12 to 15 minutes. Surround fillets with citrus slices, if desired, and serve.

4 servings
236 calories per serving

Skewered Snapper Strips with Peanut Sauce

OPTIONS: Tilefish, Grouper, Ocean perch

1¼ pounds red snapper fillets, skinless, crosscut into ½-inch strips
¾ cup plain low-fat yogurt
½ cup cracker meal or bread crumbs
1 teaspoon paprika
⅛ teaspoon cayenne pepper
¾ cup Peanut Sauce (recipe follows)

Thread fish strips lengthwise onto eight 6-inch bamboo skewers, filling each from end to end.

In a shallow bowl, coat each skewer evenly with yogurt. Mix together cracker meal or bread crumbs, paprika and cayenne on a plate. Dredge skewers in mixture. Place on a nonstick baking sheet and bake in a 450°F oven for 6 minutes. Turn skewers over and continue baking for 4 to 6 minutes, or until crispy and golden. Serve with Peanut Sauce.

4 servings
231 calories per serving

~~~~~~~~~~~~~~~~~

Peanut Sauce

¼ cup orange juice
¼ cup chicken stock
1 tablespoon peach chutney
¼ cup peanut butter
1 tablespoon lime juice
⅛ teaspoon red-hot pepper sauce

In a saucepan, combine orange juice, chicken stock and chutney. Bring to a boil. Quickly add peanut butter and stir to blend thoroughly. Remove from heat. Add lime juice and hot pepper sauce. Stir to blend. Let stand at room temperature for 30 minutes before serving.

Makes ¾ cup

Tile-Grilled Red Snapper Fillets

OPTIONS: Tilefish, Rockfish, Porgy

1 tablespoon olive oil
dash of ground white pepper
dash of ground nutmeg
1½ pounds red snapper fillets, cut into 4 equal pieces
1 lime, sliced into 8 slices
¼ teaspoon paprika

In a small bowl, combine oil, pepper and nutmeg. Place fillets, skin side down, on 4 large, square quarry tiles coated with vegetable cooking spray. Brush fillets with oil mixture, coating evenly. Place two lime slices on each portion of fish and sprinkle evenly with paprika.

Place tiles on a hot grill. Cover and cook for 6 to 10 minutes.

Remove tiles from the grill and place directly on an oak plank to serve, or remove fish to a serving plate.

4 servings
197 calories per serving

Island Chowder

OPTIONS: Grouper, Tilefish, Ocean perch

---

1 tablespoon annatto seeds (achiote)
1 tablespoon peanut oil
½ cup diced onions
¼ cup sliced scallions
¼ cup diced green peppers
¼ cup sliced celery
1 clove garlic, minced
¼ cup green peas
¼ cup corn kernels
¼ cup diced sweet potatoes
1 can (14½ ounces) whole tomatoes (including juice), coarsely chopped
1 teaspoon fresh thyme leaves or ½ teaspoon dried thyme leaves
1 tablespoon lime juice
1 teaspoon Jamaica- or Bermuda-style hot pepper sauce
5 cups chicken stock
¾ pound red snapper fillets, cut into ¾-inch cubes
¼ cup julienne of spinach leaves

In a 6- to 8-quart heavy-bottom pot, sauté annatto seeds in oil for 2 minutes. With a slotted spoon, strain and discard seeds. Add onions, scallions, peppers, celery and garlic and sauté for 5 minutes over medium heat.

Add peas, corn, sweet potatoes, tomatoes (with juice), thyme, lime juice, hot pepper sauce and chicken stock. Bring to a boil, reduce heat, cover and simmer for 10 minutes, or until sweet potatoes are tender.

Add fish cubes and spinach. Stir, remove from heat and let steep for 5 minutes. Serve hot.

4 servings
189 calories per serving

Broiled Red Snapper Fillet with Onions and Sweet Peppers

OPTIONS: Ocean perch, Tilefish, Rockfish

---

1 tablespoon olive oil
1 teaspoon red wine vinegar
2 tablespoons prepared horseradish
1 clove garlic, minced
1 teaspoon fresh thyme leaves or ¼ teaspoon dried thyme leaves
dash of ground white pepper
½ cup diced onions
½ cup diced green peppers
½ cup diced sweet red peppers
1½ pounds red snapper fillets

In a blender, puree oil, vinegar, horseradish, garlic, thyme and white pepper. Let stand for 5 minutes.

Mix together onions, green peppers and red peppers. Place fillets, skin side down, on a broiling pan sprayed with vegetable cooking spray. Spread with pepper/onion mixture and top with horseradish puree. Broil 4 to 6 inches from heat for 8 to 10 minutes, or until the topping is browned.

4 servings
208 calories per serving

Grilled Snapper Fillets with Lime–Orange Marinade

¼ cup lime juice
¼ cup orange juice
1 tablespoon olive oil
2 tablespoons minced shallots or scallions
1 tablespoon fresh tarragon or ½ teaspoon dried tarragon
⅛ teaspoon ground nutmeg
1¼ pounds red snapper fillets, cut into 4 equal pieces
1 lime, cut into ½-inch slices
1 orange, cut into ½-inch slices

In a shallow bowl, combine lime juice, orange juice, oil, shallots or scallions, tarragon and nutmeg. Place red snapper fillets in bowl, turning to coat evenly with marinade. Marinate, skin side up, covered, in the refrigerator for 1 hour.

Cook fillets on a hot grill, skin side up, for 3 minutes. Turn fillets over, baste with marinade and grill for 3 to 6 minutes.

Place lime and orange slices on grill and baste lightly with marinade. Turn once and serve with red snapper fillets.

Variation: To broil fillets and fruit, place on a flat broiling pan, skin side up, 4 inches or less from the heat for 4 minutes. Turn fillets over, baste with marinade and broil for 3 to 6 minutes.

Place fruit slices on the pan and baste lightly. Turn fruit once and serve with red snapper fillets.

4 servings
208 calories per serving

Gulf Gumbo

OPTIONS: Black drum, Grouper

½ cup sliced scallions
1 tablespoon olive oil
1 clove garlic, minced
1 tablespoon flour
5 cups chicken stock
½ cup coarsely chopped sweet red peppers
1 okra, sliced
4 small red-skin potatoes, cut into 1-inch cubes
8 pearl onions, peeled
1 carrot, sliced into ¼-inch coins
1 cup coarsely chopped cabbage
2 bay leaves
¼ cup fresh parsley
1 teaspoon fresh thyme leaves or ½ teaspoon dried thyme leaves
⅛ teaspoon cayenne pepper
8 medium shrimp, peeled, deveined and crosscut in halves
¾ pound red snapper fillets, cut into 1-inch cubes

In a 6- to 8-quart heavy-bottom pot, sauté scallions in oil for 2 minutes. Add garlic and flour, stir to blend and cook over medium-low heat for 5 to 8 minutes, or until lightly browned. Stir occasionally.

Add chicken stock, peppers, okra, potatoes, onions, carrots, cabbage, bay leaves, parsley, thyme and cayenne. Stir. Bring to a boil, lower heat, cover and simmer for 15 to 20 minutes, or until potatoes are tender. Remove bay leaves.

Add shrimp and fish cubes to hot gumbo. Stir, remove from heat and let steep for 5 minutes. Serve hot in shallow bowls.

4 servings
236 calories per serving

Red Snapper and Cucumber Salad with Lime Mayonnaise

OPTIONS: Tilefish, Ocean perch

---

4 cups water
¼ cup lime juice
¼ cup parsley sprigs
2 bay leaves
¼ teaspoon red-hot pepper sauce
1¼ pounds red snapper fillets, skinless
¼ cup reduced-calorie mayonnaise
1 tablespoon lime juice
dash of ground white pepper
½ cucumber, cut in half lengthwise, seeded and sliced

In a 4- to 6-quart pot, combine water, lime juice, parsley, bay leaves and hot pepper sauce and bring to a boil. Place fillets in one layer in hot bouillon. Be sure fillets are submerged. Bring to a boil, lower heat and barely simmer for 10 minutes. Gently remove fillets from bouillon, drain and chill in refrigerator for at least 1 hour.

In a medium bowl, mix together mayonnaise, lime juice and pepper. Add cucumbers and toss to coat.

Remove fillets from refrigerator, break into bite-size chunks and fold into cucumbers and dressing. Serve on romaine lettuce leaves, if desired.

4 servings
188 calories per serving

Stir-Fried Red Snapper and Shrimp

OPTIONS: Grouper, Tilefish

¾ pound red snapper fillets, cut into 1- × ½-inch strips
8 medium shrimp, peeled and deveined
1 tablespoon cornstarch
2 teaspoons peanut oil
1 cup diagonally sliced bok choy
¼ cup diagonally sliced scallions
1 cup diagonally sliced yellow crookneck squash (slices cut in half)
½ cup julienne of sweet red peppers
1 small slice gingerroot
1 clove garlic, crushed
1 teaspoon sesame oil
2 teaspoons low-sodium soy sauce

In a medium bowl, toss fish strips and shrimp with cornstarch, coating evenly. Set aside.

In a wok, heat 1 teaspoon peanut oil for 1 minute over medium-high heat. Add bok choy, scallions, squash and peppers and stir-fry for 3 to 5 minutes. Remove vegetables and set aside.

Add remaining peanut oil to the wok. Add ginger and garlic and stir-fry for 1 minute. Do not brown. Discard ginger and garlic. Add fish and shrimp and stir-fry for 3 to 5 minutes. Add vegetables, sesame oil and soy sauce and stir-fry for 1 minute. Cover and cook for 1 minute. Serve with rice or noodles, if desired.

4 servings
148 calories per serving

Sautéed Red Snapper Medallions with Pineapple–Pepper Sauce

OPTIONS: Grouper, Ocean perch

⅓ cup flour
1 teaspoon chili powder
¼ teaspoon garlic powder
1¼ pounds red snapper fillets, skinless, crosscut into ½-inch cutlets
2 tablespoons peanut oil
1 cup Pineapple-Pepper Sauce (recipe follows)

In a shallow bowl, mix together flour, chili powder and garlic powder. Dredge cutlets in seasoned flour, coating evenly.

In a large skillet, heat 1 tablespoon oil over medium-high heat. Add fish cutlets in batches, and sauté about 2 minutes on each side, or until lightly browned. Add more oil to the skillet as you need it. Keep fish warm in a 200°F oven until all the fillets are sautéed. Serve with Pineapple-Pepper Sauce.

4 servings
274 calories per serving

~~~~~~~~~~~~~~~~

Pineapple–Pepper Sauce

½ cup chopped fresh pineapple (including juice)
¼ cup finely chopped, seeded orange sections
2 tablespoons diced green peppers
2 tablespoons diced sweet red peppers
2 tablespoons finely chopped onions
dash of red-hot pepper sauce
1 tablespoon orange marmalade
2 tablespoons cider vinegar

In a heavy saucepan, combine all ingredients. Bring to a boil over medium-high heat. Stir, cover and remove from heat. Let stand for 30 minutes.

Spoon relish into a glass bowl or jar and refrigerate for at least 1 hour, or preferably overnight, before serving.

Makes 1 cup

Tuna

~~~~~~~~~~~~~~~~~~~~~~~~~~~~~~

If you enjoy tuna right out of the can, wait until you taste tuna fresh from the sea! It's like comparing canned corn to freshly picked corn on the cob.

In case you're one of the many tuna fish lovers who has never sampled this fish fresh, you just don't know what you're missing. Canned tuna is fine for sandwiches but fresh tuna is what you want if you're after a real meal.

Fresh tuna has a tasty, firm flesh that is great for the barbecue grill, kitchen broiler or cast-iron skillet. You should even try turning cooked, fresh tuna into salad. I'll bet you'll never want to go back to the canned product.

Like most other fish, tuna has it's particular varieties. Albacore, for example, is the only white-fleshed tuna and is traditionally used for canning. Only albacore tuna can be labeled "white meat" and carries a higher price tag to prove it. Very little albacore makes it to the fresh market.

Bluefin tuna is highly prized by the Japanese for preparing raw as sashimi. Since Japanese cuisine has become popular here in the United States, we have been seeing more fresh bluefin in the marketplace. The best-quality bluefin tuna is caught off New England at the end of its migration in late summer.

Yellowfin tuna is readily available in U.S. fish markets. Its flesh is lower in fat and lighter in color than bluefin. Yellowfin is known as *ahi* in Hawaii. Blackfin is a small tuna caught off the Florida coast.

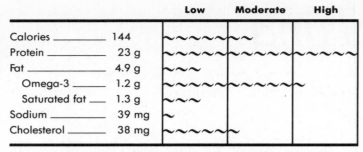

		Low	Moderate	High
Calories	144	~~~~~ ~		
Protein	23 g	~~~~~	~~~~~~~	~~~~
Fat	4.9 g	~~		
Omega-3	1.2 g	~~~~	~~~~~	
Saturated fat	1.3 g	~~		
Sodium	39 mg	~		
Cholesterol	38 mg	~~~~	~	

Source: Adapted from Agriculture Handbook No. 8–15 (Washington, D.C.: U.S. Department of Agriculture).

Bigeye tuna is fished all over the world. Next to bluefin, it is the most prized for use as sashimi.

Talking to Your Fishmonger

As the tuna reaches the northern limits of its migration along both coasts in late summer, the quality is high and the price is low. Keep an eye on the prices; they vary from season to season.

Fresh, raw tuna looks like large slabs of beef tenderloin or beef steaks. It ranges in color from light to dark red, depending on the species. For strictly personal reasons, I prefer the lighter red meat. Generally, fresh tuna is graded in two levels: "sashimi grade," for serving raw and "grill grade," for cooking. Most sashimi grade is snapped up by the Japanese restaurants.

Tuna is displayed on ice in large loins, fillets or thick steaks. I recommend an evenly cut, one-inch-thick steak. Freshly cut tuna should be glistening fresh on the surface and translucent red. If you find tuna that is grayish white on the surface, you know it has been dipped or soaked in a chemical preservative. When tuna is fresh, neither process is necessary.

I have found frozen steaks of tuna in fish markets. I recommend trying them at a price lower than fresh.

The Fillet Board

Once you bring tuna steaks or fillets home from the fish market there is little more to do to them before you cook them. You can cut the boneless steaks into individual portions and cut away any skin or dark meat, which is undesirable because of its strong flavor. The steaks can also be cut into cubes for skewers or chowder and cutlets for sautéing.

Cooking the Catch

I like to cook tuna quickly, right off the ice. Some people, however, prefer to marinate or soak it in a lemon juice solution (3 tablespoons lemon juice to 1 pint of cold water) in the refrigerator for 1 hour, no more.

The firm flesh of tuna holds together nicely when handled during cooking. Tuna steak, in fact, is perfect for the barbecue grill. Steaks 1 inch thick shouldn't be cooked longer than 10 to 12 minutes. If you don't marinate them, brush the steaks lightly with olive oil on both sides before grilling. Broiling, baking, poaching and chowdering are all suitable cooking methods for tuna.

I love to serve fresh tuna in a traditional salad; I urge you to try it because it presents such a happy surprise in flavor. First, poach or bake the tuna until just done. Let it stand at room temperature for 15 to 20 minutes, then chill it in the refrigerator until ready to be mixed with crisp or marinated vegetables. Splash on a light vinaigrette or dab with homemade mayonnaise as the crowning touch.

Do explore the culinary pleasures of fresh tuna. Tuna occupies a traditional status in cuisines of the Mediterranean and the Atlantic coasts of Portugal and Spain. Both hot and chilled, it is a fish that stands up beautifully to the savory flavors of Italian recipes. Try fresh tuna with hot marinara on a mound of freshly cooked pasta. Westward along the coast of the Riveria, tuna takes on a French accent in Salade Niçoise.

Boneless steaks or fillets can adapt easily to beef and pork recipes.

Tuna	
Market form	**Amount per person (lb.)**
Fillets	¼–⅓
Steaks	¼–⅓

~~~~~ **Galley Tips**

~~~~~ Tuna (1 lb.)

Technique Market form	Directions	Time (min.)	Temp.
Bake Fillet, steak	Use a flat nonstick pan; brush lightly with vegetable oil/juice mixture.	8–10	425°–450°F
Broil Fillet, steak	Use a flat nonstick pan; brush lightly with vegetable oil/juice mixture; broil 4 inches or less from heat; turn once.	8–12	High
Grill Fillet, steak	Cook directly on grill; baste often with vegetable oil/juice mixture; turn once.	6–12	High
Poach Fillet, steak	Use a fish poacher or deep baking pan; combine citrus juice or wine vinegar with herbs and spices in stock or water.	10–12	Simmer
Stir-fry Fillet, steak	Use a hot wok; cut fish into ½-inch strips; stir-fry fish first in small amount of hot peanut oil; remove fish; stir-fry vegetables; add fish, stir, cover and steam for 1 minute.	6–10	Med.-high to high
Chowder Fillet, steak	Cook vegetables, herbs and spices in fish stock or chicken stock; add fish chunks (boneless) last, stir and remove from heat.	5	Steep
Microwave Fillet, steak	Brush with stock, water or juice; arrange fish in 1 layer around edge of dish; cover with lid, loose plastic or paper towel; rotate often; let stand for 2 minutes after cooking.	4–6	High (100%)

Oven-Fried Tuna Sticks with Shredded Cheddar

OPTIONS: Mako shark, Cod, Pollack

1¼ pounds tuna steak, skin and dark
    meat removed
1 egg white
1 tablespoon prepared mustard
1 tablespoon water
½ cup bread crumbs
1 teaspoon dry mustard
⅛ teaspoon ground white pepper
2 ounces sharp cheddar cheese,
    finely shredded

Cut fish steak into equal sticks. In a shallow bowl, whisk together egg white, prepared mustard and water with a fork until thoroughly blended.

In another shallow bowl, mix together bread crumbs, dry mustard and pepper.

Coat a baking sheet with vegetable cooking spray. Dip fish sticks into egg white/mustard mixture and coat on all sides, then dredge in seasoned bread crumbs, coating evenly. Place on prepared baking sheet and bake in a 450°F oven for 6 minutes. Turn sticks over and continue baking for 4 minutes.

Remove sticks to a serving platter. Quickly sprinkle cheddar over tops of fish sticks and serve immediately with lemon wedges, if desired.

4 servings
251 calories per serving

Tuna Stir-Fry with Oriental Vegetables

OPTIONS: Swordfish, Mako shark

¾ pound tuna steak, skin and dark
    meat removed, cut into
    bite-size cubes or strips
3 tablespoons cornstarch
3 teaspoons peanut oil
16 snow peas
1 small carrot, sliced diagonally
    into ¼-inch slices
1 2-inch piece daikon radish, split
    lengthwise and sliced into
    ¼-inch slices
4 cups sliced bok choy or Chinese
    cabbage
½ cup fresh bean sprouts
½ cup chicken stock
½ teaspoon sesame oil
1 teaspoon low-sodium soy sauce
1 teaspoon toasted sesame seeds

Toss fish with cornstarch to coat evenly. Set aside.

Heat 2 teaspoons peanut oil in a wok or large nonstick skillet over medium-high heat for 1 minute. Add peas, carrots, radishes, bok choy or Chinese cabbage and sprouts and stir-fry for 2 minutes. Remove from wok or skillet and set aside.

Add remaining peanut oil to the wok. Toss in fish and stir-fry for about 3 minutes. Return vegetables to the wok and toss with fish. Add chicken stock, sesame oil and soy sauce. Bring to a boil, stir and remove from heat. Sprinkle with sesame seeds and serve.

4 servings
180 calories per serving

Original
Fresh Tuna Salad

1 teaspoon safflower oil
¾ pound tuna steak, skin and dark
    meat removed
½ cup finely chopped celery
2 tablespoons lemon juice
    dash of ground white pepper
½ cup reduced-calorie mayonnaise

Rub oil over all surfaces of fish steak. Place in a baking dish, cover with foil and bake in a 350°F oven for 12 to 15 minutes. Remove from oven and let stand at room temperature for 20 minutes. Wrap fish and refrigerate for at least 30 minutes.

In a bowl, mix together celery, lemon juice, pepper and mayonnaise. Whisk with a fork to blend thoroughly.

Flake chilled tuna into a medium bowl. Add dressing to coat fish. Serve on a salad plate or, if desired, on bread or crackers.

    4 servings
    174 calories per serving

Grilled
Marinated Tuna Steak
with Thousand Island
Sauce

OPTIONS: Halibut, Mako shark, Swordfish

1½ tablespoons olive oil
  3 tablespoons balsamic vinegar
1¼ pounds tuna steak, skin and
    dark meat removed
  1 cup Thousand Island Sauce
    (recipe follows)

In a shallow baking dish, mix together oil and vinegar. Cut fish steak into 4 equal pieces and place them in vinegar and oil marinade. Turn to coat all sides. Cover and refrigerate for no more than 1 hour.

Grill steaks for 4 minutes on the first side and 2 to 3 minutes on the second side.

Place steaks on serving plates and serve with Thousand Island Sauce. Garnish with red onion rings.

Variation: Arrange fish steaks on a flat broiling pan and broil no more than 4 inches from the heat for 6 to 8 minutes. Do not turn.

Place steaks on serving plates and serve with Thousand Island Sauce. Garnish with red onion rings.

    4 servings
    225 calories per serving

~~~~~~~~~~~~~~~~~~~

Thousand Island Sauce

¼ cup minced red onions
1 small clove garlic, minced
1 tablespoon red wine vinegar
1 tablespoon honey
⅓ cup tomato puree
½ cup plain low-fat yogurt, drained
    for at least 4 hours
2 tablespoons reduced-calorie
    mayonnaise
1 hard-cooked egg, coarsely
    chopped

In a saucepan, combine onions, garlic, vinegar, honey and tomato puree and cook over medium heat for 5 to 8 minutes. Transfer tomato mixture to a bowl and set aside to cool for 20 minutes.

Add yogurt, mayonnaise and eggs to tomato sauce. Stir to blend and serve immediately.

    Makes 1 cup

Tuna Steak Antipasto

OPTIONS: Shrimp, Salmon, Cod

---

2 cups chicken stock
¼ cup white wine vinegar
½ teaspoon dried oregano
¾ pound tuna steak, skin and
  dark meat removed
6 romaine or escarole leaves
1 cup roasted sweet red pepper
  strips
½ pound part-skim mozzarella
  cheese, sliced into 8 chunks
4 artichoke hearts
6 black olives, cut in halves
1 clove garlic, cut in half
2 tablespoons olive oil
3 tablespoons red wine vinegar
1 tablespoon chopped fresh basil
  or 1 teaspoon dried basil
1 tablespoon chopped fresh
  parsley
1 tablespoon freshly shredded
  Romano cheese

In a skillet, combine chicken stock, white wine vinegar and oregano. Bring to a boil, reduce heat and simmer for 5 minutes. Add fish, return to a simmer and poach for 8 to 10 minutes. Remove fish and set aside to cool. Discard stock.

Arrange romaine or escarole leaves on a large serving platter. Then arrange peppers, mozzarella, artichoke hearts and olives in mounds on the platter, leaving two spaces for the fish.

Rub a small bowl with garlic and then discard garlic. Whisk in oil, red wine vinegar, basil, parsley and Romano.

Break fish into large pieces and arrange in two mounds on the platter. Whisk dressing again and drizzle it over all. Let stand for 15 minutes before serving.

4 servings
436 calories per serving

Vince's Herbed Tuna Melt

OPTIONS: Tilefish, Freshwater trout

When I served this fresh tuna appetizer to my father, he loved it. This is sure to be a standard on the homestead menu.

2 cups water
1 tablespoon lemon juice
½ pound tuna steak, skin and dark
  meat removed
2 teaspoons olive oil
¼ teaspoon dried oregano
8 thin slices French bread
8 thin, diagonal slices plum
  tomatoes
8 fresh basil leaves
¼ pound part-skim mozzarella
  cheese, shredded or thinly
  sliced
1 tablespoon chopped fresh
  parsley

In a saucepan, combine water and lemon juice and bring to a boil. Add fish, bring to a simmer over medium heat and poach for 10 to 12 minutes. Remove fish from skillet and drain.

In a bowl, flake fish into small pieces with a fork. Add oil and oregano and mix with a fork to blend.

Spread flaked fish on bread. Lay tomato slices over fish, then add basil leaves. Top with mozzarella and sprinkle with parsley. Place open sandwiches on a baking sheet and bake in a 450°F oven until cheese melts. Serve hot from the oven.

4 servings
351 calories per serving

Tuna Steak Dionne

OPTIONS: Halibut, Swordfish, Mako shark

Dionne Warwick, one of my favorite singers, inspired this original recipe, using the technique of the classic Steak Diane, but featuring meaty tuna instead of beef.

1 pound tuna steak, skin and dark meat removed
¼ cup flour
2 teaspoons safflower oil
2 teaspoons butter
2 tablespoons minced shallots or scallions
1 tablespoon chopped capers
1 tablespoon minced fresh parsley
1 teaspoon Dijon mustard
1 teaspoon Worcestershire sauce
¼ cup clam juice or chicken stock
4 mushroom caps

Cut fish steak into 4 equal pieces and dust all surfaces with flour. Heat oil in a nonstick skillet over medium-high heat. Add fish and sauté for 3 minutes on each side. Remove and reserve steaks. Pour off oil.

Melt butter in the skillet. Add shallots or scallions and capers and sauté for 1 minute. Stir in parsley, mustard, Worcestershire sauce and clam juice or chicken stock and cook for 2 minutes.

Return fish to the skillet and cook 2 minutes on each side, coating with sauce. Remove fish to serving plates. Add mushroom caps to the skillet and quickly cook for 1 minute in remaining sauce. Pour sauce over steaks, topping each one with a mushroom cap. Garnish with fresh parsley sprigs.

4 servings
175 calories per serving

Portuguese Tuna Stew

OPTIONS: Cod, Pollack, Shrimp

¼ pound garlic sausage, thinly sliced
1 tablespoon olive oil
½ cup sliced celery
½ cup diced onions
½ cup diced sweet red peppers
1 clove garlic, minced
5 cups fish stock or chicken stock
1 large potato, cut into chunks
1 cup canned crushed tomatoes
8 black olives
1 bay leaf
2 tablespoons lemon juice
¾ pound tuna steak, skin and dark meat removed
1 cup torn fresh kale or spinach leaves
1 tablespoon minced fresh parsley

In a 6- to 8-quart, heavy-bottom pot, brown sausage slices in oil over medium-high heat for 5 minutes. Add celery, onions, peppers and garlic, stir and sauté for 3 minutes.

Add fish stock or chicken stock, potatoes, tomatoes, olives, bay leaf and lemon juice and bring to a boil. Cover, reduce heat to medium-low and simmer for 20 minutes.

Cut fish into bite-size chunks and add to stew along with kale or spinach and parsley. Stir, cover and remove from heat. Allow to steep for 10 minutes before serving.

4 servings
313 calories per serving

Tuna Torpedoes with Cucumber Tartar Sauce

OPTIONS: Cod, Tilefish, Salmon

- 2 cups water
- 2 tablespoons cider vinegar
- ¾ pound tuna steak, skin and dark meat removed
- 1 teaspoon safflower oil
- ½ cup minced celery
- 1 tablespoon minced onions
- 2 tablespoons minced pimientos
- ½ cup plain low-fat yogurt, drained overnight
- ¼ cup reduced-calorie mayonnaise
- 1 large egg, slightly beaten
  dash of ground white pepper
  dash of ground nutmeg
- ¾ cup bread crumbs
- 1 tablespoon dried parsley
- 4 Italian hard rolls, split
- ½ cup Cucumber Tartar Sauce (recipe follows)

In a deep skillet, combine water and vinegar and bring to a simmer over medium-high heat. Add fish, return to a simmer and poach for 10 minutes. Remove fish and set aside to cool.

In a small skillet, heat oil. Add celery and onions and sauté over medium heat for 3 minutes.

In a medium bowl, mix together the sautéed vegetables, pimientos, yogurt, mayonnaise, egg, pepper, nutmeg and 2 tablespoons bread crumbs and blend thoroughly. Using a fork, flake fish into the bowl and gently fold fish flakes into vegetable mixture.

In a shallow bowl, combine remaining bread crumbs and parsley. Spray a baking sheet with vegetable cooking spray. Form fish mixture into four 5-inch cylinders. Flatten torpedoes slightly and dredge in bread crumbs, coating evenly on all sides. Place on prepared baking sheet and bake in a 450°F oven for 10 to 12 minutes, or until evenly browned. Serve on Italian hard rolls with Cucumber Tartar Sauce.

4 servings
669 calories per serving

~~~~~~~~~~~~~~~~

Cucumber Tartar Sauce

- ⅓ cup finely diced cucumbers
- 4 pimiento-stuffed green olives, finely chopped
- 1 tablespoon minced onions
- 1 tablespoon Dijon mustard
- 1 teaspoon lemon juice
- 2 tablespoons reduced-calorie mayonnaise

In a bowl, mix together all ingredients and blend thoroughly. Let stand for 20 minutes before serving.

Makes ½ cup

California Tuna Broil

OPTIONS: Mako shark, Swordfish, Halibut

2 tablespoons olive oil
¼ cup orange juice
1 tablespoon minced fresh cilantro
  or 1 teaspoon dried parsley
1¼ pounds tuna steak, skin and dark
  meat removed
¼ cup Guacamole (page 269)
¼ cup Wasabi White Sauce (page
  268)
¼ cup Cocktail Sauce (page 269)

In a wide, shallow bowl, combine oil, orange juice and cilantro or parsley. Cut fish steak into 4 equal pieces and place them in marinade. Turn to coat all sides. Cover and refrigerate for no more than 1 hour.

Arrange fish on a flat broiling pan and broil no more than 4 inches from the heat for 6 to 8 minutes. Do not turn over.

To serve, cut each steak crosswise into ½-inch slices. Place fish on serving plates and serve with a tablespoon each of Guacamole, Wasabi White Sauce and Cocktail Sauce. Garnish with avocado slices and orange slices.

4 servings
312 calories per serving

Tuna Piccata

OPTIONS: Mako shark, Salmon, Swordfish

1 pound tuna steak, skin and dark
  meat removed
½ cup flour
1 clove garlic, cut in half
1 tablespoon olive oil
1 tablespoon butter
1 lemon, cut into 8 slices

Slice ½-inch cutlets on the bias from fish steak. Dredge each cutlet in flour, coating both sides evenly.

In a large nonstick skillet, sauté garlic in oil for 2 minutes over medium heat. Do not brown. Discard garlic. Add cutlets and sauté for 1 minute on each side. Be careful not to overcook. Remove fish from skillet and keep warm in a 200°F oven.

When all the fish has been cooked, discard oil and melt butter in the skillet over medium-high heat. Sauté lemon slices for 3 to 4 minutes, turning once. Pour butter and pan juices over fish cutlets and serve with sautéed lemon slices. Garnish with minced fresh parsley.

4 servings
222 calories per serving

Catfish

~~~~~~~~~~~~~~~~~~~~~~~~~~~~

At one time, catfish was the poor boy of the fish world. Restaurants, for the most part, shunned it, considering this mud lover too lowly to grace a respectable menu. Now catfish has gone upscale— thanks to some smart enterprising and a lobby of sorts known as the Catfish Farmers of America.

What you're seeing in markets today—and catfish is getting a fair shake in the display case—is actually channel catfish being grown and marketed by the U.S. aquaculture industry. You'll find it displayed fresh on ice in the most upscale fish markets and even on the menus of the finest restaurants.

And well it should be. As a youngster, I caught my fair share of this bottom feeder using a worm and sinker and I never got tired of its taste. Along with other fish lovers, I've taken full advantage of the new breed of catfish and can tell you that it too tastes great. It's firm when cooked yet tender to the bite and delicate in flavor. The small bone structure makes it simple to prepare and to eat. It is a perfect choice for fish salads, soups, chowders and stews because it doesn't flake apart when cooking or handling. Another nice thing is that it is inexpensive.

Almost 85 percent of the farmed catfish are grown in Mississippi. Farmers can raise 4,000 to 7,000 catfish per acre—and fast since fingerling (baby) catfish grow to market size (1 to 1½ pounds) in seven months.

Talking to your Fishmonger

Fresh and frozen catfish is always skinned and can appear on display in one of six market forms: whole-

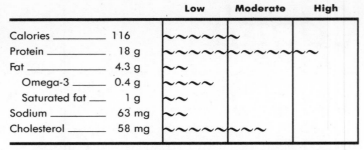

			Low	Moderate	High
Calories	————	116	~~~~~		
Protein	————	18 g	~~~~~	~~~~	~~
Fat	————	4.3 g	~~		
Omega-3	————	0.4 g	~~		
Saturated fat	——	1 g	~~		
Sodium	————	63 mg	~~		
Cholesterol	————	58 mg	~~~~~	~~	

Source: Adapted from Agriculture Handbook No. 8–15 (Washington, D.C.: U.S. Department of Agriculture).

dressed (headless, gutted and skinless), whole fillets (whole side, skinless), shank fillets (whole fillet with nugget removed), steaks (cross section of whole-dressed fish), strips (sliced shank fillet) and nuggets (belly part of whole fillet).

The market forms of catfish are unique. For example, a whole-dressed catfish is not the same as a whole-dressed flounder. Catfish terms, however, are recognized by almost everyone in the catfish industry from the processors to the retail fishmongers. Using the terms above, you can order specific cuts from your fish counter. And, with the move toward elaborate iced displays of fresh fish in supermarkets, you will probably see more fresh catfish than ever before. (In some supermarkets, catfish is usually sold frozen and vacuum-packed).

The Fillet Board

The catfish farmers have taken all the work out of preparing catfish in the home kitchen. If, however, you ever find yourself with a whole-dressed catfish, you will probably want to skin it before you cook it. (By the way, catfish has no scales.)

The easiest way to skin a catfish is to hammer a ten penny (or larger) nail through a 1- × 6-inch plank so the point protrudes straight through the back side. Lay the board flat with the nail point

Catfish	
Market form	**Amount per person (lb.)**
Fillets	¼–⅓
Nuggets and strips	¼–⅓
Steaks	⅓–½
Whole-dressed	½–¾

sticking straight up. With a sharp knife, slice the skin completely around the fish behind the head and both pectoral fins. Slam the catfish head down on the nail, impaling it until the fish sits flat, belly down, on the board. Grab the sliced skin with standard pliers. Holding the board, pull back on the skin, stripping it off the fish from head to tail. Sometimes it all comes off in one piece.

Cooking the Catch

Catfish can be cooked using just about any method. The key is to avoid overcooking; no more than 20 minutes for any market-size catfish, and less for the smaller fish and fillets.

Catfish is ideal for use in fish salads. Poach or bake the fish until just cooked, then chill it for at least 1 hour before breaking it up. That way it stays in nice, bite-size chunks and mixes well with salad dressing.

I also like to add raw pieces of catfish to hot soup or chowder at the last minute, just before I take the pot off the heat. Simply stir the fish in and let it steep for 5 minutes. (That's enough to cook it.) Catfish is also perfect for gumbos and casseroles.

Galley Tips

Catfish (1 lb.)

Technique Market form	Directions	Time (min.)	Temp.
Bake Fillet, steak, whole-dressed, nuggets and strips	Use a flat nonstick pan; brush lightly with vegetable oil/juice mixture; rub dressed fish with vegetable oil.	Fillet, steak, nuggets and strips: 8–12 dressed: 10–15	400°F
Broil Fillet, steak	Use a flat nonstick pan; brush lightly with vegetable oil; dust with seasoned flour or bread crumbs and paprika; broil 4 inches or less from heat.	8–12	High
Grill Fillet, steak, whole-dressed	Cook directly on grill; baste often with vegetable oil/juice mixture; turn once; rub dressed fish with vegetable oil.	Fillet and steak: 6–10 dressed: 10–15	High
Poach Fillet, steak, whole-dressed, nuggets and strips	Use a fish poacher or deep baking pan; combine citrus juice or wine vinegar with herbs and spices in stock or water.	Fillet, steak, nuggets and strips: 10–12 dressed: 12–15	Simmer
Stir-fry Fillet, nuggets and strips	Use a hot wok; cut fillet into ½-inch strips; stir-fry fish first in small amount of hot peanut oil; remove fish; stir-fry vegetables; add fish, stir, cover and steam for 1 minute.	5–10	Med.-high to high
Pan-fry Fillet, steak, whole-dressed, nuggets and strips	Use a nonstick skillet and no more than 1 tablespoon peanut oil; dredge in milk and egg whites, then in flour, crumbs or cornmeal.	Fillet, steak, nuggets and strips: 8–10 dressed: 10–15	Med. to med.-high
Chowder Fillet, nuggets and strips	Cook vegetables, herbs and spices in fish stock or chicken stock; add fish chunks (boneless) last, stir and remove from heat.	5	Steep
Microwave Fillet, steak, whole-dressed, nuggets and strips	Brush with stock, water or juice; arrange fish in 1 layer around edge of dish; cover with lid, loose plastic or paper towel; rotate often; let stand for 2 minutes after cooking.	Fillet, steak, nuggets and strips: 4–6 dressed: 5–8	High (100%)

Catfish, Turkey and Shrimp Casserole

OPTIONS: Tilefish, Mako shark
Red snapper

¼ cup diced onions
½ cup sliced celery
¼ cup diced sweet red peppers
½ cup diced green peppers
1 tablespoon peanut oil
1 clove garlic, minced
¾ pound catfish fillet, cut into
    2-inch chunks
¼ pound medium shrimp, peeled
    and deveined
1 cup diced smoked turkey
1 cup rice
1¼ cups chicken stock
1 cup chopped canned tomatoes,
    (including juice)
1 tablespoon lemon juice
½ teaspoon paprika
⅛ teaspoon ground allspice
¼ teaspoon dried thyme leaves
    dash of cayenne pepper
    dash of ground white pepper
1 tablespoon chopped fresh
    parsley

In a skillet, sauté onions, celery, red peppers and green peppers in oil over medium-high heat for 2 minutes. Add garlic and cook 1 minute.

In a large casserole with lid, blend together sautéed vegetables, fish chunks, shrimp, turkey and rice.

In a small saucepan, bring chicken stock and tomatoes (with juice) to a boil. Stir in lemon juice, paprika, allspice, thyme, cayenne, white pepper and parsley and then pour over rice mixture. Stir, cover and bake in a 400°F oven for 20 minutes, or until the moisture has been absorbed by rice. Serve directly from the oven.

    4 servings
    394 calories per serving

Mississippi Catfish Gumbo

OPTIONS: Yellow perch, Freshwater trout, Red snapper

5 cups chicken stock or water
1½ pounds whole catfish,
    pan-dressed and skinless
1 cup canned crushed tomatoes
¼ cup rice
1 cup fresh okra pieces
¼ cup chopped fresh parsley
1 teaspoon minced fresh chili
    peppers
½ cup diced turnips
¼ cup sliced scallions
½ cup sliced celery
¼ cup diced green peppers
2 teaspoons olive oil

In a large pot, bring chicken stock or water to a boil over medium-high heat. Add fish and poach for 10 minutes. Remove fish and set aside to cool.

Add tomatoes, rice, okra, parsley, chili peppers and turnips to poaching liquid and simmer for 20 minutes.

In a skillet, sauté scallions, celery and green peppers in oil over medium heat for 3 minutes. Add sautéed vegetables to rice mixture.

Flake cooked fish from its bone structure and add it to rice mixture. Stir and remove from heat. Serve gumbo hot in shallow bowls, garnished with chopped fresh parsley.

    4 servings
    311 calories per serving

Milk-Poached Catfish with Tomato–Mustard Sauce

OPTIONS: Red snapper, Tilefish, Yellow perch

1¼ cups chicken stock
1¼ cups skim milk
¼ cup Dijon mustard
1 tablespoon snipped dill or
    1 teaspoon dried dill
⅛ teaspoon ground white pepper
1¼ pounds catfish fillets
½ cup Tomato-Mustard Sauce
    (recipe follows)

In a deep skillet, combine chicken stock, milk, mustard, dill and pepper. Stir and bring to a simmer over medium heat. Add fish fillets, return to a simmer and poach for 8 to 10 minutes.

Transfer fillets to a serving platter, spoon Tomato-Mustard Sauce over all and serve.

4 servings
190 calories per serving

~~~~~~~~~~~~~~~

Tomato-Mustard Sauce

1 tablespoon minced onions
½ teaspoon olive oil
¼ cup tomato puree
2 tablespoons Dijon mustard
2 tablespoons low-fat cottage
    cheese
1½ teaspoons skim milk

In a saucepan, sauté onions in oil over medium heat for 3 minutes, or until soft. Add tomato puree and mustard and continue to cook for 3 minutes. Stir frequently.

Place cottage cheese and milk in a blender and puree until smooth. Add to pan, stir, remove from heat and serve.

Makes ½ cup

Spicy Smoked Catfish

OPTIONS: Red snapper, Tilefish, Shrimp

1 teaspoon red-hot pepper sauce
¼ cup catsup
1 teaspoon red wine vinegar
1 teaspoon olive oil
1 teaspoon white wine
    Worcestershire sauce
1 pound catfish fillets
2 tablespoons whole mixed
    pickling spice

In a shallow bowl, combine hot pepper sauce, catsup, vinegar, oil and Worcestershire sauce. Add fish fillets and turn to coat evenly on all surfaces. Cover bowl and place in refrigerator to marinate for 1 hour.

Spoon pickling spice onto the bottom of a wok. Pat fish dry with a paper towel and place fillets on a metal steaming rack in wok and cover with a dome lid.

Smoke fish for 10 minutes over medium-high heat. *Do not lift lid.*

Turn off heat and allow to stand for 10 minutes before removing lid. Vent range area well.

Test doneness by gently probing flesh with the tip of a paring knife. It should be opaque. If necessary, finish cooking in a 400°F oven for a few minutes (this step is needed if fish is unusually thick). Serve hot from the wok or chilled.

4 servings
157 calories per serving

Cagey Catfish Salad

OPTIONS: Yellow perch, Red snapper, Salmon

  ¾ pound catfish fillet
  1 teaspoon safflower oil
  1 cup thinly sliced celery
  1 tablespoon minced scallions
    dash of ground white pepper
  1 tablespoon lime juice
  4 red-leaf lettuce leaves
  1 cup alfalfa sprouts

Lightly rub fish with oil. Place fish on a baking sheet and bake in a 400°F oven for 8 to 10 minutes, then chill in the refrigerator for at least 30 minutes.

In a bowl, combine celery, scallions, pepper and lime juice. Break chilled fish into pieces and toss lightly with celery/scallion mixture. Spoon equal amounts of salad onto each lettuce leaf. Place a tuft of sprouts next to salad and garnish with lime twists.

  4 servings
  122 calories per serving

Greek-Style Catfish

OPTIONS: Red snapper, Tilefish, Grouper

---

  2 tablespoons olive oil
  ¼ cup chopped, seeded lemon
    sections
  1 tablespoon minced scallions
  1 tablespoon minced black olives
  1 tablespoon minced fresh parsley
  1 teaspoon minced fresh oregano
    or ¼ teaspoon dried oregano
  1 small clove garlic, minced
  1¼ pounds catfish fillets

In a bowl, combine oil, lemons, scallions, olives, parsley, oregano and garlic.

Lightly spray a broiling pan with vegetable cooking spray. Place fish fillets on the pan and spoon lemon/scallion mixture evenly over fillets. Broil 4 inches from heat for 6 to 8 minutes, or until topping just starts to brown.

Transfer fish to a platter and spoon any remaining topping from the pan onto fillets. Garnish with lemon slices, black olive slices and fresh parsley sprigs.

  4 servings
  208 calories per serving

Baked Catfish Fillets with Spiced Topping

OPTIONS: Red snapper, Tilefish, Grouper

  ¼ cup bread crumbs
  ¼ teaspoon ground coriander
  ¼ teaspoon ground cumin
  ⅛ teaspoon garlic powder
    dash of ground white pepper
  1¼ pounds catfish fillets
  1 tablespoon lemon juice
  1 tablespoon olive oil

In a small bowl, combine bread crumbs, coriander, cumin, garlic powder and pepper.

Spray a baking sheet with vegetable cooking spray. Place fish fillets on the baking sheet and brush with lemon juice and then oil. Spoon bread crumb mixture evenly over the top of the fillets and pat gently. Bake in a 400°F oven for 12 to 14 minutes, or until topping begins to brown. Serve with lemon wedges, if desired.

  4 servings
  222 calories per serving

Sizzlin' Catfish with Tomato–Orange Relish

OPTIONS: Salmon, Red snapper, Tilefish

¼ cup sliced scallions
1 teaspoon olive oil
1 tablespoon red wine vinegar
1 tablespoon honey
½ cup drained, chopped canned whole tomatoes
½ cup diced, seeded orange sections
½ cup flour
1 teaspoon paprika
¼ teaspoon garlic powder
⅛ teaspoon ground white pepper
¼ teaspoon dried thyme leaves
1 teaspoon rubbed sage
1¼ pounds catfish fillets
1 tablespoon peanut oil

In a small saucepan, sauté scallions in olive oil for 1 minute. Stir in vinegar and honey and cook for 1 minute.

Remove pan from heat. Add tomatoes and oranges and mix thoroughly. Set aside.

In a wide, shallow bowl, mix together flour, paprika, garlic powder, pepper, thyme and sage. Dredge fish fillets in seasoned flour, coating all surfaces.

In a large, heavy skillet, heat peanut oil over medium-high heat for 1 minute. Add fillets to the pan, cover and cook for 6 to 8 minutes, turning once. Serve with tomato-orange relish and garnish with orange slices.

4 servings
319 calories per serving

Catfish Bits with Curried Mayonnaise

OPTIONS: Red snapper, Tilefish, Grouper

½ cup plain low-fat yogurt
1 tablespoon orange marmalade
½ teaspoon dry mustard
¼ cup bread crumbs
¼ cup cornmeal
1¼ pounds catfish fillets, cut into bite-size pieces
¼ cup Curried Mayonnaise (recipe follows)

In a shallow bowl, combine yogurt, marmalade and mustard and blend thoroughly. In another shallow bowl, combine bread crumbs and cornmeal.

Coat a baking sheet with vegetable cooking spray. Dip fish into yogurt mixture and then into crumb mixture, coating all sides evenly. Place on the baking sheet and bake in a 450°F oven for 8 to 10 minutes, or until lightly browned, turning once. Serve with Curried Mayonnaise on the side.

4 servings
300 calories per serving

~~~~~~~~~~~~~~~

Curried Mayonnaise

1 teaspoon olive oil
½ teaspoon lemon juice
½ teaspoon curry powder
¼ cup reduced-calorie mayonnaise

In a saucepan, combine oil, lemon juice and curry powder and cook over medium heat for 2 minutes.

Pour curry mixture into a small bowl. Allow to cool for 2 minutes. Add mayonnaise and blend thoroughly.

Makes ¼ cup

Swordfish

~~~~~~~~~~~~~~~~~~~~~~~~~~~~~~~~~~~~

Next to a shark, there is one deep-water fish that's recognized by virtually everyone: swordfish. Its large, imposing body and long, swordlike beak that juts from its upper jaw makes snagging this ocean wonder an angler's dream. In the last few years, this awesome catch has become the diner's dream as well.

Forget the high market price or the scare years ago about high mercury levels. The Food and Drug Administration inspects all imported swordfish for prohibitive mercury levels. So don't worry fish lovers. Swordfish ranks right near the top of the list of popular seafood. And it's no wonder because there is plenty to admire: no bones; easy, even cooking; firm texture and, most important of all, memorable flavor.

Most imported swordfish comes to the fish store frozen. Buy the Japanese version for highest quality. You can get fresh swordfish, landed in Florida, New England and California, from late spring to early fall. Domestic fishermen concentrate on the smaller swordfish, which are safe in terms of mercury levels.

No matter where in the world swordfish comes from, it is always the same fish. Quality can only differ in handling procedures. Prices fluctuate greatly during the summer, when the U.S. catch is peaking.

Talking to Your Fishmonger

Swordfish steak *is* expensive but, unlike beef steak, what you see is what you get. There is no waste

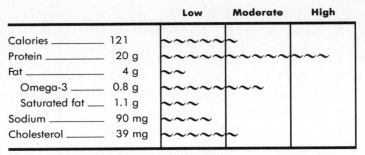

		Low	Moderate	High
Calories	121	~~~~~		
Protein	20 g	~~~~~~~~~~~~		
Fat	4 g	~~		
Omega-3	0.8 g	~~~~~~		
Saturated fat	1.1 g	~~~		
Sodium	90 mg	~~~~		
Cholesterol	39 mg	~~~~~		

Source: Adapted from Agriculture Handbook No. 8-15 (Washington, D.C.: U.S. Department of Agriculture).

since swordfish steaks are often sliced from a boneless and skinless loin.

The flesh can vary in color, but color is not a sign of quality as much as it is a sign of the fish's diet. Nevertheless, for some reason, pink is preferred on the East Coast and white is preferred on the West Coast.

The most important factor in choosing swordfish steak is freshness. Once again, ask your seafood clerk to let you sniff it for a fresh seawater aroma that says "buy me."

Next, be sure the clerk has not mistaken mako shark for swordfish. Mako shark is less expensive and should not be passed off as swordfish. There are a couple of signs to verify the genuine article: Swordfish has a smooth skin and shark has a rough skin like coarse sandpaper; the dark meat on swordfish appears as small, distinct, winglike shapes, while the dark meat on shark steaks tends to appear more round shaped.

The summer months offer the cheaper prices on fresh steaks caught off both the East Coast and the West Coast. Fortunately, this is just in time for the barbecue season when, in my opinion, swordfish reigns supreme. The thick, firm steaks cooperate more than most fish on the barbecue grill. Have your steaks for grilling cut 1 inch thick. It allows easy handling on the grill and, of course, even cooking.

The Fillet Board

If you're fussy, you can cut off the skin and remove the dark meat from the steaks when you bring them home from the store. This really isn't necessary, however. You'll find the dark meat lightens when cooked and is perfectly edible.

Cooking the Catch

Since swordfish is low in saturated fat, I suggest you marinate the steaks and cook them quickly over (or under) high heat. They are easy to turn and don't fall apart. Don't be afraid to turn them over on the broiler pan and baste them often to keep them moist.

Swordfish works particularly well on skewers. It stays put and cooks at the same rate as the accompanying vegetables or fruit.

I like to take advantage of firm-fleshed fish like swordfish for use in salads. Poach or bake the fish until it is just done and then chill it in the refrigerator. Swordfish is ideal for fish salads because it doesn't flake away into tiny, mushy pieces when mixed with dressing. It is a great substitute for tuna in salads and antipasto platters.

Swordfish	
Market form	**Amount per person (lb.)**
Steaks	¼–⅓

Galley Tips

Swordfish (1 lb.)

Technique Market form	Directions	Time (min.)	Temp.
Bake Steak	Use a flat nonstick pan; brush lightly with vegetable oil/juice mixture.	8–10	425°–450°F
Broil Steak	Use a flat nonstick pan; brush lightly with vegetable oil/juice mixture; broil 4 inches or less from heat; turn once.	8–12	High
Grill Steak	Cook directly on grill; baste often with vegetable oil/juice mixture; turn once.	6–12	High
Stir-fry Steak	Use a hot wok; cut steak into ½-inch strips; stir-fry fish first in small amount of hot peanut oil; remove fish; stir-fry vegetables; add fish, stir, cover and steam for 1 minute.	6–10	Med.-high to high
Pan-fry Steak	Use a nonstick skillet and no more than 1 tablespoon peanut oil; splash with stock or juice; turn once.	8–12	Med. to med.-high
Microwave Steak	Brush with stock, water or juice; arrange fish in 1 layer around edge of dish; cover with lid, loose plastic or paper towel; rotate often; let stand for 2 minutes after cooking.	4–6	High (100%)

Flaming Red Swordfish

OPTIONS: Mako shark, Tuna

---

  1 cup thin carrot slices
1¼ pounds swordfish
  1 cup tomato puree
  ¼ cup chopped pimientos
  1 tablespoon olive oil
  4 or 5 saffron threads

In a small saucepan, blanch carrots, covered, in simmering water for 6 to 8 minutes. Drain.

Coat a shallow baking dish with vegetable cooking spray. Spread carrots on bottom of dish. Set fish on top of carrots.

In a small saucepan, combine tomato puree, pimientos, oil and saffron. Cover and cook over medium-low heat for 10 minutes. Transfer sauce to a blender and puree for 1 minute, or until smooth. Pour sauce over fish and bake in a 400°F oven for 12 to 15 minutes.

  4 servings
  217 calories per serving

Grilled Swordfish Steaks with Tangy Citrus Butter

OPTIONS: Mako shark, Tilefish fillet

---

  1 tablespoon butter, softened
  1 tablespoon olive oil
  1 tablespoon lemon juice
  1 tablespoon lime juice
  ¼ teaspoon ground white pepper
1¼ pounds swordfish, cut into 4 equal pieces

In a small bowl, combine butter, oil, lemon juice, lime juice and pepper and blend thoroughly with a fork.

Place fish on a hot grill. Spread about 1 teaspoon citrus butter on each piece and grill for 3 minutes. Turn and spread with remaining butter and grill for 4 to 6 minutes more. Serve with lemon and lime slices, if desired.

Variation: Broil fish 4 inches from heat for 8 to 12 minutes, turning once after 3 minutes and spreading with remaining butter. Serve with lemon and lime slices, if desired.

  4 servings
  210 calories per serving

Open-Face Swordfish Sandwich with Italian Catsup

OPTIONS: Flounder fillet, Tuna, Tilefish fillet

---

  1 pound swordfish, cut into 4 equal pieces
  2 teaspoons olive oil
  4 slices crusty Italian bread
  1 teaspoon grated Parmesan cheese
  1 cup thinly sliced romaine lettuce leaves
  4 thin, large tomato slices
  ¼ cup Italian Catsup (page 269)

Rub fish with oil on all sides. Grill or broil steaks 4 inches from heat for 7 to 10 minutes, turning after 4 minutes.

Lightly toast bread and sprinkle with Parmesan while hot. Place ¼ cup of romaine on each piece of bread. Add a slice of tomato, then a fish steak and top with a tablespoon of catsup.

  4 servings
  242 calories per serving

Salad
of Swordfish Ribbons

OPTIONS: Mako shark, Tuna

1½ cups chicken stock
1 teaspoon white wine vinegar
¾ pound swordfish, crosscut into
     ¼-inch strips
½ cup julienne of celery
½ cup julienne of carrots
½ cup julienne of scallions
2 tablespoons olive oil
1 tablespoon lemon juice
1 tablespoon orange juice
¼ teaspoon dried oregano
     dash of ground white pepper
4 radicchio or escarole leaves

In a large nonstick skillet, combine chicken stock and vinegar. Bring to a boil and then reduce to a simmer. Drop in fish strips and poach for 3 to 5 minutes. Remove fish and set aside.

Return stock to a simmer and poach celery and carrots for 3 to 5 minutes. Drain and reserve stock, if desired. Add vegetables to fish and chill for 30 minutes.

In a bowl, combine scallions, oil, lemon juice, orange juice, oregano and pepper. Add chilled fish and vegetables and toss to coat evenly. Serve immediately on radicchio or escarole leaves, or marinate in the refrigerator for 30 minutes before serving.

4 servings
164 calories per serving

Poached Swordfish
with Herbs

OPTIONS: Halibut, Mako shark

3 cups chicken stock
1 tablespoon white wine vinegar
1 small clove garlic, cut in half
1 tablespoon fresh rosemary or
     1 teaspoon dried rosemary
2 teaspoons fresh thyme leaves or
     1 teaspoon dried thyme
¼ teaspoon coarsely ground black
     pepper
1¼ pounds swordfish, cut into
     4 equal pieces
½ cup chopped fresh parsley
½ cup sliced roasted sweet red
     peppers or pimientos

In a nonstick skillet, combine chicken stock, vinegar, garlic, rosemary, thyme and black pepper. Bring to a boil over medium-high heat and cook for 5 minutes.

Drop fish into stock, bring to a simmer and poach for 8 to 10 minutes. Remove fish from skillet and keep warm in a 200°F oven.

Strain stock into a bowl and discard herbs and garlic. Return stock to the skillet and bring to a rolling boil over high heat. Reduce stock to ½ cup, 6 to 8 minutes.

Place parsley in a blender. Pour in reduced stock and puree until smooth.

Arrange peppers or pimientos on a platter. Set fish on top and spoon herb sauce over steaks. Serve immediately.

4 servings
167 calories per serving

Sizzling Swordfish with Broccoli and Peanuts

OPTIONS: Mako shark, Tuna

¾ pound swordfish, cut into
     1- × 2-inch strips
2 tablespoons cornstarch
½ pound fresh broccoli, cut into
     2-inch strips
½ cup julienne of carrots
¼ cup low-sodium soy sauce
1 teaspoon sesame oil
1 small clove garlic, minced
1 teaspoon minced gingerroot or
     ½ teaspoon ground ginger
1½ tablespoons peanut oil
¼ cup unsalted peanuts

In a small bowl, toss fish strips with cornstarch to coat evenly.

In another small bowl, combine broccoli, carrots, soy sauce, sesame oil, garlic and ginger.

In a wok or large nonstick skillet, heat 1 tablespoon peanut oil over medium-high heat for 1 minute. Add fish and stir-fry until lightly browned, about 5 minutes. Remove fish and set aside.

Heat remaining peanut oil and stir-fry vegetable mixture and peanuts over medium-high heat for 4 minutes.

Add fish, stir, cover and heat for 1 minute. Serve over steamed rice, if desired.

    4 servings
    239 calories per serving

Cheesy Swordfish Steaks

OPTIONS: Mako shark, Tuna

1 egg white
2 tablespoons skim milk
½ cup bread crumbs
1 tablespoon grated Parmesan
     cheese
1 tablespoon grated Romano
     cheese
⅛ teaspoon ground white pepper
1 teaspoon dry mustard
1 teaspoon paprika
1¼ pounds swordfish, cut into 4
     equal pieces

Slightly whisk egg white in a wide, shallow bowl. Add milk and mix thoroughly.

In another wide, shallow bowl, combine bread crumbs, Parmesan, Romano, pepper, mustard and paprika. Mix to blend.

Coat a baking sheet with vegetable cooking spray. Dip each fish steak into egg white mixture to coat evenly. Then dredge in seasoned bread crumbs, place on the baking sheet and bake in a 450°F oven for 8 to 10 minutes, or until lightly browned. Garnish with lemon and lime wedges.

    4 servings
    225 calories per serving

Broiled Swordfish Steaks
à la Capri

OPTIONS: Mako shark, Tuna

3 tablespoons olive oil
2 tablespoons balsamic vinegar
1 clove garlic, minced
1 teaspoon minced fresh rosemary
  or ½ teaspoon dried rosemary
1¼ pounds swordfish, cut into
  4 equal pieces

In a small bowl, combine oil, vinegar, garlic and rosemary.

Place fish on a large, shallow platter. Spoon marinade over steaks, turn to coat both sides, cover with plastic wrap and marinate in the refrigerator for 30 minutes.

Place steaks on a broiling pan and broil 4 inches from heat for 6 to 8 minutes, turning once after 3 minutes and basting with marinade. Serve with broiling pan juices for dipping.

4 servings
239 calories per serving

Swordfish Provençale

OPTIONS: Mako shark, Tuna

1 clove garlic, cut in half
1 tablespoon olive oil
1 pound swordfish, cut into
  bite-size pieces
¼ cup flour
1 cup coarsely chopped plum
  tomatoes
½ cup black olives
2 tablespoons chopped fresh
  parsley
1 tablespoon lemon juice
2 teaspoons grated Parmesan
  cheese

Dredge fish in flour, coating evenly.

In a nonstick skillet, sauté garlic in oil over medium-high heat for 1 minute. Press garlic with the back of a fork, remove and discard.

Add fish and sauté for 8 to 10 minutes, or until browned on all sides.

Stir in tomatoes, olives, parsley and lemon juice, cover and cook for 1 minute. Serve topped with Parmesan.

4 servings
196 calories per serving

Shark

~~~~~~~~~~~~~~~~~~~~~~~~~~~~~~~~~~~

I'm sure you have heard of fish-and-chips, the number one fast food in Great Britain. By tradition, the fish half of that famous combination is shark that has been dipped in batter and deep-fried.

Today shark is making its mark in the American retail market and at very reasonable prices. Sample this tasty, firm-fleshed fish now, before popularity pushes its prices out of the bargain range.

In my opinion, mako shark steaks are just as good, if not better, than swordfish steaks—and they are usually a dollar or two cheaper per pound. Blacktip shark from Florida and Gulf waters is gaining in popularity and availability in the East. Thresher shark from Pacific waters is becoming more popular on the West Coast.

Talking to Your Fishmonger

Mako shark and thresher shark are sold fresh on retail ice displays as steaks or large loin slabs. If your fishmonger slices steaks to order, request that they be cut 1 inch thick. It's the ideal cooking thickness. You'll notice that these steaks look a lot like swordfish steaks. The most noticeable difference is the skin. Shark skin is rough and swordfish skin is smooth.

Mako and thresher have pinkish white flesh. The closer to white, the better. Blacktip shark has translucent white flesh. Avoid shark meat that is dark. All shark steaks should have glistening skin with firm flesh and no hint of ammonia odor.

Keep fresh shark on ice and cook it within 24 hours of purchase. Shark meat turned gray with

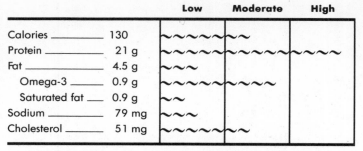

		Low	Moderate	High
Calories	130	~~~~~~		
Protein	21 g	~~~~~~	~~~~~~	~~~~~~
Fat	4.5 g	~~~		
Omega-3	0.9 g	~~~~~~		
Saturated fat	0.9 g	~~~		
Sodium	79 mg	~~~		
Cholesterol	51 mg	~~~~~~		

Source: Adapted from Agriculture Handbook No. 8-15 (Washington, D.C.: U.S. Department of Agriculture).

time is tough when cooked, no matter how quickly you cook it.

The Fillet Board

Here's what you should know about preparing shark:

- Remove the skin and any dark spots from the steaks with a sharp fillet knife before cooking.
- Cut large steaks into individual portions or cubes for skewering.

One nice thing about shark is that it has no bones except for a cartilaginous backbone that you might find in the center of small shark steaks. It can be, but doesn't have to be, removed before cooking.

Cooking the Catch

Be careful! Do not overcook shark meat. This lean fish has little fat to keep it moist. I cook it just before it is time to serve the meal. Quick cooking techniques like grilling, broiling and high-heat baking are best for this fish.

Shark can develop an ammonia odor quickly. I preempt any chance of that by marinating shark meat. A few tablespoons of lemon juice in a pint of water is fine for this, but here is your chance to be creative. Use vinegars and other citrus juices with herbs and spices for a complementary marinade and basting sauce. Marinate shark steaks in the refrigerator for 1 hour prior to cooking.

Shark	
Market form	**Amount per person (lb.)**
Steaks	¼–⅓

Galley Tips

Shark (1 lb.)

Technique Market form	Directions	Time (min.)	Temp.
Bake Steak	Use a flat nonstick pan; brush lightly with vegetable oil/juice mixture.	8–10	425°–450°F
Broil Steak	Use a flat nonstick pan; brush lightly with vegetable oil/juice mixture; broil 4 inches or less from heat; turn once.	8–12	High
Grill Steak	Cook directly on grill; baste often with vegetable oil/juice mixture; turn once.	6–12	High
Stir-fry Steak	Use a hot wok; cut steak into ½-inch strips; stir-fry fish first in small amount of hot peanut oil; remove fish; stir-fry vegetables; add fish, stir, cover and steam for 1 minute.	6–10	Med.-high to high
Pan-fry Steak	Use a nonstick skillet and no more than 1 tablespoon peanut oil; splash with stock or juice; turn once.	8–12	Med. to med.-high
Microwave Steak	Brush with stock, water or juice; arrange fish in 1 layer around edge of dish; cover with lid, loose plastic or paper towel; rotate often; let stand for 2 minutes after cooking.	4–6	High (100%)

Shark, Citrus
and Avocado Salad

1 egg white, slightly beaten
1 teaspoon honey
1 pound mako shark steak,
    trimmed of skin and dark meat
1 tablespoon cornstarch
½ teaspoon dry mustard
    dash of ground white pepper
2 tablespoons peanut oil
1 avocado, thinly sliced
2 oranges, thinly sliced and halved
1 small head Bibb or Boston
    lettuce
½ cup orange juice
2 tablespoons lime juice
1 tablespoon olive oil
¼ teaspoon coarsely ground black
    pepper

In a small bowl, combine egg white and honey.

Cut steak into bite-size chunks and toss to coat evenly with egg white. Sprinkle with cornstarch, mustard and white pepper and toss to blend.

Heat peanut oil in a wok over medium-high heat for 1 minute. Add fish and cook for 4 to 6 minutes, stirring frequently. Do not brown. Drain fish on paper towels and let stand for 3 minutes.

Arrange avocado and orange slices over lettuce leaves on four plates. Top with fish cubes and drizzle each serving with orange juice, lime juice and olive oil in that order. Sprinkle with black pepper and garnish with radish slices.

4 servings
341 calories per serving

Shark Steak Bake
with Herbs

OPTIONS: Swordfish, Halibut

¼ cup water
1 tablespoon white wine vinegar
1¼ pounds mako shark steaks,
    trimmed of skin and dark meat
⅓ cup bread crumbs
¼ cup chopped fresh parsley
1 teaspoon chopped fresh sage or
    ½ teaspoon rubbed sage
1 teaspoon fresh thyme leaves or
    ½ teaspoon dried thyme leaves
½ teaspoon paprika
1 tablespoon safflower oil

In a shallow bowl, combine water and vinegar.

Cut fish into four equal pieces. Add fish to marinade and toss to coat. Marinate in the refrigerator for 1 hour.

Toss bread crumbs, parsley, sage, thyme and paprika into a blender and whiz until thoroughly blended. Pour into a small bowl, add oil and blend until bread crumbs are moistened.

Drain steaks and discard marinade. Place steaks in a baking dish, spoon crumb mixture onto each and bake in a 450°F oven for 8 to 10 minutes. Garnish with orange wedges.

4 servings
239 calories per serving

Pan-Fried
Shark Steak Italiano
with Linguine

OPTIONS: Swordfish, Halibut

¼ cup flour
⅛ teaspoon ground white pepper
½ teaspoon paprika
1 pound mako shark steak, trimmed of skin and dark meat
3 teaspoons olive oil
½ cup sliced onions
½ cup sliced green peppers
1 clove garlic, minced
1 zucchini, sliced into ¼-inch slices
1 small eggplant, cut into 2-inch strips
1 can (28 ounces) plum tomatoes (including juice), sliced
¼ cup chopped fresh parsley
1 tablespoon chopped fresh basil or 1 teaspoon dried basil
½ pound linguine, cooked

In a shallow bowl, combine flour, white pepper and paprika.

Cut fish into four equal pieces and dredge each piece in seasoned flour.

Heat 2 teaspoons oil in a nonstick skillet over medium-high heat. Add steaks to skillet and brown for 2 minutes on each side. Remove from pan and set aside.

Add remaining oil to pan. Stir-fry onions and peppers for 2 minutes. Stir in garlic, zucchini and eggplant and cook for 2 minutes. Add tomatoes (with juice), parsley and basil and stir. Cover and cook for 5 minutes.

Place fish steaks on top of vegetables, cover and cook for 5 to 7 minutes.

Place fish steaks on a bed of freshly cooked linguine and spoon vegetables over all.

4 servings
474 calories per serving

Shark, Turkey
and Mushroom Brochettes

OPTIONS: Swordfish, Tuna

½ cup orange juice
1 tablespoon olive oil
1 teaspoon dry mustard
1 small clove garlic, minced
¾ pound mako shark steak, trimmed of skin and dark meat
8 fresh button mushrooms
2 slices (4 ounces each) smoked turkey, each cut into 4 equal strips

In a small mixing bowl, combine orange juice, oil, mustard and garlic. Blend thoroughly with a fork.

Cut fish steak into 12 equal cubes. Add fish cubes to orange juice mixture and toss. Marinate in the refrigerator for 1 hour.

Soak four 6-inch bamboo skewers in water for 30 minutes. Trim mushroom stems close to button. Skewer fish cubes, mushrooms and turkey alternately on the skewers.

Spray a broiler pan with vegetable cooking spray. Place skewers on pan and broil at least 4 inches from the broiler for 6 to 8 minutes, turning 3 times and basting with marinade as they cook. If desired, serve each brochette on a bed of 3 thin orange slices.

4 servings
250 calories per serving

Peppered Shark Steak

OPTIONS: Swordfish, Halibut

¼ cup lemon juice
1 tablespoon lime juice
1 tablespoon olive oil
¼ teaspoon ground white pepper
¼ teaspoon paprika
⅛ teaspoon cayenne pepper
1 small clove garlic, minced
1¼ pounds mako shark steaks,
  trimmed of skin and dark meat

In a shallow bowl, combine lemon juice, lime juice, oil, white pepper, paprika, cayenne and garlic.

Cut fish into four equal pieces and place in marinade, turning to coat both sides. Marinate in the refrigerator for 1 hour.

Broil steaks at least 4 inches from broiler for 4 minutes on one side and 4 to 6 minutes on the other side, basting with marinade. Garnish with lemon wedges.

  4 servings
  205 calories per serving

Roast Fish-and-Chips

OPTIONS: Blue shark, Cod

---

1 egg white
½ cup plain low-fat yogurt
½ cup flour
½ teaspoon paprika
¼ teaspoon ground white pepper
¾ cup bread crumbs
1 pound mako shark steak,
  trimmed of skin and dark meat
4 baking potatoes, each cut lengthwise into 8 wedges
2 teaspoons safflower oil
¼ teaspoon red-hot pepper sauce
1 teaspoon peanut oil

In a shallow bowl, whisk egg white with a fork for 30 seconds. Add yogurt and combine thoroughly.

In another shallow bowl, mix together flour, paprika and pepper.

Place bread crumbs in a third shallow bowl.

Cut fish steaks into eight equal pieces. Dredge fish pieces in seasoned flour. Transfer to yogurt/egg mixture and coat thoroughly. Next, dredge fish in bread crumbs until evenly coated. Set aside.

Toss potato wedges in a bowl with safflower oil and hot pepper sauce. Arrange on a baking sheet and bake in a 425°F oven for a total of 25 minutes.

Lightly coat a large cast-iron skillet with peanut oil. Over medium-high heat, lightly brown breaded fish on 1 side for 1 minute. Turn fish over and place the skillet in a 425°F oven for 8 to 10 minutes.

Remove fish and potatoes from the oven and serve, if desired, with malt vinegar and/or catsup.

  4 servings
  442 calories per serving

Grilled Mako Shark with Tomato–Orange Marinade

OPTIONS: Swordfish, Tuna

1 can (6-ounces) no-salt V-8 juice
¼ cup frozen orange juice concentrate
¼ cup minced onions
1 small clove garlic, minced
1¼ pounds mako shark steak, trimmed of skin and dark meat

In a bowl, combine V-8 juice, orange juice concentrate, onions and garlic and allow to stand at room temperature for 15 minutes.

Cut fish into four equal pieces.

Pour marinade into a shallow baking dish. Add steaks to marinade and turn to coat evenly on both sides. Cover and marinate in the refrigerator for 1 hour. Remove steaks and reserve marinade.

Grill fish for 4 minutes on one side and 2 to 3 minutes on the other side.

In a small saucepan, bring reserved marinade to a boil, stirring constantly, and boil for 2 minutes. Strain sauce over fish. Garnish with orange wedges.

4 servings
219 calories per serving

Stir-Fried Shark Sticks

OPTIONS: Swordfish, Tuna

¼ cup low-sodium soy sauce
1 teaspoon sesame oil
1 teaspoon minced gingerroot or ½ teaspoon ground ginger
1 small clove garlic, minced
¾ pound mako shark steak, trimmed of skin and dark meat
3 teaspoons peanut oil
3 cups small fresh broccoli florets

In a shallow bowl, combine soy sauce, sesame oil, ginger and garlic. Cut steak into ½- × 2-inch strips. Add fish to soy sauce and toss to coat. Marinate in the refrigerator for 1 hour.

Heat 1 teaspoon peanut oil over medium-high heat in a wok or large nonstick skillet for 1 minute. Add broccoli and stir-fry for 3 minutes. Remove broccoli and set aside.

Drain fish strips and discard marinade. Add remaining peanut oil to the hot wok or skillet. Add fish and stir-fry for 3 to 4 minutes.

Return broccoli to wok or skillet and stir. Cover and steam for 1 to 2 minutes. Serve garnished with sweet red pepper rings.

4 servings
161 calories per serving

Monkfish

~~~~~~~~~~~~~~~~~~~~~~~~~~~~~

Monkfish was the ugly duckling of the fish counter until some clever promoter turned this sweetly succulent whitefish into a swan by dubbing it the "poor man's lobster." Now monkfish is no longer the poor man's anything. It has earned another, more celebrated identity: "marvelous monkfish."

French bouillabaisse and other European fish stews and soups feature monkfish as a traditional ingredient. I like to use it in fish salads and for stir-frying. Monkfish is perfect for all these uses because of its firm flesh. The cooked meat doesn't flake and disintegrate in a hot soup. Nor does it break apart as it's tossed in a salad or hot wok.

Talking to Your Fishmonger

At times you might find a whole monkfish tail, sometimes called monktail, with the backbone still intact. But most often, you'll find fillets displayed on ice.

There's one thing to look out for when buying monkfish fillets: the tough, inedible membrane. While you'll almost always find the fillets skinned, they often still have a thin, blue-gray membrane covering most of the flesh. Some people unfamiliar with monkfish have made the unfortunate mistake of cooking the monkfish with the membrane still attached, making for a sadly unforgettable eating experience. So, make sure you ask your fishmonger to remove the membrane for you.

The Fillet Board

You also can remove the membrane yourself. Done correctly, it is an easy task. The membrane looks like a bluish, cloudy plastic wrapped tightly to the

		Low	Moderate	High
Calories _____	76	~~~~		
Protein _____	14 g	~~~~~~~~~		
Fat _____	1.5 g	~		
Omega-3 _____	—			
Saturated fat ___	—			
Sodium _____	18 mg	~		
Cholesterol _____	25 mg	~~~~		

Source: Adapted from Agriculture Handbook No. 8-15 (Washington, D.C.: U.S. Department of Agriculture).

flesh. Puncture the membrane with the point of a slim, sharp fillet knife. Slide the blade flatly under the membrane, across the fillet. Gripping the fillet end closest to you, strip the membrane from the flesh as you slide the blade with a sawing motion toward the opposite end. Remember, keep the blade flat.

Monkfish is easy to fillet. It has no pin bones and is completely boneless. Just cut and peel the two fillets off each side of the one long backbone.

Cooking the Catch

When broiling or baking monkfish fillets, I like to butterfly and brush them with a spicy dressing or marinade. I also crosscut scallops or small steaks from the fillet loin.

The thin scallops can be quickly stir-fried or breaded and sautéed in a flash. The thicker steaks can be poached, broiled or wok-smoked. It is easy to portion and display the steaks for a family dinner.

To create "poor man's lobster," butterfly a 4- to 5-inch-long, thick fillet. Poach it for about 10 minutes in simmering water with a few tablespoons of lemon juice. Serve it with browned butter on the side. Or you can brush the raw, butterflied fillet with lemon butter, sprinkle with paprika and broil close to the heat for 6 to 8 minutes.

My favorite way to eat monkfish is in fish salads. Very simply, poach or bake the fillets until fully cooked. Chill in the refrigerator for at least 1 hour. Cut the cooked, chilled fillet into bite-size chunks

Monkfish	
Market form	**Amount per person (lb.)**
Fillets	¼–⅓

and toss with your favorite dressing, vegetables and herbs. Chill and serve on a leaf of romaine lettuce or escarole. Substitute the cooked, chilled monkfish for tuna in your favorite tuna fish salad recipe. You will be pleasantly surprised.

~~~~~~ ~~~~~~

Galley Tips
Monkfish (1 lb.)

Technique Market form	Directions	Time (min.)	Temp.
Bake Fillet	Use a flat nonstick pan; brush lightly with vegetable oil or butter; sprinkle with citrus juice.	10–15	400°F
Broil Fillet	Use a flat nonstick pan; brush lightly with vegetable oil; dust with seasoned flour or bread crumbs and paprika; broil 4 inches or less from heat	8–12	High
Grill Fillet	Cook directly on grill; turn once; baste often with vegetable oil/juice mixture.	6–12	High
Poach Fillet	Use a fish poacher or deep baking pan; combine citrus juice or wine vinegar with herbs and spices in stock or water.	10–12	Simmer
Sauté Fillet	Use a nonstick skillet; mix vegetable oil with stock to moisten while sautéing; turn once; sprinkle with citrus juice in pan.	8–12	Med. to med.-high
Stir-fry Fillet	Use a hot wok; cut fillet into ½-inch strips; stir-fry fish first in small amount of hot peanut oil; remove fish; stir-fry vegetables; add fish, stir, cover and steam for 1 minute.	5–10	Med.-high to high
Microwave Fillet	Brush with stock, water or juice; arrange fish in 1 layer around edge of dish; cover with lid, loose plastic or paper towel; rotate often; let stand for 2 minutes after cooking.	4–6	High (100%)

Brochettes of Monkfish with Zucchini and Artichokes

OPTIONS: Tilefish, Ocean pout, Ocean catfish

- 1 pound monkfish fillet, membrane removed
- 1 tablespoon brown mustard
- 1 tablespoon olive oil
- 2 tablespoons white wine vinegar
- ½ teaspoon minced garlic
- 1 zucchini, sliced into 8 equal slices
- ¼ teaspoon paprika
- ½ teaspoon ground mustard seeds or ¼ teaspoon dry mustard dash of ground white pepper
- 4 artichoke hearts

Soak eight 9-inch bamboo skewers in water for 1 hour.

Cut fish into 16 equal chunks. In a medium bowl, combine brown mustard, oil, vinegar and garlic. Add fish chunks, toss and marinate for 10 to 15 minutes.

In a gallon-size, plastic food-storage bag, combine paprika, mustard seeds or dry mustard and pepper. Add zucchini slices and shake until slices are fully coated.

Alternate fish and zucchini on double skewers (two skewers keep the pieces stable) with an artichoke in the center.

Spray a broiler pan with vegetable cooking spray. Place skewers on pan, spoon remaining marinade on vegetables and broil 4 inches or less from heat for 6 minutes. Rotate skewers a half turn, baste with pan liquids and broil for another 6 minutes.

4 servings
141 calories per serving

Poached Monkfish with Browned Citrus Butter

OPTIONS: Tilefish, Ocean pout, Ocean catfish

- 1 quart water
- ¼ cup plus 1 tablespoon lemon juice
- 6 sprigs of parsley
- 12 black peppercorns
- 2 bay leaves
- 1¼ pounds monkfish fillet, membrane removed
- 1 tablespoon orange juice
- 1 tablespoon lime juice
- 1 tablespoon butter

In a 3- or 4-quart pot, combine water, ¼ cup lemon juice, parsley, peppercorns and bay leaves. Bring to a boil over high heat. Reduce heat and simmer for 5 minutes.

Add fish, return to a simmer and cook for 10 to 15 minutes, or until white through center of fish. Lift out fish and remove to a warm platter.

In a cup, combine orange juice, remaining lemon juice and lime juice. In a small skillet, melt butter over medium-high heat. Just as butter begins to brown, add citrus juice mixture and sizzle for 20 to 30 seconds. Pour hot sauce over fish and serve immediately.

4 servings
131 calories per serving

Browned Scallops of Monkfish

OPTIONS: Tilefish, Ocean pout, Ocean catfish

½ cup flour
1 teaspoon ground cumin
⅛ teaspoon cayenne pepper
¼ teaspoon garlic powder
1¼ pounds monkfish fillet,
        membrane removed
3 tablespoons safflower oil

Combine flour, cumin, cayenne and garlic powder in a shallow bowl. Cut fish into ½-inch-thick scallops and dust 2 or 3 at a time with seasoned flour. Sauté in a large skillet, using 1 tablespoon oil at a time, over medium heat. Drain on paper towels. Garnish with lime wedges.

4 servings
250 calories per serving

Monkfish Stew with Anise

OPTIONS: Tilefish, Ocean pout, Ocean catfish

½ cup sliced leeks
1 tablespoon olive oil
1 large clove garlic, minced
2 cups canned crushed plum
        tomatoes (including juice)
1 cup chicken stock
¼ cup chopped fresh parsley
¼ teaspoon anise seeds
8 saffron threads
1¼ pounds monkfish fillet,
        membrane removed
¼ cup Parmesan cheese

In a 3- to 4-quart pot, sauté leeks in oil for 2 to 3 minutes. Add garlic and sauté for 30 seconds. Add tomatoes (with juice), chicken stock, parsley, anise seeds and saffron. Bring to a boil, reduce heat and simmer for 15 minutes, stirring occasionally.

Cut fish into equal pieces and add to simmering stew. Return to a gentle simmer and cook for 10 minutes. Serve in shallow soup bowls topped with Parmesan.

4 servings
199 calories per serving

Skillet-Steamed Monkfish on Vegetables

OPTIONS: Tilefish, Cod, Haddock

1¼ pounds monkfish fillet,
        membrane removed
1 tablespoon Italian dressing
½ cup julienne of zucchini
½ cup julienne of carrots
½ cup julienne of celery
½ cup thinly sliced fresh
        mushroom caps
1 tablespoon olive oil
½ cup chicken stock

Coat fish fillet with Italian dressing and let stand for 15 minutes.

In a large skillet, sauté zucchini, carrots, celery and mushrooms in oil for 2 minutes over medium-high heat. Add chicken stock, then place fillet on vegetables, cover and steam for 10 to 12 minutes. Serve fish topped with vegetables.

4 servings
164 calories per serving

Bay-Smoked Monkfish Scallops with Green Herb–Mustard Dressing

OPTIONS: Tilefish, Ocean pout, Ocean catfish

- 10 bay leaves
- 1 pound monkfish fillet, membrane removed
- 1 teaspoon olive oil
- ⅓ cup Green Herb-Mustard Dressing (recipe follows)

Toss bay leaves onto the bottom of a wok.

Cut fish into 1-inch scallops. Place fish on metal steaming rack coated with vegetable cooking spray in wok. Cover with a dome lid and smoke fish for 5 to 6 minutes over medium-high heat. *Do not lift lid.*

Turn off the heat. Let stand for 1 minute before removing lid. Vent range area well.

Spread oil evenly on a flat baking dish. Arrange smoked scallops in the dish and bake in a 450°F oven for 4 to 5 minutes. Serve hot or chilled with Green Herb-Mustard Dressing.

4 servings
137 calories per serving

~~~~~~~~~~~~~~~~~~

Green Herb– Mustard Dressing

- 2 tablespoons chopped watercress leaves
- 2 tablespoons chopped fresh parsley
- 2 tablespoons orange juice
- 1½ teaspoons Dijon mustard
- ¼ cup reduced-calorie mayonnaise

In a blender, combine watercress, parsley and orange juice and puree on high until smooth.

In a small bowl, mix together pureed herbs, mustard and mayonnaise and blend thoroughly. Cover and refrigerate for at least 1 hour before serving.

Makes ⅓ cup

Maritime Monkfish Soup

OPTIONS: Tilefish, Cod, Haddock

- 1 tablespoon olive oil
- ½ cup diced onions
- ½ cup diced carrots
- 1 cup sliced cabbage
- ½ cup diced potatoes
- 3 cups chicken stock
- 1 cup clam juice
- 1 tablespoon cider vinegar
- 1 tablespoon minced fresh parsley
- ¼ teaspoon dried thyme leaves
- ¼ teaspoon freshly ground black pepper
- ¾ pound monkfish fillet, membrane removed

In a large, heavy pot, heat oil over medium-high heat. Add onions, carrots and cabbage and sauté for 5 minutes. Stir in potatoes, chicken stock, clam juice, vinegar, parsley, thyme and pepper and bring to a boil. Reduce heat and simmer for 15 minutes, or until potatoes are tender.

Cut fish fillet into small chunks and gently stir into soup. Remove from heat, cover and steep for 10 minutes. Serve immediately.

4 servings
148 calories per serving

Stir-Fried Monkfish with String Beans

OPTIONS: Tilefish, Catfish, Ocean pout

1 tablespoon peanut oil
1 dried red chili pepper
1 tablespoon sliced gingerroot
1 cup whole green beans
1 cup whole wax beans
¼ cup unsalted whole cashews
¾ pound monkfish fillet,
    membrane removed
2 tablespoons cornstarch
¼ cup chicken stock
1 teaspoon low-sodium soy sauce

In a wok, heat oil for 1 minute over medium-high heat. Add pepper and ginger and stir-fry for 1 minute. Remove and discard pepper and ginger.

Stir-fry green beans, wax beans and cashews for 2 to 3 minutes. Remove and reserve.

Cut fish into 1-inch scallops. Dust fish with cornstarch, coating evenly, and stir-fry for 5 minutes. Add chicken stock, stir and cook for 1 minute. Stir in beans, cashews, soy sauce and heat for 1 minute. Serve hot.

4 servings
174 calories per serving

Light Lunch Monkfish Salad

⅓ cup plain low-fat yogurt, drained
    for 1 hour
2 tablespoons reduced-calorie
    mayonnaise
2 tablespoons tomato paste
2 tablespoons orange juice
1 pound monkfish fillet,
    membrane removed
1 quart water
2 tablespoons rice wine vinegar
1 cup chopped, seeded cucumbers
1 hard-cooked egg, coarsely
    chopped

In a small bowl, combine yogurt, mayonnaise, tomato paste and orange juice and whisk with a fork until smooth. Cover and refrigerate for 30 minutes.

Slice monkfish fillet into ½-inch cutlets.

In a large skillet, combine water and vinegar and bring to a boil over medium-high heat. Add fish, reduce heat to low and simmer for 3 to 5 minutes. Drain and pat fish dry with paper towels. Then refrigerate for 30 minutes.

Spoon yogurt mixture onto four serving plates. Top with fish cutlets and sprinkle cucumbers and eggs around fish. Garnish with chopped watercress and serve with water crackers, if desired.

4 servings
150 calories per serving

Shrimp

~~~~~~~~~~~~~~~~~~~~~~~~~~~~~~

Shrimp is simply the most popular seafood in the United States. People are unabashed about their love for shrimp. Just try putting a tray of shrimp out on a buffet table—they're gone in a wink! There's something about shrimp that can bring out the glutton in the most reserved person.

And I guess we could say that something is flavor. Shrimp is something that just about everyone loves to eat, whether it's cold in a cocktail, steamed from the pot or transformed into a savory entrée like scampi. It's the one fish that people don't seem to mind breaking the bank over.

Yes, without a doubt, shrimp *is* expensive. But, although it's expensive, portions are easy to control. You can purchase them by the count, as well as by the pound.

The kind most likely to appear on display in your fish market and on most restaurant menus is tropical shrimp, fished from warm climates throughout the world. These common shrimp are always sold by size, which is determined by the number of shrimp per pound.

Shrimp of a different species, freshwater prawns, are imported from Asia and can be purchased live and whole. But be prepared to pay a premium price for this delicacy.

Rock shrimp tails have hard shells that look just like lobster tail. They even taste like lobster. But these small crustaceans are difficult to peel and the shell is half the weight. You'll work hard for the tiny morsels of meat in inexpensive rock shrimp.

Contrary to popular belief, almost all shrimp

167

**School
of Nutrients**

Shrimp
3½ oz. raw

168
~~~~~
Super Seafood

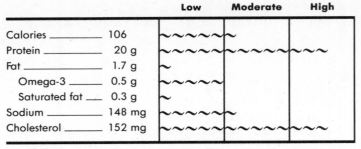

		Low	Moderate	High
Calories	106	~~~~~		
Protein	20 g	~~~~~	~~~~	~~~~
Fat	1.7 g	~		
Omega-3	0.5 g	~~~~		
Saturated fat	0.3 g	~		
Sodium	148 mg	~~~~~		
Cholesterol	152 mg	~~~~~	~~~~	~~~~

Source: Adapted from Agriculture Handbook No. 8-15 (Washington, D.C.: U.S. Department of Agriculture).

on the U.S. market arrives frozen at the retail store or restaurant. Freezing the shrimp quickly at harvest guarantees superior quality because shrimp is highly perishable and is shipped great distances from native waters. If you're lucky enough to live in the right area, some local harvests in Maine, Florida, Alaska and the Gulf Coast provide fresh shrimp to nearby communities.

Talking to Your Fishmonger
You will always find shrimp, with the shell on and the head removed, in at least two or three different sizes at the fish counter. This is the most common market form. Many fishmongers also offer cooked shrimp with the shell on or peeled and deveined. When shrimp is peeled, deveined and cooked, expect to pay a premium price for the convenience and high yield per pound.

I prefer to buy shrimp with the shell on because I believe it is most likely the freshest in the display case. I even go a step further, if I expect to be serving a lot of shrimp (and if I can afford it), I will ask my fishmonger to sell me a 5-pound box of frozen shrimp. Sometimes there is a discount on the pound price, because I'm saving the fishmonger time and labor.

If I don't intend to prepare the whole 5 pounds, I defrost only what I plan to use quickly, under cold running water. I return the remaining frozen shrimp

to the freezer for future use. Shrimp is highly perishable in the raw state and doesn't last long at
normal refrigerator temperatures. It isn't wise to
keep raw shrimp thawed for more than 24 hours
under refrigeration. Cooked shrimp lasts longer —
but no more than three days.

Once again, your nose knows best. Sniff raw or
cooked shrimp for the odor of iodine before you
buy. If it's there, forget it.

Shrimp is marketed in a least 11 different grada-
tions of large, medium or small. The larger the size,
the higher the price per pound. Such variety offers
you a size to suit all your recipe and appetite needs.
Although you may find discrepancies at your local
retail market, these are the industry standards.

I recommend extra large shrimp (26 to 30 per
pound) as a good, all-around size for home cooking.
A good value for steaming with the shell on is medium shrimp (43 to 50 per pound). Of course, if you
want to treat your family or guests to shrimp stuffed
with crabmeat, extra jumbo (16 to 20 per pound) or
colossal (10 to 15 per pound) are the best. For very
special occasions, "force" yourself to enjoy 2 or 3 of
the extra colossal shrimp (under 10 per pound).

Try to purchase your shrimp by count per
pound. This way you can communicate with your
fishmonger on the same level.

Shrimp	
Market form	**Amount per person (lb.)**
Cooked, shell on	⅓–½
Shell on	⅓–½
Cooked, peeled and deveined	¼–⅓

Sizing Up the Shrimp

Name	Count per Pound (in the shell)	Name	Count per Pound (in the shell)
Extra colossal	Under 10	Medium large	36 to 42
Colossal	10 to 15	Medium	43 to 50
Extra jumbo	16 to 20	Small	51 to 60
Jumbo	21 to 25	Extra small	61 to 70
Extra Large	26 to 30	Tiny	Over 70
Large	31 to 35		

The Fillet Board

Clean shrimp while it's raw. Cooked shrimp is slightly more difficult to clean. Cleaning raw shrimp without fancy gadgets is easy. I peel shrimp with two strokes if I leave the tail on. Three strokes if I remove the tail.

1. Holding the shrimp by the tail with one hand, peel the front half of the shell up and over with your thumb, removing the legs with the shell.

2. Repeat with the back half. Leave the tail attached.

3. To remove the tail, hold the shrimp meat with one hand. Pull straight back on the tail with the thumb and forefinger of the other hand.

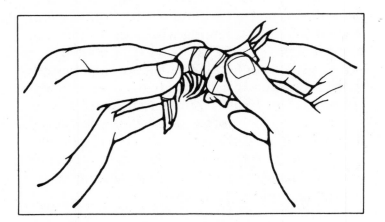

When handling shrimp, be careful not to puncture the skin on your finger with the sharp, spiny tip of the tail.

Devein raw shrimp easily by slicing a ¼-inch-deep cut down the center of the back, from head to tail.

Spread the cut open using the knife to pull out the vein. The cut blooms (spreads) when cooked.

To back-butterfly shrimp, just slice a deeper cut down the center of the back. Cut a little over halfway through the shrimp so that two sides can lay apart. Be careful not to cut the shrimp through.

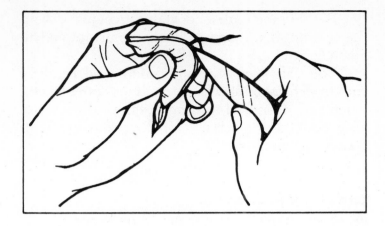

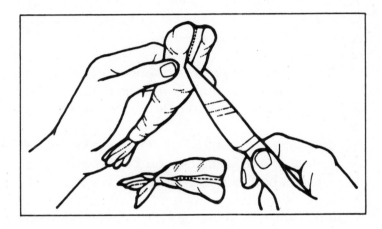

Back-butterflied shrimp blooms with beautiful white flesh when cooked, but it curls tightly. Don't back-butterfly for dipping shrimp. Use this method for sautéed, poached or steamed shrimp. When stuffing extra large shrimp or larger, butterfly on the belly, or underside, not down the back. Spread the side out flat. Place a mound of stuffing under or on top of the flattened shrimp.

I like to wing-cut shrimp for sautéed dishes. The wings spread out on both sides and make a few shrimp look like a large, snowy white pile with accents of pink. Just split the shrimp into two sides, from head end to the tail, before cooking. Leave the tail attached. Or you can just split it 1 inch on the head end and still use it for dipping.

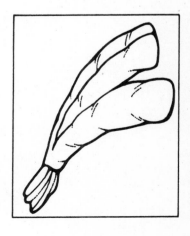

For dipping with a cocktail sauce, just devein the shrimp. It will be less likely to curl into a ball when cooked.

You can keep shrimp straight and rigid by running a bamboo skewer through the entire length, when raw, from tail to head. Remove the skewer after cooking, or serve it on the skewer for an elegant oriental touch.

Cooking the Catch

Fresh or thawed shrimp needs no more than 5 minutes to cook completely. If the shrimp is cut in any way, it will cook in 1 or 2 minutes. Jumbo and colossal shrimp might need the full 5 minutes, but no more.

The simplest way, and to some the best way, is boiled shrimp in the shell. If you can boil water and read spice labels, you can enjoy boiled shrimp any time.

Just take 2 cups of water, 3 tablespoons of red wine vinegar and a tablespoon of pickling spice. Bring it to a boil, add the shrimp, cover and cook.

The best advice I can give you on cooking shrimp in any way, shape or form is this: Undercook it. By the time it reaches the table, it will be perfectly cooked. Do not start cooking shrimp until just before it is scheduled to be served.

Sometimes, if it is part of a larger-volume dish like soup, stew or casserole, the liquid will temper the heat and soften its effect on the shrimp. However, just like mushrooms, I recommend that you hold the raw shrimp back until just before serving—then add it.

Create Your Own
Shrimp Boil

There are hundreds of combinations for brewing up a shrimp boil. Here are some I've used in the past. Create your own signature shrimp boil.

In Place of Pickling Spice

crab boil mix
bay leaves
ground white or black pepper
dry mustard
thyme
parsley
garlic powder
paprika
cayenne pepper
coriander seeds
celery seeds

In Place of Water

chicken stock
vegetable stock
fish stock
beer
weak orange juice

In Place of or with Vinegar

lemon juice
lime juice
frozen orange juice concentrate
citrus fruit slices
hot pepper sauce
Worcestershire sauce

Rock shrimp, with its small yield of meat, is certainly sensitive to overcooking. Try not to cook rock shrimp for more than 1 minute. That will guarantee you tasty, plump morsels of crustacean that resemble lobster meat.

Properly cooked shrimp will bring smiles to the faces of the people who dine at your table.

~~~~~~ **Galley Tips**

~~~~~~ Shrimp (1 lb.)

Technique Market form	Directions	Time (min.)	Temp.
Boil Shell on, peeled and deveined	Use a large pot; boil spicy stock for 5 minutes; add shrimp and return to simmer; stir; when finished, drain and serve hot or chilled.	3–5	High
Bake Shell on, peeled and deveined	Use a flat nonstick pan; brush lightly with vegetable oil/juice mixture.	3–5	425°–450°F
Broil Peeled and deveined	Use a flat nonstick pan; brush lightly with vegetable oil/juice mixture; broil 4 inches or less from heat; stir once.	2–4	High
Grill Shell on, peeled and deveined	Cook large shrimp directly on the grill; baste often with vegetable oil/juice mixture; turn once.	2–4	High
Sauté Peeled and deveined	Use a nonstick skillet; sauté in small amount of vegetable oil and citrus juice; stir often.	3–5	Med.-high
Stir-fry Peeled and deveined	Use a hot wok; stir-fry shrimp in small amount of peanut oil; remove shrimp; stir-fry vegetables; add shrimp, stir, cover and steam for 1 minute.	3–5	Med.-high
Microwave Shell on, peeled and deveined	Brush with stock, water or juice; arrange shrimp in 1 layer around edge of dish, tails pointing in; cover with lid, loose plastic or waxed paper; rotate often; let stand for 1 minute after cooking.	3–5	Med. (70%)

Shrimp-Stuffed Zucchini

OPTIONS: Crabmeat, Scallops

2 zucchinis, cut in half lengthwise
¾ pound medium large shrimp, peeled and deveined
1 cup boiling water
¼ cup minced red onions
¼ cup chopped fresh mushrooms
¼ cup shredded carrots
1 tablespoon olive oil
1 tablespoon chopped fresh tarragon or 1 teaspoon dried tarragon
3 tablespoons bread crumbs

Slightly scoop out each zucchini half with a spoon. Chop scooped-out pulp and set aside.

In a saucepan, poach shrimp in water for 2 minutes. Drain and set aside.

In a large bowl, combine zucchini pulp, onions, mushrooms, carrots, oil, tarragon and bread crumbs. Toss to blend. Coarsely chop cooked shrimp and toss with stuffing mixture.

Spoon stuffing into zucchini halves and place stuffed zucchini in a square baking dish that has been coated with vegetable cooking spray. Cover with foil and bake in a 350°F oven for 20 minutes. Uncover and bake an additional 10 to 15 minutes to crisp stuffing. Serve immediately.

4 servings
140 calories per serving

Spicy Boiled Shrimp with Two Raspberry Dipping Sauces

OPTIONS: Scallops, Crab claws

2 cups water
½ cup red wine vinegar
1 teaspoon red-hot pepper sauce
2 tablespoons crab boil mix
½ lemon, sliced into 4 equal slices
2 bay leaves
1¼ pounds extra large shrimp, peeled and deveined, tail on
½ cup seedless raspberry jam or preserves
1 tablespoon raspberry vinegar
1 tablespoon grated fresh horseradish
1 tablespoon sour cream

In a large saucepan, combine water, red wine vinegar, hot pepper sauce, crab boil mix, lemon slices and bay leaves. Bring to a boil, reduce heat, cover and simmer for 10 minutes.

Place shrimp in boiling bouillon. Stir, bring to a boil, cover and cook for 2 minutes. Stir and cook for 1 minute more. Drain.

In a small bowl, mix together raspberry jam or preserves, raspberry vinegar and horseradish to make first raspberry sauce.

In another small bowl, combine ¼ cup first raspberry sauce with sour cream and blend thoroughly to make second raspberry sauce.

Arrange shrimp on a platter. Serve hot or chilled with two raspberry dipping sauces.

4 servings
242 calories per serving

Yellow Shrimp Barbecue

OPTIONS: Scallops, Lobster meat

2 tablespoons safflower oil
1 teaspoon curry powder
1 teaspoon grated lemon peel
1 tablespoon lemon juice
1 tablespoon low-sodium soy sauce
1 pound colossal shrimp, peeled,
    deveined and butterflied,
    tail on

In a small saucepan, heat oil over medium heat for 1 minute. Stir in curry powder and cook for 2 minutes more. Remove from heat and let stand for 1 minute. Add lemon peel, lemon juice and soy sauce and blend.

Place shrimp in a gallon-size, plastic food-storage bag. Pour curry marinade over shrimp, twist-tie shut and gently knead shrimp to coat evenly. Marinate in the refrigerator for 1 to 2 hours.

Arrange shrimp on a hot grill and barbecue for 1 to 2 minutes on each side, or broil at least 4 inches from the heat for 2 to 3 minutes on each side. Serve hot with lemon wedges, if desired.

4 servings
164 calories per serving

Shrimp and Cucumber Salad

OPTIONS: Lobster meat, Scallops

1 pound medium large shrimp,
    peeled and deveined
1 cup boiling water
¼ cup reduced-calorie mayonnaise
½ cup plain low-fat yogurt, drained
    overnight
1 tablespoon lemon juice
    dash of ground white pepper
½ teaspoon dried dill
¾ cup thinly sliced, seeded
    cucumbers
1 scallion, sliced
2 cups shredded romaine lettuce

In a saucepan, poach shrimp in water for 3 to 4 minutes. Drain and chill shrimp for 1 hour.

In a large bowl, combine mayonnaise, yogurt, lemon juice, pepper, dill, cucumbers and scallions. Cut chilled shrimp into large chunks and fold into dressing. Mound salad on lettuce and serve.

4 servings
162 calories per serving

Lemon Sautéed Shrimp Wings

OPTIONS: Scallops, Lobster medallions

1 tablespoon butter
1 tablespoon olive oil
1 small clove garlic, crushed
1 lemon, sliced into 8 equal slices
⅛ teaspoon red-hot pepper sauce
1¼ pounds extra large shrimp, peeled
    and deveined, tail on, split
    1-inch on head end

In a large skillet, combine butter and oil over low heat. Rub garlic over bottom of pan and cook for 2 minutes. Do not brown. Discard garlic.

Turn heat to medium-high. Place lemon slices and hot pepper sauce in pan and sauté for 5 minutes turning once and pressing juice from slices with a spoon. Remove and set aside.

Place shrimp in the pan and sauté over medium-high heat for 5 to 6 minutes. Add lemon slices and sauté for 1 minute more. Serve immediately.

4 servings
181 calories per serving

Grilled Sweet-and-Tart Shrimp

    2 tablespoons coarse Dijon
        mustard
    2 tablespoons white wine vinegar
        or rice wine vinegar
    2 tablespoons vegetable oil
    2 tablespoons honey
    1¼ pounds jumbo shrimp, peeled
        and deveined, tail on

In a shallow bowl, combine mustard, vinegar, oil and honey. Stir to blend. Add shrimp and toss to coat. Cover and marinate in refrigerator for 1 hour.

Place shrimp on a hot grill and barbecue for 3 to 5 minutes, turning once and basting often with marinade. Serve warm with orange and lime wedges, if desired.

Variation: Broil 4 inches from the heat for 4 to 6 minutes, turning once and basting often with marinade.

Serve warm with orange and lime wedges, if desired.

4 servings
234 calories per serving

Shrimp and Chicken Calico Stew

OPTIONS: Scallops, Lobster meat, Crabmeat

    1 teaspoon olive oil
    ¼ cup chopped scallions
    ¼ cup sliced carrots
    ½ pound boneless chicken breast,
        cut in quarters
    1 small clove garlic, minced
    ½ cup corn kernels
    1 cup diced tomatoes
   12 snow peas
    1 tablespoon fresh parsley
    ¼ teaspoon dried thyme leaves
    1 cup chicken stock
   12 extra large shrimp, peeled and
        deveined
    ½ cup milk

Heat oil in a large, heavy-bottom pot. Add scallions and carrots and sauté over medium heat for 3 to 4 minutes. Add chicken and garlic. Stir and sauté for 4 to 5 minutes. Add corn, tomatoes, peas, parsley, thyme and chicken stock. Bring to a boil and simmer for 10 minutes. Add shrimp, stir in milk, return to a simmer and cook for 2 to 3 minutes. Serve steaming hot.

4 servings
172 calories per serving

Stir-Fried Shrimp and Vegetable Cylinders

OPTION: Crab leg pieces

1 tablespoon plus 1 teaspoon peanut oil
½ cup diagonally cut green beans
½ cup diagonally cut wax beans
½ cup diagonally cut asparagus
½ cup peeled carrot tips
½ cup diagonally cut scallions
¾ pound extra large shrimp, peeled and deveined
1 tablespoon cornstarch
¼ cup chicken stock
1 small clove garlic, minced
1 teaspoon minced gingerroot or ½ teaspoon ground ginger
1 teaspoon low-sodium soy sauce

In a wok, heat 1 tablespoon oil for 1 minute over medium-high heat. Add green beans, wax beans, asparagus, carrots and scallions and stir-fry for 3 to 4 minutes. Remove vegetables and set aside.

Dust shrimp with cornstarch and stir-fry in remaining oil for 3 to 4 minutes. Add chicken stock, garlic, ginger, soy sauce and vegetables. Stir, cover and cook for 3 to 5 minutes. Stir and remove from heat. Serve immediately.

4 servings
145 calories per serving

Peppered Herb Shrimp

3 teaspoons olive oil
1 green pepper, sliced into ½-inch strips
1 sweet red pepper, sliced into ½-inch strips
1 onion, core removed, sliced into thin strips
1 clove garlic, minced
1 pound extra large shrimp, peeled and deveined
1 tablespoon sliced fresh sage or 1 teaspoon rubbed sage
1 teaspoon fresh thyme leaves or ¼ teaspoon dried thyme leaves
¼ teaspoon freshly ground black pepper
¼ cup lime juice

In a large, deep nonstick skillet or heavy pot, heat 2 teaspoons oil. Add green peppers, red peppers and onions and sauté, stirring often, over medium-high heat for 3 to 4 minutes. Stir in garlic and cook for 1 to 2 minutes more. Remove vegetables from skillet and set aside.

Add remaining oil and sauté shrimp, stirring often, for 2 to 3 minutes. Stir in sage, thyme and black pepper and cook for 1 minute.

Return vegetables to skillet, add lime juice, toss to mix, cover and cook for 1 to 2 minutes. Garnish with lime slices and sage sprigs and serve.

4 servings
154 calories per serving

Shark Steak Bake with Herbs
page 156

179

Maritime Monkfish Soup
page 165

Spicy Boiled Shrimp
with Two Raspberry Dipping Sauces
page 175

Stir-Fried Pepper Scallops
page 190

Shrimp Pouches

OPTIONS: Scallops, Lobster meat

¾ pound medium large shrimp,
    peeled and deveined
¼ cup plus 1 tablespon sliced
    scallions
1 small clove garlic, minced
1½ teaspoons sesame oil
¼ cup plus 1 teaspoon low-sodium
    soy sauce
24 round or square wonton
    wrappers

In a food processor, chop shrimp into a paste with ¼ cup scallions, garlic, 1 teaspoon oil and 1 teaspoon soy sauce.

Moisten edge of each wonton wrapper with water. Place a small spoonful of shrimp paste in the middle, gather wrapper into a small pouch with a small amount of shrimp paste exposed. Press pouch lightly to form a neck. Place on the racks of a bamboo steamer, set over water in a hot wok and steam each batch for 5 minutes.

Combine remaining soy sauce with remaining oil and scallions in a small dipping bowl. Serve shrimp pouches on a tray or a steamer rack with dipping sauce.

    4 servings
    209 calories per serving

Louisiana Hot-Broiled Shrimp

¼ cup red-hot pepper sauce
2 tablespoons red wine vinegar
2 tablespoons olive oil
2 tablespoons hickory-smoked
    barbecue sauce
1 tablespoon Worcestershire
    sauce
½ teaspoon garlic powder
1¼ pounds extra large shrimp,
    peeled and deveined

In a small bowl, combine hot pepper sauce, vinegar, oil, barbecue sauce, Worcestershire sauce and garlic powder. Stir to blend thoroughly with a fork.

Place shrimp in a double gallon-size, plastic food-storage bag. Pour marinade over shrimp. Squeeze air out of bag and twist-tie shut. Knead bag to coat shrimp evenly and marinate in refrigerator for 1 hour.

Drain shrimp, catching marinade in a bowl. Place shrimp on a flat broiling pan and broil 4 inches from heat for 3 to 5 minutes. Turn once and baste both sides with marinade. Serve with lemon wedges, if desired.

Variation: Barbecue on a hot grill for 3 or 4 minutes, turning once and basting with marinade. Serve with lemon wedges, if desired.

    4 servings
    196 calories per serving

Skewered Shrimp with Scallion–Orange Relish

OPTIONS: Bay scallops or sea scallops

¼ teaspoon prepared wasabi green horseradish or 1 tablespoon grated fresh horseradish
½ cup low-sodium soy sauce
¼ cup frozen orange juice concentrate
28 extra large shrimp, peeled and deveined, tail on
¼ cup sliced scallions
½ cup diced, seeded orange sections
¼ cup julienne of dried apricots
2 tablespoons minced fresh cilantro or parsley
1 tablespoon orange juice
1 teaspoon honey
1 tablespoon peanut oil

Soak eight 6-inch bamboo skewers in water for 1 hour.

In a shallow bowl, combine horseradish with soy sauce and orange juice concentrate. Add shrimp to marinade and toss to coat evenly. Cover and marinate in refrigerator for 1 hour.

Meanwhile, in a small bowl, combine scallions, oranges, apricots, cilantro or parsley, orange juice and honey. Let stand at room temperature for 45 minutes to blend flavors.

Drain marinade from shrimp and discard. Slide shrimp onto double skewers. (Two skewers keep the pieces stable). Arrange shrimp closely, alternating the direction. Six should fit on each skewer.

Pour oil into a hot, flat skillet and sauté shrimp quickly, 1 to 2 minutes on each side. Serve hot with scallion-orange relish.

4 servings
172 calories per serving

Hot Potted Shrimp

OPTIONS: Lobster meat, Scallops

24 extra large shrimp, peeled and deveined
1 cup boiling water
1 whole egg
1 egg white
¼ cup skim milk
1 tablespoon catsup
1 teaspoon prepared horseradish
1 tablespoon lemon juice
1 tablespoon olive oil

In a saucepan, poach shrimp in water for 2 minutes. Drain shrimp and set aside.

In a medium bowl, slightly whisk whole egg and egg white together. Stir in milk, catsup, horseradish, lemon juice and oil, one at a time. Blend thoroughly.

Coat four custard cups with vegetable cooking spray, arrange six shrimp in each and pour custard mixture over shrimp. Place cups in a baking pan of hot water and bake in a 300°F oven for 25 to 30 minutes, or until a toothpick inserted in the center comes out clean. Let stand 5 minutes before serving.

4 servings
154 calories per serving

Scallops

~~~~~~~~~~~~~~~~~~~~~~~~~~~~~~~~~~~~~

Scallops are the ultimate plain or fancy fast food. Portioned by nature into bite-size pieces, they need only moments to cook, and that means they're perfect for those meals you make on the run. They fall right into any plan—broil, stir-fry, poach, bake or sauté—and in 5 or 6 minutes you're sitting down to a treat that's terrific.

The large sea scallops familiar to most of us are fished from the North Atlantic and shucked from the shell at sea. European fishermen keep the roe to sell at market, but Americans generally discard it. The roe from scallops is a gourmet delicacy; I urge you to try it if you see it in the display case.

Speaking of delicacies, the tinier bay scallop fits that category to perfection. This gem found only in bays and harbors, from Long Island to Cape Cod, is sometimes sold as cape scallop. But whether it's called bay or cape, the flavor and texture are superior to all other small scallops. This includes calico scallops, fished from the warm waters off the Carolinas to South America and generally smaller than bay scallops. When you buy them in the store, you'll find that the calicos are usually slightly cooked; that's due to the steam process that is used to shuck them.

Unlike other bivalves such as clams, oysters and mussels, scallops can propel themselves through the water by opening and closing their shells. This helps them escape from predators. More important to you, this mobility helps scallops to get away from pollutants the immobile bivalves sometimes have to live with.

185

**School
of Nutrients**

Scallops
3½ oz. raw

186

Super Seafood

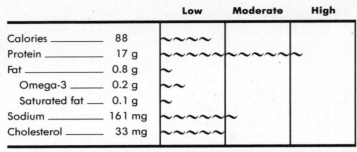

	Low	Moderate	High
Calories ——— 88	~~~~		
Protein ——— 17 g	~~~~~~~	~~~~~~	
Fat ——— 0.8 g	~		
Omega-3 ——— 0.2 g	~~		
Saturated fat — 0.1 g	~		
Sodium ——— 161 mg	~~~~		
Cholesterol ——— 33 mg	~~~~		

Source: Adapted from Agriculture Handbook No. 8–15 (Washington, D.C.: U.S. Department of Agriculture).

Talking to Your Fishmonger

Scallops of one kind or another are generally available year-round, but be prepared for prices that fluctuate wildly according to harvest and demand. The highest prices are commanded by bay scallops because they are only available fresh in late fall and early winter. Don't be taken in by the tiny calicos sometimes passed off as bay scallops. Bay scallops are always a translucent cream color; calicos are usually white and smaller than bay scallops. The much larger sea scallops are also a cream color. All fresh scallops should be shiny and plump, with the scent of sweet seawater.

Frozen scallops are sometimes thawed for the retail display case. They are usually white and less tender than fresh scallops when cooked. Frozen scallops should also cost less than the fresh ones.

You really can't depend on size claims when it comes to scallops. However, I think this range of counts per pound is reasonable:

sea scallops: 20 to 40 per pound
bay scallops: 50 to 90 per pound
calico scallops: 70 to 200 per pound

The Fillet Board

Keep scallops on ice when refrigerated, and use them within 24 hours. I don't recommend freezing

Scallops, Bay, Sea and Calico	
Market form	**Amount per person (lb.)**
Shucked	¼–⅓

scallops bought at a retail fish market or fish counter. Buy only what you need, when you need it.

Wash scallops just before you are ready to cook them. If a recipe calls for thin scallop disks, you can slice sea scallops in half across the cylinder; the disks cook twice as fast.

Cooking the Catch

Always undercook scallops slightly. They will finish cooking by the time they reach the table. A good rule of thumb is 1 to 4 minutes for bay scallops and calico scallops; no more than 5 to 6 minutes for sea scallops. This short, convenient exposure to heat guarantees moist, tender seafood morsels that are full of flavor. Don't overcook scallops; if you do, they turn into shrunken, tough, white balls with diminished flavor. To me, that's a culinary tragedy.

~~~~~ **Galley Tips**

~~~~~ Scallops (1 lb.)

Technique Market form	Directions	Time (min.)	Temp.
Bake Bay, sea, calico	Use a flat nonstick pan; brush with vegetable oil/juice mixture.	Bay and calico: 1–4 sea: 3–6	425°– 450°F
Broil Bay, sea, calico	Use a flat nonstick pan; brush lightly with vegetable oil/juice mixture; broil 4 inches or less from heat; do not stir.	Bay and calico: 1–4 sea: 3–5	High
Poach Bay, sea, calico	Use a deep skillet or large saucepan; combine citrus juice with water or stock.	Bay and calico: 1–4 sea: 3–6	Med. to med.-high
Sauté Bay, sea, calico	Use a nonstick skillet; sauté in small amount of vegetable oil and citrus juice; stir once.	Bay and calico: 1–4 sea: 3–6	Med.-high
Stir-fry Bay, sea, calico	Use a hot wok; stir-fry scallops first in small amount of hot peanut oil; remove scallops; stir-fry vegetables; add scallops, stir, cover and steam for 1 minute.	Bay and calico: 1–4 sea: 3–6	Med.-high to high
Microwave Bay, sea, calico	Brush with stock, water or juice; arrange scallops in 1 layer around edge of dish; cover with lid, loose plastic or waxed paper; rotate often; let stand for 1 minute after cooking.	Bay and calico: 2–5 sea: 3–6	High (100%)

Scallops Santa Cruz

OPTIONS: Shrimp, Lobster meat

---

2 teaspoons olive oil
1 pound bay scallops or sea
    scallops
½ cup finely diced onions
1 small clove garlic, minced
1 jar (4 ounces) roasted sweet red
    pepper or pimiento strips
1 can (4 ounces) peeled mild green
    chili peppers
1 package (10 ounces) frozen
    whole bay corn, thawed
    dash of ground white pepper
1 tablespoon minced fresh parsley

In a large skillet, heat 1 teaspoon oil. Add scallops and sauté for 2 minutes. Drain pan juices, remove scallops and set aside.

In remaining oil, sauté onions and garlic for 1 minute. Add red peppers or pimientos, chili peppers, corn, white pepper and parsley. Stir and cook for 1 minute. Stir in scallops and continue cooking, uncovered, for 2 to 3 minutes. Serve over steamed rice if desired.

    4 servings
    162 calories per serving

Broiled Scallops Provençale

OPTIONS: Shrimp, Lobster meat,
Lump crabmeat

1¼ pounds bay scallops or calico
    scallops
1 tablespoon butter
1 tablespoon olive oil
1 tablespoon lemon juice
1 small clove garlic, minced
1 tablespoon fresh bread crumbs
1 tablespoon grated Parmesan
    cheese or Romano cheese

Divide scallops among 4 individual broiling dishes. In a small saucepan, melt butter with oil, lemon juice and garlic. Spoon butter mixture evenly over scallops, sprinkle with bread crumbs and Parmesan or Romano and broil 4 inches from heat for 2 to 3 minutes.

    4 servings
    195 calories per serving

Crouton-Stuffed Scallops

OPTIONS: Shrimp, Lobster meat

---

3 cups croutons
½ cup chicken stock
½ cup skim milk
1 tablespoon minced fresh sage or
    1 teaspoon rubbed sage
2 tablespoons minced fresh
    parsley
    dash of ground white pepper
1 teaspoon olive oil
½ cup minced onions
½ cup minced celery
1 pound sea scallops
1 tablespoon bread crumbs
⅛ teaspoon paprika

In a large bowl, toss croutons in chicken stock, milk, sage, parsley and pepper. Let stand for 15 minutes.

In a skillet, heat oil. Add onions and celery and sauté until soft, then combine with crouton mixture. Spread crouton stuffing evenly on the bottom of a large, shallow baking dish. Arrange scallops in a single layer on top of the stuffing.

Combine bread crumbs and paprika and sprinkle evenly over scallops. Bake, uncovered, in a 450°F oven for 10 to 12 minutes. Serve immediately.

    4 servings
    214 calories per serving

Stir-Fried Pepper Scallops

OPTION: Shrimp

---

1 tablespoon peanut oil
1 cup thinly sliced sweet red
 peppers or yellow peppers
1 cup thinly sliced green peppers
1 cup thinly sliced onions
1 pound sea scallops
1 teaspoon sesame oil
1 tablespoon low-sodium soy sauce

Heat peanut oil in a wok for 1 minute over medium-high heat. Stir-fry peppers and onions until just cooked, about 5 minutes. Remove vegetables and set aside.

Stir-fry scallops for 3 minutes. Return vegetables to the wok and toss with scallops. Add sesame oil and soy sauce. Toss, cover and cook for 1 to 2 minutes. Serve immediately over oriental ramen noodles, if desired.

 4 servings
 168 calories per serving

Sea Scallops Baked in Spinach Leaves

OPTIONS: Lobster meat, Shrimp

---

1 cup chicken stock
2 tablespoons lemon juice
¼ teaspoon dried thyme leaves
 dash of ground white pepper
¼ cup reduced-calorie mayonnaise
1 tablespoon Dijon mustard
1 pound sea scallops
1 jar (4 ounces) pimientos, sliced
 into ¼-inch strips
½ pound fresh spinach leaves

In a small saucepan, combine chicken stock, lemon juice, thyme and white pepper. Bring to a boil, reduce heat

to low and simmer for at least 10 minutes. Set aside.

In a cup, combine mayonnaise and mustard and place a drop on each scallop. Top with a pimiento strip. Wrap each in a spinach leaf, folding edges under, and place in a shallow baking dish.

Pour ½ cup stock mixture over spinach-wrapped scallops, cover with foil and bake in a 400°F oven for 10 to 12 minutes.

 4 servings
 162 calories per serving

Broiled Scallop and Shrimp Kabobs

OPTIONS: Crab leg chunks, Lobster medallions

---

1 tablespoon minced onions
1 tablespoon safflower oil
½ cup tomato juice
½ cup frozen orange juice
 concentrate
⅛ teaspoon red-hot pepper sauce
12 sea scallops (about ½ pound)
8 extra large shrimp, peeled and
 deveined
1 green pepper, cut into eighths

In a gallon-size, plastic food-storage bag, combine onions, oil, tomato juice, orange juice concentrate and hot pepper sauce. Blend thoroughly. Add scallops, shrimp and green peppers to the bag. Twist-tie shut and gently knead bag to coat fish and peppers with marinade. Refrigerate for 1 to 2 hours.

Soak eight 6-inch bamboo skewers in water for 1 hour.

Alternate scallops and peppers on double skewers (two skewers keep the pieces stable). Finish by placing a shrimp on either end of the skewers.

Place marinade in a small saucepan and bring to a boil over high heat. Simmer for 5 minutes and set aside for basting.

Place kabobs on a broiling pan and baste with some marinade. Broil for 3 to 5 minutes, no more than 4 inches from heat. Turn kabobs over, baste and broil for another 2 to 3 minutes, or until fish is fully cooked. Serve over rice pilaf, if desired.

4 servings
164 calories per serving

Skillet-Seared Scallops on Skewers

---

    24 sea scallops (about 1¼ pounds)
     1 large sweet red pepper, cut into
          16 ½-inch squares
     1 tablespoon flour
     1 tablespoon paprika
     1 teaspoon chili powder
     3 teaspoons peanut oil
     1 cup chunky salsa
     1 tablespoon red wine vinegar
     2 tablespoons frozen orange juice
          concentrate

Soak eight 9-inch bamboo skewers in vinegar for 30 minutes.

Alternate scallops and peppers (using two scallops for each pepper) on double skewers (two skewers keep the pieces stable), beginning and ending each with a pepper square.

On a plate, mix together flour, paprika and chili powder. Dry each skewer of scallops with a paper towel. Press all four sides of each skewer into seasonings.

In a large, well-seasoned, cast-iron skillet, heat 1 teaspoon oil to smoking over medium-high heat. Sear each side of the skewers for 1 to 2 minutes on each side, or until browned. Add remaining oil as needed. Remove to serving plate.

Reduce heat to medium. Add salsa, vinegar and orange juice concentrate to the pan. Bring to a boil and pour over scallop skewers to serve.

4 servings
208 calories per serving

Scallops with Mushrooms, Leeks and Tarragon

---

     1 cup sliced leeks
     1 tablespoon olive oil
     2 cups sliced fresh mushrooms
     2 teaspoons fresh tarragon or
          ½ teaspoon dried tarragon
     1 tablespoon lemon juice
    1¼ pounds sea scallops
     2 teaspoons grated Parmesan
          cheese
     ¼ teaspoon paprika

In a large nonstick skillet, sauté leeks in oil over medium-high heat for 1 to 2 minutes. Add mushrooms and sauté for 3 to 4 minutes. Stir in tarragon and lemon juice and remove from heat. Drain pan juices into a small bowl.

Coat a shallow casserole dish or pie plate with vegetable cooking spray. Spoon sautéed mushrooms and leeks onto the bottom and arrange scallops in a single layer on top. Spoon pan juices over all and sprinkle with Parmesan, then paprika. Broil scallops 4 to 6 inches from the heat for 6 to 8 minutes, or until cheese begins to brown. Serve hot, garnished with mushroom caps.

4 servings
191 calories per serving

Baby Scallop Burritos

OPTIONS: Crabmeat, Lobster meat

1 tablespoon olive oil
¼ cup sliced scallions
¼ cup sliced black olives
¼ cup corn kernels
1 small clove garlic, minced
1 teaspoon minced chili peppers
    or ⅛ teaspoon cayenne pepper
⅛ teaspoon ground cumin
1 pound bay scallops or calico
    scallops
4 9- or 10-inch flour tortillas
½ cup chunky salsa
½ cup sour cream

In a large skillet, heat oil. Add scallions, olives, corn, garlic and chili peppers or cayenne and sauté over medium heat for 2 minutes. Add cumin and scallops and sauté for 3 minutes.

In another skillet, soften flour tortillas over medium heat. Spoon scallop mixture onto tortillas, roll to wrap and fold under ends. Serve immediately with salsa and sour cream.

4 servings
313 calories per servings

Scallops and Shells Marinara

OPTION: Shrimp

1 tablespoon olive oil
½ cup diced onions
1 cup sliced mushrooms
1 small clove garlic, minced
1 cup chopped plum tomatoes
1 cup tomato puree
½ teaspoon fennel seeds
    dash of cayenne pepper
1 pound bay scallops or sea
    scallops
½ pound small pasta shells, cooked
1 tablespoon grated Parmesan
    cheese

In a 3- to 4-quart heavy pot, heat oil. Add onions and mushrooms and sauté over medium heat for 2 minutes. Add garlic and tomatoes and sauté for another minute. Stir in tomato puree, fennel seeds and cayenne, reduce heat to low, cover and simmer for 10 minutes, stirring occasionally.

Add scallops, cover and simmer over low heat for 3 to 5 minutes.

Spoon scallops and sauce over individual servings of pasta. Sprinkle with grated Parmesan and serve immediately.

4 servings
393 calories per serving

New England Scallop Stew

OPTIONS: Shrimp, Lobster meat

1 tablespoon olive oil
½ cup diced onions
½ cup sliced leeks
½ cup thinly sliced celery
½ cup diced green peppers
½ cup chopped tomatoes
1 small clove garlic, minced
2 cups chicken stock
1 cup clam juice
½ teaspoon dried thyme leaves
⅛ teaspoon ground white pepper
1 teaspoon Dijon mustard
1 teaspoon Worcestershire sauce
1 tablespoon minced fresh parsley
2 bay leaves
¾ pound bay scallops or calico
    scallops
1 cup milk

In a large, heavy pot, heat oil. Add onions, leeks, celery and peppers and sauté until soft, about 5 minutes. Add tomatoes and garlic and sauté for 1 minute.

Add chicken stock, clam juice, thyme, white pepper, mustard, Worcestershire sauce, parsley and bay leaves. Bring to a boil, reduce heat and simmer for 15 to 20 minutes.

Add scallops to the pot, remove from heat and let steep 2 to 3 minutes.

Warm milk. Add to the pot, stir, remove bay leaves and serve.

4 servings
190 calories per serving

Baked Scallops with Mushroom Crust

OPTION: Lobster meat

2 tablespoons minced shallots or scallions
1 tablespoon olive oil
1 cup finely chopped fresh mushrooms
  dash of cayenne pepper
¼ cup bread crumbs
1¼ pounds sea scallops

In a large skillet, sauté shallots or scallions in oil for 1 minute. Add mushrooms and sauté for 2 minutes. Stir in cayenne and bread crumbs and sauté for 1 minute more.

Arrange scallops in a single layer on a broiling pan or individual broiling dishes. Spoon mushroom mixture evenly over all scallops and bake in a 450°F oven for 5 to 7 minutes. Pass under the broiler for 1 minute to brown crust and serve immediately.

4 servings
187 calories per serving

Scallop and Cuke Salad

OPTION: Shrimp

1 cup chicken stock
¼ cup plus 1 tablespoon lime juice
⅛ teaspoon red-hot pepper sauce
1 pound bay scallops or calico scallops
¼ cup chopped, seeded cucumbers
  dash of ground white pepper
¼ cup reduced-calorie mayonnaise
¾ cup sliced, seeded cucumbers
4 romaine lettuce leaves

In a medium saucepan, combine chicken stock, ¼ cup lime juice and hot pepper sauce. Bring to a boil and remove from the heat. Add scallops and let stand for 2 minutes. Drain. (Stock may be used in a soup recipe.) Chill scallops for at least 1 hour.

In a blender, puree chopped cucumbers, remaining lime juice and white pepper.

In a mixing bowl, combine cucumber puree, mayonnaise, sliced cucumbers and toss to blend. Fold in chilled scallops. Spoon on lettuce leaves to serve.

4 servings
148 calories per serving

Crabs

~~~~~~~~~~~~~~~~~~~~~~~~~~~~

Crabs are truly the imperial members of the shell-fish family. The sweet flavor and delicate texture (not to mention the high price) can transform any dining occasion into a royal feast.

The yield of meat in most crabs is about one-quarter the crab's total weight. And breaking through those hard shells to get out the meat is no easy task. But on those rare occasions when you have the opportunity to get fresh crabs. I believe it's well worth the effort. Crabmeat can also be purchased pasteurized or frozen.

Blue crabs are the number one crab seller in the United States, probably because they have the widest geographical range (Cape Cod to Florida and the Gulf Coast waters) and because they have the most delicate textured crabmeat. They are swimming crabs that maneuver with their flat rear "legs" called the backfins. In comparison to their cousins, blue crabs are small.

As it grows, a blue crab sheds its hard shell (molts) many times during its growth cycle of 18 months. All types of crabs molt, but only blue crab is meaty enough to be edible during the molting stage. Live soft-shell crabs readily reach the marketplace during the molting season in June, July and August. They are available frozen during the rest of the year. You eat the entire soft-shell crab, calcium-rich shell and all, after minimal cleaning.

My introduction to whole soft-shell crab was in a sandwich. I didn't know quite what to expect and was aghast to see little legs and claws hanging off the side of the kaiser roll. But I'm not one to turn

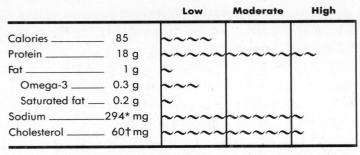

		Low	Moderate	High
Calories	85	~~~		
Protein	18 g	~~~~~~~~~~		
Fat	1 g	~		
Omega-3	0.3 g	~~		
Saturated fat	0.2 g	~		
Sodium	294* mg	~~~~~~~~~		
Cholesterol	60† mg	~~~~~~~~~		

**School
of Nutrients**

Crab, blue, king and
Dungeness
3½ oz. raw

195
~~~~
Crabs

Source: Adapted from Agriculture Handbook No. 8–15 (Washington, D.C.: U.S.
Department of Agriculture).
*The exception is Dungeness with a sodium value of 830 mg.
†This figure is an average.

down an eating adventure. That sandwich was great
and I have been hooked on soft-shells ever since!

Blue crabs are a popular East-Coast delicacy
during the summer when they are sold steamed
and whole and usually by the piece or dozen in crab
houses and take-out restaurants near the shore
points. The taste is so perfect it needs no dipping
sauce, as lobster and clams often do. People can
literally spend hours cracking crabs and picking
them clean of meat.

West Coasters think a lot bigger when it comes
to their love affair with crab. Dungeness crab is
their idea of good eating. Dungeness is a large rock
crab normally weighing between 1½ to 2½ pounds
on the market. One to a customer is usually more
than plenty. One of my most memorable meals
included performing delicate surgery on a steamed
dungeness crab to expose the tender meat for picking. That was preceded by a bowl of perfect she-
crab soup.

Then there is king crab, truly the giant of its
kingdom. King crab spans up to 6 feet across and is
primarily fished off Alaska. It is prized for its giant
legs, which are sold frozen at the market. King crab
is a popular appetizer item but is also served steamed
as a main course. Though much smaller, the snow
crab from waters around the continental United
States is sometimes offered as an alternative when

king crab is in short supply, and it's quite acceptable. The meat is firm but doesn't quite come up to the lobsterlike quality of the king crab.

The claws of the stone crab, which lives in the waters from Florida to Texas, are a gourmet's delight. These black-tipped claws must be cooked immediately after harvest. You can sometimes find them frozen for the marketplace.

Talking to Your Fishmonger

Generally, crabs are sold as live whole, cooked whole and parts or crabmeat picked clean from the shell.

Live hard-shell blue crabs are sold by the dozen or bushel. Males are called "jimmies" and are larger than females, called "sooks." Never accept dead raw crabs. They should be sold either live or cooked.

Male, hard-shell blue crabs are preferred. The females are smaller and their shell is harder, which makes them more difficult to pick for meat.

Blue crabmeat is picked professionally and sold pasteurized in cans. Jumbo lump or backfin crabmeat are large pieces of meat and are the premier buy (also at a premier price). But it's all pure eating: There is no waste. Flake meat or special meat denotes smaller pieces from the body. Claw meat is browner and cheaper and is used for dishes where the crabmeat is not exposed.

Blue crab cocktail claws are also available.

Soft-shell blue crabs are sold live by the dozen or frozen by the pound. Size is not a sign of quality with soft-shell crabs. However, they are graded by the width of their shell (carapace):

whales: over 5½ inches
jumbos: 5 to 5½ inches
primes: 4½ to 5 inches
hotels: 4 to 4½ inches
mediums: 3½ to 4 inches

All snow crab is cooked immediately after harvest and is sold on the market cooked. Generally, it appears as clusters, which include three legs and

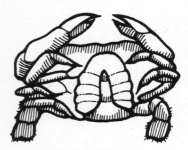

Male hard-shell blue crab

Female hard-shell blue crab

one claw attached to a shoulder. Cocktail claws and snow crabmeat are also available.

Dungeness crabs are available in West-Coast port cities. They are marketed mostly as fresh cooked (whole) or frozen cooked. You can also find clusters, legs, claws and frozen meat. All of these parts have been cooked.

King crab also is cooked immediately after harvest. And it is offered as clusters, legs, claws or as picked king crabmeat. Sometimes you can find split legs and claws.

Stone crab claws are cooked upon harvest and the shell is cracked at the knuckle. Stone crab claws are primarily a Florida treat, but they are shipped frozen all across North America.

Crab, Blue Hard-Shell

Market form	Amount per person
Cocktail claws	½ lb.
Crabmeat	¼ lb.
Whole	3

Crab, Blue Soft-Shell

Market form	Amount per person
Whole	2

Crab, Dungeness

Market form	Amount per person
Claws	¾–1 lb.
Clusters	¾–1 lb.
Crabmeat	¼ lb.
Legs	¾–1 lb.
Whole	½

Crab, King and Snow

Market form	Amount per person (lb.)
Claws	¾–1
Clusters	¾–1
Crabmeat	¼
Legs	¾–1

Crab, Stone

Market form	Amount per person (lb.)
Claws	¾–1
Cocktail claws	½

The Fillet Board

Hard-shell blue crabs need no preparation before they are boiled. The real work starts after they are cooked.

First, remove the legs (leaving the backfin attached), claws and belly apron from the body. At the front of the body, either use a paring knife to cut between the shells at the mouth, or puncture the mouth with your thumb tip. Using two thumbs, pry the top shell from the bottom shell. Discard the top shell. Scoop out the light gray, spongy gills, also know as "dead man's fingers." Crab gills are not edible. Scoop out the intestines. Break the body in half. Twist off the back fins and attached meat. With a dowel or mallet, break the claw shell. Pick the meat out of the body, claw and claw arm with a cocktail fork or your fingers.

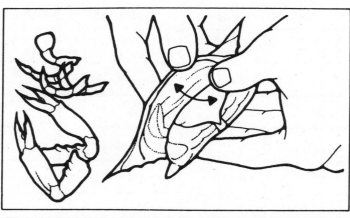

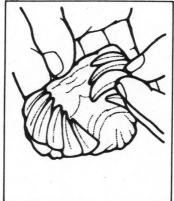

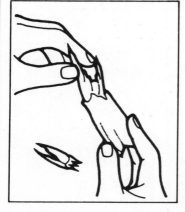

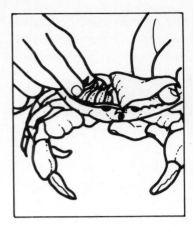 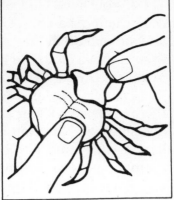 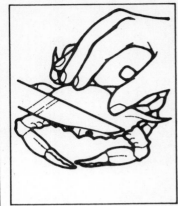

Soft-shell blue crabs need to be cleaned and dressed *before they are cooked.*

First, lift up each side of the upper shell (it is soft). Pull out the light gray, spongy gills. Turn the crab on its back and tear off the apron from the rear of the belly. Either cut off or pull off the face, including the eyes and mouth. Rinse the cleaned soft-shell crab with cold water and pat dry.

Do not clean live, soft-shell crabs unless you are ready to cook them or freeze them.

Snow crab legs can be opened with a metal nutcracker or a sharp, heavy knife. You need the nutcracker for the claws.

Cooked Dungeness crab can be cleaned by hand with the help of a nutcracker for the claws and legs.

A heavy knife or nutcracker can get through the shell on king crab legs. Claws need the cracker.

Stone crab claws need a nutcracker or hammer if the shells have not been precut.

Cooking the Catch

A hard-shell crab boil is a fun time, though messy. Plan a crab boil when you and your guests have lots of leisure time. Boiled hard-shells are not suitable for a 1-hour lunch.

Cover your picnic table with lots of newspaper and have a full roll of paper towels handy. Provide wooden dowels or mallets for cracking the claw shells.

If you have a lot of crabs, you might want to cook them in batches. Use a large pot for each batch and submerge all the crabs in boiling bouillon and then remove from the heat to finish cooking for 5 minutes. Do not overcook.

I pan-fry or sauté cleaned soft-shell crabs. Dredge them in seasoned flour and pan-fry in a small amount of peanut oil. I also sauté soft-shells in olive oil with lemon slices and garlic. Either way, do not cook them more than 4 minutes on each side.

Remove all shell particles from the crabmeat before it's served. Blue crabmeat is pasteurized and need not be cooked for a long time. You should, however, locate and pick out any remaining shell pieces in it. Spread the pasteurized crabmeat on a baking sheet in a thin layer. Place the sheet under the broiler, 4 to 6 inches from the heat. Broil for 30 to 40 seconds.

The shell pieces will turn bright white or red under the broiler and are easy to spot. Simply pick and discard them to clean the meat completely.

Dungeness crab can be prepared in the same manner as blue crab. If the crab is precooked, it can be warmed, heated for a short time in hot water or chilled.

Snow crab will be precooked. You can warm it to serving temperature or serve it cold.

King crab and stone crab claws are both precooked. They can be warmed, steamed for a short time or chilled.

Technique Market form	Directions	Time (min.)	Temp.
Boil Whole, cluster, legs, claws	Boil spicy stock for 10–15 minutes; add crabs, return to boil, remove from heat and let stand for 5 minutes.	5–8	High
Broil Crabmeat	Use a flat nonstick pan; brush lightly with vegetable oil; sprinkle with citrus juice; broil 4–6 inches from heat.	2–4	High
Steam Whole, cluster, legs, claws	Use a shellfish steam kettle or a steamer rack in a wok; combine water and crab boil mix; bring to a rolling boil; cover tightly.	10–12	Med. to med.-high
Sauté Whole soft-shell blue crabs, crabmeat	Use a nonstick skillet; sauté in small amount of vegetable oil and citrus juice; turn crabs once.	Whole: 6–10 crabmeat: 3–5	Med. to med.-high
Microwave Crabmeat	Brush with stock, water or juice; arrange crabmeat in 1 layer around edge of dish; cover with lid, loose plastic or waxed paper; rotate often; let stand for 1 minute after cooking.	1–3	Med. (70%)

Club 18 Crab Cakes with Tommy's Cocktail Sauce

OPTIONS: Dungeness crabmeat, King crabmeat, Snow crabmeat, Cod, Surimi

I concocted this easy crab cake recipe for my friend, Tommy O'Reilly, to serve when I visit his restaurant, Club 18, in Pottsville, Pennsylvania. The cakes are zippy and the sauce has made a name for itself because of the fresh orange it contains.

- 1 teaspoon olive oil
- ½ cup minced celery
- ¼ cup minced onions
- ¼ cup minced green peppers
- 2 tablespoons minced pimientos
- ½ teaspoon dry mustard
  dash of ground white pepper
- 1 tablespoon lemon juice
- ⅓ cup reduced-calorie mayonnaise
- 1½ cups lump backfin crabmeat, shell pieces removed (page 200)
- ¾ cup bread crumbs
- 1 cup Tommy's Cocktail Sauce (recipe follows)

In a small skillet, heat oil. Add celery, onions and green peppers and sauté over medium heat for 3 to 4 minutes.

In a medium bowl, combine sautéed vegetables, pimientos, mustard, white pepper, lemon juice and mayonnaise. Fold in crabmeat and 2 tablespoons bread crumbs until well blended. Form mixture into four round cakes.

Place remaining bread crumbs in a shallow bowl. Dredge crab cakes in crumbs and place on a baking sheet that has been coated with vegetable cooking spray. Bake in a 450°F oven for 8 to 10 minutes, turning once, or until cakes are browned. Garnish with lemon wedges and serve with Tommy's Cocktail Sauce.

4 servings
252 calories per serving

~~~~~~~~~~~~~~~~~~

Tommy's Cocktail Sauce

- ⅓ cup finely chopped, seeded orange sections
- 1 teaspoon grated orange peel
- ½ cup chili sauce
- 1 teaspoon Worcestershire sauce
- 1 teaspoon Dijon mustard
- 3 tablespoons prepared horseradish

In a bowl, combine all ingredients. Stir to blend thoroughly. Cover and let stand in refrigerator overnight.

Makes 1 cup

Sautéed Crab with Linguine and Vegetables

OPTIONS: Dungeness crabmeat, King crabmeat, Snow crabmeat, Surimi

- 1 pound linguine
- 4 quarts water
- 1 tablespoon olive oil
- 1 pound lump backfin crabmeat, shell pieces removed (page 200)
- 2 cloves garlic, minced
- 1½ cups sliced fresh mushrooms
- ½ pound fresh asparagus, cut into ½-inch pieces
- 1 jar (4 ounces) roasted sweet red peppers, cut into slivers
- 1 teaspoon dried thyme leaves
- ½ teaspoon crushed dried red pepper
- 3 tablespoons Parmesan cheese

Cook linguine in 4 quarts boiling water for 9 to 11 minutes, or until desired tenderness.

Meanwhile, in a large nonstick skillet, heat half of the oil over medium heat. Add crabmeat and sauté for 4 to 5 minutes. Remove from skillet and set aside.

Add remaining oil to the skillet and sauté garlic for 1 to 2 minutes. Stir in mushrooms, asparagus and peppers and continue cooking for another 5 to 6 minutes. Add thyme and dried pepper and cook for 1 minute more. Set skillet aside.

Drain linguine and place in a large serving bowl. Toss with Parmesan. Add vegetables and lightly toss. Spoon crabmeat over top of pasta and serve immediately.

> 6 servings
> 403 calories per serving

Crabmeat-Stuffed Zucchini

OPTIONS: Dungeness crabmeat, King crabmeat, Snow crabmeat, Scallops, Lobster meat

---

- 2 zucchinis
- ¼ cup shredded carrots
- 2 tablespoons minced scallions
- 1 teaspoon snipped dill or ½ teaspoon dried dill
- 2 tablespoons finely chopped, seeded lemon sections
- ¼ teaspoon dry mustard
- 2 tablespoons reduced-calorie mayonnaise
- 1½ cups lump backfin crabmeat, shell pieces removed (page 200)
- 1 tablespoon bread crumbs
- ¼ teaspoon paprika

Blanch whole zucchinis in boiling water for 2 minutes. Remove zucchinis and set aside to cool.

In a bowl, combine carrots, scallions, dill, lemons, mustard and mayonnaise. Fold in crabmeat until well blended.

Cut zucchinis in half lengthwise. With a spoon, scoop out seeds and discard. Mound crab mixture on zucchini halves and sprinkle with bread crumbs and paprika. Place on a baking sheet and bake in a 400°F oven for 8 to 10 minutes. Serve hot.

> 4 servings
> 101 calories per serving

Cool Crabmeat Salad

OPTIONS: Dungeness crabmeat, King crabmeat, Snow crabmeat, Scallops, Shrimp, Lobster meat

---

- 1 cup boiling water
- ½ cup thinly sliced celery
- 1 cup sliced, seeded cucumbers
- 1 tablespoon lime juice
- 2 tablespoons orange juice
- 1 teaspoon Dijon mustard
- ¼ cup reduced-calorie mayonnaise dash of ground white pepper
- 1½ cups lump backfin crabmeat, shell pieces removed (page 200)
- 4 romaine lettuce leaves

In a small bowl, pour water over celery. Stir, let stand for 1 minute, drain and cool.

In a medium bowl, combine celery, cucumbers, lime juice, orange juice, mustard, mayonnaise and pepper. Stir to blend thoroughly. Fold in crabmeat, cover and refrigerate for at least 1 hour. When ready to serve, spoon crabmeat salad onto lettuce leaves and garnish with lime and carrots.

> 4 servings
> 124 calories per serving

Blue Claw
Hard-Shell Crab Boil
with Mustard–Mayo Sauce

OPTIONS: Dungeness crab, Shrimp

1 tablespoon mustard seeds
1 1-inch piece vanilla bean
1 tablespoon coriander seeds
1 teaspoon celery seeds
1 teaspoon dried thyme leaves
1 teaspoon paprika
4 bay leaves
2 whole cloves
½ teaspoon freshly ground black
  pepper
¼ teaspoon cayenne pepper
½ teaspoon garlic powder
1 tablespoon minced gingerroot or
  1 teaspoon ground ginger
1 lemon, sliced
2 quarts water
1 dozen live male blue crabs,
  washed
½ cup Mustard-Mayo Sauce (recipe
  follows)

In a large steamer pot, combine mustard seeds, vanilla bean, coriander seeds, celery seeds, thyme, paprika, bay leaves, cloves, black pepper, cayenne, garlic powder, ginger, lemon slices and water. Bring to a boil. Cover, reduce heat and simmer for 15 minutes.

Uncover, bring to a boil again and add crabs. Stir and return to a boil. Cover, remove pot from heat and let stand for 5 minutes. Remove crabs from pot with long tongs. Garnish with lemon wedges and serve with Mustard-Mayo Sauce.

2 servings
288 calories per serving

~~~~~~~~~~~~~~~~~

Mustard–Mayo Sauce

1 tablespoon Dijon mustard
½ cup reduced-calorie mayonnaise
1 tablespoon lemon juice

In a small bowl, combine all ingredients. Cover and let stand in the refrigerator for at least 1 hour to blend flavors.

Makes ½ cup

California
Crabmeat Cocktail

OPTIONS: King crabmeat, Snow crabmeat, Shrimp, Scallops

2 cups sliced iceberg lettuce
1 ripe avocado, quartered
¼ cup lime juice
1 cup lump backfin crabmeat,
  shell pieces removed
  (page 200)
2 hard-cooked eggs, cut into
  wedges
2 plum tomatoes, sliced
1 lime, cut into wedges
1 cup chili salsa
1 tablespoon chopped fresh
  cilantro or 1 teaspoon dried
  parsley flakes

Divide lettuce among four serving dishes. Sprinkle avocados with 1 tablespoon lime juice. Mound crabmeat on lettuce. Arrange avocados, eggs, tomatoes and lime wedges in a decorative fashion on the dishes.

In a small bowl, combine salsa, remaining lime juice and cilantro or parsley. Stir to blend. Spoon salsa onto lettuce, next to crabmeat. Garnish each plate with three roasted whole almonds and serve.

4 servings
216 calories per serving

Blue Crab Claws with Creole Cocktail Sauce

OPTION: Stone crab claws, Shrimp

---

2 pounds blue crab cocktail claws, meat exposed
¼ cup lemon juice
4 leaves red-leaf lettuce
1 hard-cooked egg, sliced
1 tablespoon julienne of pimientos
1 cup Creole Cocktail Sauce (recipe follows)

In a large bowl, toss claws with lemon juice to coat. Lay lettuce leaves flat on a serving platter. Arrange claws in overlapping spiral rows, working from outer edge toward center. Leave room for two custard cups.

Place egg slices around the edge of the platter with one in the center. Arrange two pimiento slivers in an X on each slice. Place two small custard cups of Creole Cocktail Sauce on the platter and serve.

4 servings
230 calories per serving

~~~~~~~~~~~~~~~~~~

Creole Cocktail Sauce

2 tablespoons minced scallions
1 tablespoon minced pimientos
1½ teaspoons minced fresh parsley
¼ teaspoon paprika
dash of red-hot pepper sauce
½ teaspoon Chinese mustard
1½ teaspoons red wine vinegar
½ teaspoon molasses
½ cup tomato puree

In a bowl, combine all ingredients. Stir to blend thoroughly. Cover and let stand in refrigerator overnight to blend flavors.

Makes 1 cup

Pea–Crab Soup

OPTIONS: Dungeness crabmeat, King crabmeat, Snow crabmeat, Shrimp, Scallops

---

1 tablespoon safflower oil
½ cup chopped celery
½ cup slivered snow peas
¼ cup sliced scallions
1 clove garlic, minced
2 cups chicken stock
1 tablespoon minced fresh parsley
1 tablespoon prepared mustard
dash of ground white pepper
¾ cup peas
1½ cups lump backfin crabmeat, shell pieces removed (page 200)
3 cups hot milk
1 hard-cooked egg, coarsely chopped
⅛ teaspoon paprika

In a 4-quart pot, heat oil. Add celery, snow peas and scallions and sauté over medium heat for 3 to 4 minutes. Stir in garlic and sauté for 1 minute. Add chicken stock, parsley, mustard and pepper. Bring to a simmer and cook for 10 minutes.

Add peas, crabmeat and milk. Stir, cover and remove from heat. Let stand for 5 minutes. Ladle soup into shallow soup bowls, top with eggs and paprika and serve.

4 servings
267 calories per serving

Mediterranean Crab Casserole

OPTIONS: Dungeness crabmeat, King crabmeat, Snow crabmeat, Scallops, Shrimp, Lobster meat

¼ pound fresh spinach leaves
1 tablespoon olive oil
¼ cup diced plum tomatoes
1 tablespoon minced shallots or scallions
1 tablespoon minced fresh parsley
2 tablespoons sliced pimiento-stuffed green olives
1½ cups lump backfin crabmeat, shell pieces removed (page 200)
2 large eggs, slightly beaten
¼ cup skim milk
1 tablespoon tomato paste

Blanch spinach in boiling water for 1 minute. Remove and set aside to cool. Coat four 6-ounce custard cups with vegetable cooking spray and line with spinach leaves.

In a nonstick skillet, heat oil. Add tomatoes and shallots or scallions and sauté over medium heat for 2 minutes. Remove from heat. Add parsley, olives and crabmeat. Stir to mix. Spoon crab mixture into spinach-lined custard cups.

In a medium bowl, whisk together eggs, milk and tomato paste. Pour over crab mixture and bake in a 325°F oven for 20 to 25 minutes. Serve hot, garnished with tomato slices and parsley sprigs.

4 servings
120 calories per serving

Crabmeat-Stuffed Jumbo Mushroom Caps

OPTIONS: Dungeness crabmeat, Scallops, Lobster meat

8 large or 16 medium fresh mushrooms
1 teaspoon butter, melted
1 tablespoon olive oil
1 tablespoon minced scallions
1 tablespoon white wine Worcestershire sauce
¼ cup low-fat cottage cheese
2 tablespoons bread crumbs
1 cup lump backfin crabmeat, shell pieces removed (page 200)

Remove stems from mushroom caps. Finely mince stems and set aside.

Coat a broiling pan with vegetable cooking spray. Place caps upside down on the pan and brush with butter.

In a skillet, heat oil. Add minced stems and scallions and sauté over medium heat for 4 to 5 minutes. Remove from heat. Add Worcestershire sauce, cottage cheese and 1 tablespoon bread crumbs. Stir to blend, then fold in crabmeat. Mound mixture on mushroom caps, sprinkle with remaining bread crumbs and broil at least 4 inches from heat for 6 to 8 minutes, or until browned on top. Serve hot.

4 servings
120 calories per serving

Clams, Oysters and Mussels

~~~~~~~~~~~~~~~~~~~~~~~~~~~~~

I bet I have cleaned and steamed hundreds of thousands of littleneck clams in my life. I've shucked tens of thousands of cherrystones and turned them into clams casino. I have scars on my left palm to prove that I've opened at least 100,000 live chowder clams, the giants of the hard-shell family. And I'm not tired of it yet. I just love the ritual of opening or cooking clams.

I like to eat clams too. If they are small clams, I like to eat lots of them. One of the things I miss about living by the sea is eating the calms dug from the waters of New Jersey's Little Egg Harbor Bay. I worked as a chef at the Boathouse Restaurant in Beach Haven, New Jersey, in the early 1970s, and my favorite clammer used to brave the rough waters of the inlet there to pick the finest-tasting littlenecks I have ever steamed. In those days I paid two cents per clam, wholesale for any size. Fish houses now are paying about ten times that for the clams they serve! Clams are still plentiful in that area because they quickly grow to legal size, which is 1½ to 2 inches across (or the breadth of a standard book of matches measured at the striker). This is because the fresh seawater rushes back and forth through the inlet twice a day with the tide.

In my years as a seafood chef, I've also shucked my share of oysters. And I've treated myself to more than a few. Cold and glistening fresh on the half shell, they're hard to resist.

Oysters develop a signature appearance and flavor. It is a result of their region of origin, and that's how they are identified: blue point are from

Long Island; Chincoteague are from Virginia; Apalachicola are from Florida, and so on.

Each kind has its champions, but I urge you to make up your own mind. If your fishmonger has a selection, buy some of each and see which is your favorite.

It was fairly easy for me to dive right into dealing with clams and oysters in the kitchen. From sea to stove, handling them was a familiar experience that went back to my childhood days. But my meeting with mussels as a novice chef gave new meaning to the phrase "lots to learn."

My first Memorial Day weekend at the Boathouse Restaurant, the owner, Lewis Starr, told me it was my job as the new guy to bounce the mussels. I said, "Sure!" but I had no idea what I was supposed to do. We were ready to open the doors Friday evening when Lew discovered the mussels had not been bounced.

I was handed over to the local bay man who took the mussels and me out onto the bay in Lew's flat-bottom, wooden garvey. Upon reaching clean water, he stopped the boat. We split a bushel of mussels between two burlap bags, tied each of them to an 8-foot length of line and tied the other end of the lines to cleats at the rear of the boat. He cranked up the throttle until the outboard motor had the garvey planing full-speed across the bay. We threw the bags of mussels overboard and the taut lines kept them at the perfect place to "bounce" on the surface of the boat's wake. From that day on I was a bay man, bouncing mussels across the bay just before dusk. It was a great way to start a tense evening of cooking seafood for 300 people.

Why did we bounce the mussels?

Well, it is the easiest way of opening mud mussels before they reach the steam pot and the best way to scrape big, ugly barnacles from the mussel shells.

The next season, a clammer supplied us with clean, fresh, smaller, more delicately flavored mus-

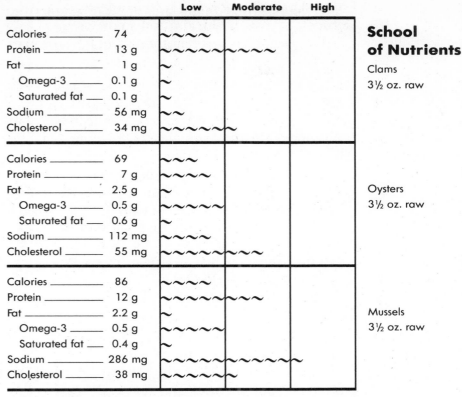

	Low	Moderate	High
Clams — 3½ oz. raw			
Calories — 74	~~~~		
Protein — 13 g	~~~~	~~~~	
Fat — 1 g	~		
Omega-3 — 0.1 g	~		
Saturated fat — 0.1 g	~		
Sodium — 56 mg	~~		
Cholesterol — 34 mg	~~~~~		
Oysters — 3½ oz. raw			
Calories — 69	~~~		
Protein — 7 g	~~~		
Fat — 2.5 g	~		
Omega-3 — 0.5 g	~~~		
Saturated fat — 0.6 g	~		
Sodium — 112 mg	~~~~		
Cholesterol — 55 mg	~~~~~	~~~	
Mussels — 3½ oz. raw			
Calories — 86	~~~		
Protein — 12 g	~~~~~	~~~	
Fat — 2.2 g	~		
Omega-3 — 0.5 g	~~~~		
Saturated fat — 0.4 g	~		
Sodium — 286 mg	~~~~	~~~~	~~
Cholesterol — 38 mg	~~~~	~	

Source: Adapted from Agriculture Handbook No. 8–15 (Washington, D.C.: U.S. Department of Agriculture).

sels that he just picked from our nearby bay. We no longer needed to deal with the cruddy-shelled mussels shipped from Long Island. And, I'm sorry to say, with the cleaner, local product, bouncing the mussels was no longer necessary.

Talking to your Fishmonger

Clams are primarily an East-Coast treasure, but they're harvested and shipped throughout the country in every season.

Hard-shell clams are available in three basic sizes. Littlenecks are the smallest. They are the most expensive but are perfect for steaming. Littlenecks are also shucked raw and eaten on the half shell. Cherrystones are medium size. They can be eaten raw on the half shell or broiled. Chowder clams are large and tough. They are best chopped for stuffed clams or chowder.

It is essential that clams be harvested from clean, pure water. Each batch of clams is tagged upon harvesting and that follows them to the consumer. The tag tells where and when the clams were harvested and who did the harvesting. You are protected because this allows a bad batch of clams to be traced to the source. You can ask your fishmonger to show you the tag for your batch of clams before you buy them.

Generally clams are wholesome and good for you. Just remember that clams must be alive until you are ready to cook and eat them. You can tell quickly if a clam is dead. Its shell will be gaping open, and no matter how much you squeeze the two halves together, it won't close. Fresh, live clams will clam up at the slightest touch.

Soft-shell clams have a firm neck that sticks out of the shell when they are alive and fresh. Don't buy them if that neck hangs limp; it means the clam is dead.

Oysters are widely cultivated on both the Atlantic and Pacific coasts and are available shucked and unshucked from September through May. However, they are so difficult to open that you can usually find one or two sizes of shucked oysters at your fish market. Shucked oysters are sold on the East Coast as selects (large) or standards. On the West Coast, the shucked oysters appear as large, medium, small, extra small or yearlings. Be sure to get some oyster liquor (juice) with each dozen of shucked oysters that you buy.

Mussels are also harvested on both coasts; the season for them runs from March through December. Fresh, live mussels should have a beard attached and the shells should be clamped tightly shut. Beards are little threads used by the mussels to attach themselves to rocks and pilings along the coast. If a mussel dies, it's shell will open just as a clam's does. The shells of a live mussel should close in response to a quick squeeze.

When open, fresh mussel meat normally varies

in color from cream to orange. Two surprises might await you inside wild mussel shells. Along with the meat, you might find either minuscule pearls, the same type as in oysters, or tiny pea crabs. Discard the former because they are valueless and a nuisance. Gather, cook and eat the latter. They are a bonus.

A mud mussel can really be troublesome. It looks just like a live, closed mussel, but it is packed full of a dark, inklike mud. It can totally ruin a pot of steamed mussels or a seafood stew. The best protection you have against a mud mussel is your thumb and forefinger. Briefly twist the two shells of *every* mussel in opposite directions when cleaning. Mud mussels will open at the slightest pressure from the twisting.

The Fillet Board

Soft-shell clams can be shucked with your fingers but the simplest way to open them is to steam them. Pull the skin off the neck before eating or breading them.

Hard-shell clams require a clam knife for shucking. To do this, rinse off the clams well with cold water. Then submerge the clams in cold water, scrub them and let them soak for an hour or two. But be aware that they start to lose flavor when siphoning your tap water.

I use a flexible-blade clam knife to shuck a clam. If serving on the half shell, be careful to retain the clam liquor in the shell with the meat. To open large, tough, chowder clams, I use a rigid-blade clam knife. A clam knife should be fairly dull since its function is merely to slip between the shells and sever the clam's adductor muscles.

The secret to opening fresh, live clams is ice and stealth. Ice down clams and let them rest for 1 hour. Sneaking up on them is a little trickier. You must try to simulate the calmness of the bed in the bay. That means no stirring, no bumping and no knocking. Do not jostle the chilled clams.

Clams

Market form	Amount per person
Cherrystones	4–8
Chowder clams	1–2
Littlenecks	12–24
Soft-shell steamers	12–24

Oysters

Market form	Amount per person
In-the-shell	4–8
Shucked	4–8

Mussels

Market form	Amount per person
In-the-shell	8–18
Shucked, cooked	8–18

Gently pick up the top clam and place it flat in your hand with the hinge toward your thumb. Sneak up on the outer edge with your clam knife. Don't touch the clam with your knife until you are ready to slip the blade between the two shells with a bit of pressure.

Slide the broad, sharper edge between the shells in the front. Push the blade flatly through to the hinge on your thumb side. Now the adductor is severed on that side.

Pull the tip of the knife inside the clam, angle it up into the upper shell and sweep across the inside of the upper shell, cutting the adductor muscle on the back side and separating the meat from the upper shell.

Clamp down on the upper shell with your knife-hand thumb and the blade of the knife. Keeping the blade inside the clam, twist the top shell off, the bottom shell with a horizontal, flat motion away from you. Discard the top shell.

With the tip of your clam knife, sever the adductor muscles from the bottom shell with one sweep of the blade.

As for shucking oysters, leave that to the professionals. The knife is pointed and dangerous in the hand of a novice.

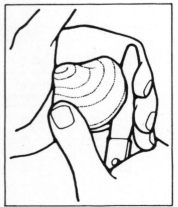
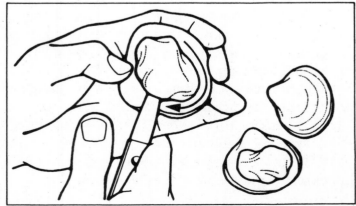

To clean mussels, soak them in cold water for 30 minutes. Use a clam knife to scrape any barnacles off. Use the clam knife blade and your thumb to grab the beard on each mussel and pull it out of the shell. Twist the shells gently in opposite directions to test for mud mussels. Cook the mussels quickly, because they don't live long after you remove the beard.

Cooking the Catch

Clams don't take long to cook. Eight to 10 minutes is the general rule of thumb for any method—whether you are steaming them in their shells, broiling or baking them on the half shell or cooking minced clams for chowder.

When steaming clams, you know they are finished cooking once all the clams open. Some say don't eat a clam that hasn't opened. I say that is the hardiest of the bunch. Either steam it until it does open, or pry it open with a clam knife.

I wait until the last few minutes of cooking chowder before adding minced raw clams. Add the clams to soup while simmering. Stir and remove the pot from the heat. Let the chowder steep for 5 minutes and serve. That way, the clams cook perfectly and don't get gummy. If you should happen to overcook clams slightly, keep cooking them for 30 more minutes and they will get tender again.

Oysters don't take long to cook either. When I see the edges curling, that signals me that the oyster is ready to eat. Usually that takes no more than 5 to 6 minutes. Baked oysters, however, take a little longer.

The best way to cook mussels is to steam them. In fact, no matter how I plan to use mussels, I usually steam them first. They shouldn't be plucked from the shell raw.

Mussels are quick cooking. It takes no longer than 8 to 10 minutes to steam mussels open. I like to steam them with a small amount of spicy broth. As far as I'm concerned, fresh mussels from the bay are the finest steaming shellfish of all.

Lewis Starr, my seafood mentor, taught me a basic rule: The fewer the hands between the water and you, the better the shellfish. I never learned a better lesson, so I pass it on to you.

~~~~~ Galley Tips
~~~~~ Clams, oysters, mussels (1 doz.)

Technique Market form	Directions	Time (min.)	Temp.
Bake Half-shell	Use a flat baking dish or small muffin tin; brush lightly with vegetable oil.	6–10	425°–450°F
Broil Half-shell	Use a flat nonstick pan or small muffin tin, brush lightly with vegetable oil; broil 4–6 inches from heat.	6–10	High
Steam Whole	Use a large pot; add water or stock to ½ inch deep; add cleaned shellfish; cover tightly.	7–10	Med.-high
Chowder Shucked	Cook vegetables, herbs and spices in clam stock, fish stock or chicken stock; add chopped shellfish last, stir and remove from heat.	5	Steep

Lewis Street Clam Chowder

OPTIONS: Cod, Scallops

True chowders are thick with fish and vegetables, not thickened with a starch. Bisques are thickened seafood soups. This version of my white clam chowder surfaced on the debut menu at my former restaurant, the Lewis Street Chowderhouse, in Greenwich, Connecticut, in 1975. I was in my "mustard period," so, of course, the signature ingredient here is . . . Dijon.

    1 tablespoon olive oil
  1½ cups sliced leeks
    1 cup diced onions
    1 cup sliced celery
    1 clove garlic, minced
    2 cups clam liquor
    2 cups chicken stock
    1 teaspoon Dijon mustard
    2 teaspoons Worcestershire sauce
  ⅛ teaspoon ground white pepper
    1 teaspoon fresh thyme leaves or
        ½ teaspoon dried thyme leaves
    2 bay leaves
    1 tablespoon minced fresh parsley
    1 cup diced potatoes
    1 dozen live chowder clams,
        shucked, drained and chopped
        or 2 cans (6½ ounces each)
        chopped clams, drained
    2 cups hot milk

In a 3- to 4-quart heavy-bottom pot, heat oil. Add leeks, onions and celery and sauté for 5 minutes. Stir in garlic and cook for 1 minute.

Add clam liquor, chicken stock, mustard, Worcestershire sauce, pepper, thyme, bay leaves and parsley and blend thoroughly. Stir in potatoes. Bring to a boil, reduce heat and simmer for 20 minutes, or until potatoes are tender.

Stir in clams. Bring to a boil and remove pot from heat. Remove bay leaves. Stir in milk. Serve in shallow soup bowls, garnished with parsley sprigs.

    4 servings
    257 calories per serving

Steamed Shellfish Combo

This recipe was created by Lewis Starr, chef-owner of the Boathouse Restaurant in Beach Haven, New Jersey. It is simply my favorite.

    1 cup sliced leeks or scallions
    1 tablespoon olive oil
    2 cloves garlic, minced
    1 teaspoon freshly ground black
        pepper
    1 teaspoon fresh thyme leaves or
        ½ teaspoon dried thyme leaves
    2 cups water
  12 extra large shrimp, peeled and
        deveined, tail on
  16 sea scallops
  ¾ pound cod fillet
    2 dozen live mussels, cleaned
        (page 213)
    2 dozen live littleneck clams,
        cleaned

In a large, heavy pot, sauté leeks or scallions in oil over medium heat for 5 minutes. Do not brown. Add garlic, pepper and thyme and sauté for 1 minute.

Pour in water and bring to a boil. Add shrimp, scallops, cod, mussels and clams. Return to a boil, cover and steam for 10 minutes, or until all the clams open.

Spoon seafood into shallow bowls and serve.

    4 servings
    242 calories per serving

Oyster and Potato–Corn Pie

OPTIONS: Clams, Scallops, Mussels

> 1 cup oyster liquor
> 1½ cups cubed potatoes
> ½ cup sliced celery
> ½ cup diced onions
> 1 tablespoon cornstarch
> ½ cup corn kernels
> ⅛ teaspoon ground nutmeg
> ⅛ teaspoon ground white pepper
> 1 tablespoon minced fresh parsley
> 1 tablespoon minced pimientos
> 2 dozen shucked oysters, drained
>   pastry for 1 9-inch pie crust
> 1 egg
> 1 tablespoon water

In a large saucepan, combine ¾ cup oyster liquor, potatoes, celery and onions. Bring to a boil, reduce heat, cover and simmer for 15 to 20 minutes, or until potatoes are tender.

Combine cornstarch with remaining oyster liquor and blend. Add cornstarch mixture to vegetables and stir to blend. Bring to a boil, stirring constantly. Remove from heat and stir in corn, nutmeg, pepper, parsley and pimientos.

Pour vegetables into a 9-inch pie dish and top with oysters. Cover with pastry.

Beat egg and water with a fork. Brush egg mixture over crust and bake in a 425°F oven for 15 to 20 minutes. Remove from oven and let stand for 5 minutes. Slice and serve.

4 servings
391 calories per serving

Scalloped Oysters Orndorf

"Orny" Orndorf could never get enough oysters during our four good years on the Virginia coast in the late 1960s. I put together this easy casserole so he could satisfy his craving with minimal fuss.

> 2 dozen shucked oysters, drained
>   with liquor reserved
> 2 hard-cooked eggs, coarsely
>   chopped
> ¾ cup oyster liquor
> ¾ cup skim milk
> 1 teaspoon white wine
>   Worcestershire sauce
> ¼ teaspoon freshly ground black
>   pepper
> 2 tablespoons minced fresh
>   parsley
> 1½ cups crushed soda crackers or
>   matzos
> ¼ teaspoon paprika

Coat a shallow dish with vegetable cooking spray. Arrange oysters in one layer in the dish. Spoon eggs evenly over oysters.

In a small bowl, combine oyster liquor, milk and Worcestershire sauce and pour over oysters. Sprinkle with pepper and parsley, then spread soda crackers or matzos evenly over all. Sprinkle with paprika and bake in a 425°F oven, uncovered, for 8 to 10 minutes. Garnish with parsley sprigs and serve.

4 servings
307 calories per serving

Neopolitan Clam Bake

OPTIONS: Mussels, Oysters, Scallops

---

4 quarts water
1 pound spaghetti
½ cup diced onions
1 tablespoon olive oil
2 cloves garlic, minced
1 can (28 ounces) plum tomatoes, drained and sliced
1 teaspoon minced fresh oregano or ½ teaspoon dried oregano
2 tablespoons minced fresh parsley
1 dozen shucked cherrystone clams, with liquor
1 whole egg, slightly beaten
4 ounces part-skim mozzarella cheese, shredded
2 tablespoons grated Parmesan cheese
¼ cup Italian bread crumbs

In a large pot, bring 4 quarts of water to a rolling boil. Break spaghetti in half and add to water a quarter portion at a time. Return water to a rolling boil, stir and cook for 10 minutes.

Meanwhile, sauté onions in oil over medium heat for 3 to 4 minutes. Do not brown. Add garlic and cook 1 minute.

Stir in tomatoes, oregano and parsley and cook for 3 to 4 minutes. Pour tomato mixture into a large bowl.

Chop clams with liquor in a blender for a short time using the pulse button. Do not puree. Add clams and beaten egg to tomato mixture and stir to blend.

Drain spaghetti. Toss spaghetti and mozzarella with tomato mixture until thoroughly combined. Spoon into a 2½- to 3-quart casserole dish that has been coated lightly with vegetable cooking spray. Spread Parmesan and bread crumbs evenly over casserole and bake in a 400°F oven for 25 to 30 minutes, or until the top is golden brown.

4 servings
648 calories per serving

Oyster Stew

OPTIONS: Littleneck clams,

Mussels, Scallops

---

2 cups oyster liquor
2 cups milk or buttermilk
½ teaspoon Dijon mustard
1 teaspoon Worcestershire sauce
¼ teaspoon red-hot pepper sauce dash of ground white pepper
1 teaspoon butter
1 teaspoon safflower oil
¼ cup minced scallions
1 tablespoon minced celery leaves
4 dozen shucked oysters, drained

Combine oyster liquor, milk or buttermilk, mustard, Worcestershire sauce, hot pepper sauce and pepper in a 2-quart saucepan. Blend thoroughly and heat to just under boiling point. Do not boil.

In a heavy 6- to 8-quart pot, melt butter in oil. Add scallions and celery and sauté over medium heat for 2 minutes. Stir in oysters and cook for 3 to 4 minutes, or until edges curl.

Add hot milk mixture and remove from heat. Serve hot in shallow bowls, sprinkled with paprika and dry mustard, if desired.

4 servings
256 calories per serving

Jackpot Broiled Clams

OPTIONS: Oysters, Mussels

This recipe has yet to show up in Atlantic City's casinos, but my version of clams casino is a winner due to the chili peppers, plum tomatoes and smoked turkey I put in it.

- 2 dozen littleneck clams, raw on the half shell
- 1 tablespoon olive oil
- 2 tablespoons minced scallions
- 1 clove garlic, minced
- 1 tablespoon minced fresh chili peppers
- ¼ cup minced fresh plum tomatoes
- 1 tablespoon grated Parmesan cheese
- 1 slice (4 ounces) smoked turkey, cut into 24 equal strips

Place clams on each cup opening of two mini-muffin pans or on a broiling pan. Add 2 drops oil to each clam.

In a small bowl, combine scallions, garlic, chili peppers and tomatoes. Place 1 teaspoon vegetable mixture on each clam, sprinkle each with Parmesan and top each with a strip of turkey. Broil 4 inches from heat for 6 to 8 minutes. Remove to serving tray or serve the hot pans on a trivet at the table.

2 servings
234 calories per serving

Oven-Fried Oysters with Jamaican Tartar Sauce

OPTIONS: Clams, Mussels, Scallops

- 2 teaspoons corn oil
- ¼ teaspoon red-hot pepper sauce
- 1 cup cracker meal
- ¼ cup fine cornmeal
- 2 dozen large frying oysters
- ⅔ cup Jamaican Tartar Sauce (recipe follows)

In a shallow bowl, combine oil and hot pepper sauce. Whisk with a fork until thoroughly blended. In another shallow bowl, combine cracker meal and cornmeal.

Toss oysters in oil mixture. Then dredge in cracker/cornmeal blend, coating all sides evenly. Place oysters flat on a nonstick baking sheet and bake in a 450°F oven for 10 to 15 minutes, or until coating becomes crispy brown. Serve hot with Jamaican Tartar Sauce.

4 servings
403 calories per serving

~~~~~~~~~~~~~~~~~~

Jamaican Tartar Sauce

- ¼ cup thinly sliced scallions
- 1 tablespoon minced fresh cilantro or 1 teaspoon dried parsley flakes
- 2 tablespoons finely chopped, seeded lime sections
- ⅓ cup finely chopped fresh papaya
- ⅓ cup reduced-calorie mayonnaise
- ½ teaspoon Jamaica-style hot pepper sauce

Combine all ingredients and blend thoroughly. Refrigerate for at least 1 hour before serving.

Makes ⅔ cup

Presto Paella-in-a-Pot

OPTIONS: Clams, Scallops

___

1 tablespoon olive oil
½ cup sliced leeks or scallions
1 cup sweet red pepper strips
1 can (14½ ounces) plum tomatoes, drained
2 cups chicken stock
2 tablespoons chopped parsley
¼ teaspoon chili powder
1 bay leaf
4 or 5 saffron threads
¼ pound lean pork sausage, cut into 4 equal pieces
½ pound boneless, skinless chicken breast, cut into 8 equal pieces
½ cup green peas
½ cup fresh or frozen sugar snap peas
1 cup rice
1 dozen live mussels, cleaned (page 213)
8 large shrimp, peeled and deveined

In a large, enameled, cast-iron pot, heat oil. Add leeks or scallions and peppers and sauté for 3 to 4 minutes. Add tomatoes, chicken stock, parsley, chili powder, bay leaf, saffron, sausage, chicken, peas, sugar snap peas and rice. Bring to a boil, reduce heat to low, cover and simmer for 10 minutes, stirring occasionally to prevent sticking.

Add mussels and shrimp. Do not stir. Cover and continue to simmer for 10 minutes. Remove bay leaf and serve from the pot at the table.

4 servings
517 calories per serving

Mediterranean Mussel Salad

OPTIONS: Clams, Scallops, Oysters

___

¼ cup minced shallots or scallions
1 clove garlic, minced
2 tablespoons olive oil
1 cup chicken stock
6 dozen live mussels, cleaned (page 213)
2 tablespoons red wine vinegar
1 tablespoon chili sauce or catsup
1 teaspoon minced fresh oregano or ⅓ teaspoon dried oregano
1 tablespoon minced fresh parsley
½ cup thinly sliced celery
1 tablespoon minced onions
4 Bibb lettuce leaves

In a 4- to 6-quart, heavy-bottom pot, sauté shallots or scallions and garlic in oil for 2 minutes. Do not brown.

Add chicken stock and mussels. Cover tightly, bring to a boil and steam mussels for 8 to 10 minutes, or until all the mussels are opened. Remove from heat. Lift mussels from the pot, reserving stock. Remove mussel meat from shells and discard shells.

Add vinegar, chili sauce or catsup, oregano, parsley, celery and onions to the stock and blend. Add mussels, toss and refrigerate for at least 1 hour. Serve chilled in Bibb lettuce leaves.

4 servings
193 calories per serving

Lobster

~~~~~~~~~~~~~~~~~~~~~~~~~~~~~~~~~~

True lobster is an American original, and it's as feisty and independent as the fishermen who trap it along the northeast coast of the United States.

Technically, only the shellfish found in those American waters can be called lobster. Spiny lobsters from water off Florida, Brazil, Australia, New Zealand and South Africa are really crawfish and are called rock lobster on the market. They lack the huge claws of *Homarus americanus.*

This northern lobster is caught close to shore in traps built to allow illegal small-size lobsters to escape and grow larger. (It takes a lobster seven years to grow to a weight of 1 pound.) The harvest of lobsters is strictly regulated by state governments to protect against exhausting the supply. That's one reason they're so expensive.

Lobster is the crown jewel of all seafood. Because of its rarity and high price, lobster seldom appears at any but the most glittering occasions. I hope you'll find an occasion that warrants a lobster dinner very soon.

The texture and flavor of lobster is best when it is kept alive until cooking time. Freezing lobster causes the flavor to fade and the texture to toughen.

Talking to Your Fishmonger

The first rule in buying live, whole lobster is this: Pick a lively rascal. A lobster away from its ocean floor feeding grounds for a long time (or one that has been mishandled) will be slow and lethargic. By all means, never buy a lobster that doesn't move. Observe the lobster as it comes out of the tank. (New technology allows for lobster tanks in most

		Low	Moderate	High
Calories	90	~~~~~		
Protein	19 g	~~~~~	~~~~~~	~~
Fat	0.9 g	~		
Omega-3	—			
Saturated fat	—			
Sodium	—			
Cholesterol	95 mg	~~~~~	~~~~~	~

School of Nutrients

Lobster
3½ oz. raw

Source: Adapted from Agriculture Handbook No. 8-15 (Washington, D.C.: U.S. Department of Agriculture).

fish markets and restaurants.) Ask the plucker to hold the lobster up for your inspection. The best buy is the lobster that holds its claws up, spread eagle, and kicks its tail forward in defiance.

Be sure both claws are pegged or banded, and keep them that way until cooked. The small, thin claw is a quick pincher that considers a finger fair game. The large claw is a little slower but it can be a real bone cruncher.

My personal favorite is a female lobster because it contains the richly flavored coral or roe that turns brilliant red when cooked. I pick female lobsters by looking for delicate hairs on the small paddle fins under the tail end. The male tail end is comparatively hairless. The hairs on the female hold the clinging eggs before hatching.

Don't pick a live lobster from the tank until the day (or a few hours before) you plan to cook it. Call a few days ahead to reserve your lobster by size. I recommend 1- to 2-pound live lobsters. Price increases with size. Be sure to get home quickly with live lobsters.

Few retailers or restaurateurs make money on live lobsters. They are stocked to accommodate the fish lover on that special occasion. Watch for lobster promotions in the newspaper food section. Believe it or not, pricey lobsters are sometimes used as loss leaders to attract your business.

Cold-water lobster tails from Florida, Australia, New Zealand and South Africa are more desirable than warm-water tails from Brazil and the Caribbean. They are usually priced according to market demand.

The main factor to consider when purchasing frozen lobster tails is handling. If the tail was frozen properly and kept frozen solid until you pick it from the freezer, the meat will be tender and sweet when thawed and cooked. Look for a thin ice glaze over the exposed meat. That is normal. However, don't pay for a big chunk of ice at lobster tail prices.

The telltale sign of mishandled lobster tails is odor. If after the tail is thawed, it gives off a distinct ammonia odor, I return it to the market immediately with the receipt. Good fishmongers know the smell of a bad lobster tail and will gladly replace it. For your information: Return a cooked lobster tail in a restaurant if it has a distinct odor of iodine.

The Fillet Board

Even if you live in the part of the country where buying live lobster now and then is a part of the warm-weather tradition, you may find dealing with them a bit difficult, especially when a recipe calls for killing it before cooking it. But it shouldn't be a job too big for you to handle. Cooking a live lobster can be quite painless (for you and the lobster). If baking or broiling, the lobster should be killed first. (When boiling, it's not necessary.)

Here's how it's done:

1. Lay the whole lobster on its back with the tail toward you. Insert a sharp chef's knife into the middle of the head using a good bit of force. This kills the lobster instantly.

2. Continue cutting back to the tail, through the center of the body between the legs, to the end of the tail. Cut deep, through to the back shell.

3. Press the two sides down and out with your hands or cut through the back shell for two separate halves.

4. Remove the gritty stomach sack and the black digestive tract from the body cavity on the head end. Discard both. Remove and reserve the liver and the roe.

Lobster	
Market form	**Amount per person (lb.)**
Meat	¼
Tail	¼-½
Whole	¾-1¼

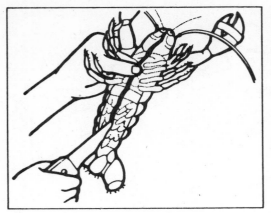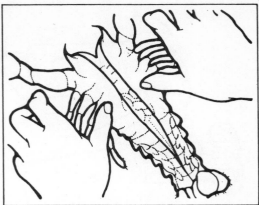

In most parts of the country, lobster tail is what most people are familiar with and can readily find. If not done properly, removing tail meat can be a real challenge. Learning the correct way to cut a tail is very easy and can give you, in a matter of seconds, a clean and beautiful piece of flesh intact with no wasted meat.

I suggest doing this in the kitchen (either before or after cooking) so your diners can enjoy this wonderful delicacy without having to wrestle with a shell. While the method of cutting may be easy, it makes for mighty messy hands!

Here's how it's done:

1. Using sturdy kitchen shears, cut down the center of the back shell of each lobster tail. Raw, frozen tails must be thawed first.

2. To broil, pull the raw meat up through the split by pressing down on the sides of the shell and pushing the meat up through the center, perching it on top of the shell. The shell is a perfect support for broiling the tail meat. This method can also be used to finish off a cooked lobster under the broiler.

3. For the easiest access to a cooked tail, cut down both sides of the belly shell with kitchen shears. Remove and discard the belly shell and serve the opened, cooked tail.

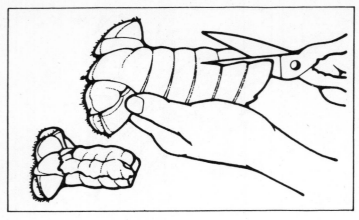
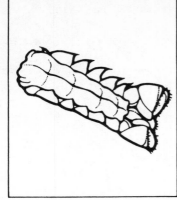

Cooking the Catch

I've heard many tales about anesthetizing lobsters before cooking, for more tender meat. One method described French chefs intoxicating the creatures in a bath of sherry for 1 hour before cooking. I never tried it, but something tells me it's a waste of time and sherry.

A rolling boil of plenty of water in a huge pot has always done the trick for me. It is quick to kill and no one has ever sent a whole lobster back to me because the meat was tough. Just be sure that you don't overcook or undercook it. Some prefer to steam lobsters, but I consider it too slow in the killing and the cooking.

Bring enough water to cover the lobsters to a rolling boil. Be generous with the water and use a very large pot. Quickly immerse the live lobsters, head first, into the boiling water. The shells turn red immediately, but that is no indication of doneness.

Split, whole lobsters can be baked just as quickly as when boiling whole lobsters. Times for the items on the facing page are calculated on a 400°F oven. As you can see, broiling is quicker. The lobster halves should be no farther than 6 inches from the heat.

Packaged lobster meat is already cooked and needs only to be heated or lightly cooked with other ingredients.

Lobster tails can be steamed, poached, broiled

Lobster Cooking Times

Each lobster should be timed separately unless they are close in weight.

Weight (lb.)	Boiling, Whole (min.)	Baking, Split whole (min.)	Broiling, Split whole (min.)
1	10	10	6–8
1¼	12	12	6–8
1½	13	13	7–9
1¾	14	14	7–9
2	15	15	8–10
2½	17	17	9–11
3	19	19	10–12
3½	20	20	11–13
4	21	21	12–14
4½	22	22	13–15
5	23	23	14–16

or barbecued. The meat can be removed from the shell and just cooked like any other fish flesh. Tails should be thawed completely in the refrigerator, or quickly under cold running water before cooking.

Split the tail, or at least cut the shell before cooking. It is very difficult to crack the shell of a hot tail at the table.

Always cook tails quickly. Avoid baking lobster tails for a long time in a slow oven. Long cooking times toughen lobster tails.

~~~~~~ **Galley Tips**

~~~~~~ Lobster (1 lb.)

Technique Market form	Directions	Time (min.)	Temp.
Bake Split tail	Use a shallow baking dish; brush lightly with vegetable oil/juice mixture.	6–10	425°–450°F
Broil Split tail	Use a sturdy broiling pan; brush lightly with vegetable oil/juice mixture; dust with paprika, flour or bread crumbs; broil 4–6 inches from heat.	6–10	High
Poach Split tail	Use a deep skillet or a large soup pot; combine citrus juice with water.	6–10	Med. to med.-high
Microwave Split tail	Brush with stock, water or juice; arrange lobster in 1 layer around edge of dish, thinnest end pointing in; cover with lid, loose plastic or waxed paper; rotate often; let stand 1 minute after cooking.	4–6	Med. (70%)

Broiled Lobster Tail
with Dill–Lime Butter

OPTIONS: Shrimp, Monkfish, Scallops

---

2 tablespoons butter, softened
1 tablespoon olive oil
1 tablespoon lime juice
1 tablespoon snipped dill or
    1 teaspoon dried dill
¼ teaspoon paprika
4 frozen lobster tails (8 ounces
    each), thawed

In a small bowl, combine butter, oil, lime juice, dill and paprika. Stir to blend thoroughly.

Split lobster tails (page 222). Brush lobster meat with ½ tablespoon dill-lime butter, coating evenly. Heat remaining butter in a small saucepan over low heat for 4 to 5 minutes.

Place lobster tails on a broiler pan, meat side up, and broil 4 inches or less from heat for 6 to 8 minutes, or until browned.

To serve, pour heated butter over tails and garnish with lime wedges and fresh dill.

4 servings
157 calories per serving

Creamed Lobster
and Mushrooms

OPTIONS: Shrimp, Crab, Scallops

---

1 cup chopped onions
2 tablespoons olive oil
2 tablespoons flour
1 cup hot milk
¼ teaspoon dry mustard
    dash of ground white pepper
1½ cups sliced fresh mushrooms
1 tablespoon minced pimientos
1 cup chunked, cooked lobster
    meat

In a nonstick skillet, sauté onions in 1 tablespoon oil for 3 to 4 minutes. Stir in flour and cook for 3 to 4 minutes. Add milk and stir quickly to thicken. Stir in mustard and pepper. Transfer to a blender and puree until smooth.

In a clean skillet, heat remaining oil. Add mushrooms and sauté over medium heat for 3 to 4 minutes, or until soft. Stir in pimientos and lobster. Pour creamed onions over lobster mixture, stir and cook for 1 minute. Serve hot.

4 servings
168 calories per serving

Lobster Sandwich
with Tarragon

OPTIONS: Shrimp, Crab, Scallops

---

1 teaspoon chopped fresh tarragon
    or ½ teaspoon dried tarragon
1 teaspoon tarragon vinegar
    dash of ground white pepper
2 tablespoons reduced-calorie
    mayonnaise
8 thin slices French bread
4 Bibb or Boston lettuce leaves
¼ cantaloupe, rind removed, thinly
    sliced
12 ounces cold cooked lobster meat,
    preferably sliced from the tail

In a small bowl, combine tarragon, vinegar and pepper. Add mayonnaise and stir to blend thoroughly. Spread on each slice of bread. Place a leaf of lettuce on four of the slices. Arrange cantaloupe slices on lettuce leaves. Place lobster on cantaloupe and top with remaining four slices of bread, mayonnaise side down. Slice sandwiches in half on the diagonal and serve.

4 servings
304 calories per serving

My Bouillabaisse

1 cup chopped leeks
1 cup chopped onions
3 cloves garlic, minced
2 tablespoons olive oil
1 can (28 ounces) plum tomatoes
  (including juice)
¼ teaspoon crushed saffron
  threads
½ cup chopped fresh parsley
1 tablespoon fresh thyme leaves or
  ½ teaspoon dried thyme leaves
1 teaspoon freshly ground black
  pepper
½ teaspoon anise seeds or fennel
  seeds
2 cups fish stock or chicken stock
2 live female lobsters (1 pound
  each)
½ pound cod fillet, cut into 4 equal
  pieces
12 extra large shrimp, peeled and
  deveined
12 sea scallops
32 live mussels, cleaned (page 213)
2 dozen live littleneck clams,
  cleaned

In an 8-quart, heavy-bottom pot, sauté leeks, onions and garlic in oil over medium-high heat for 2 minutes. Coarsely chop tomatoes (with juice) in a blender using the pulse button. Add to sautéed vegetables. Stir in saffron, ¼ cup parsley, thyme, pepper, anise seeds or fennel seeds and fish stock or chicken stock. Bring to a boil, cover, reduce heat and simmer for 30 minutes. Stir occasionally.

Split each lobster to the beginning of the tail (page 222). Cut the tail from the body. Remove and discard the gritty sack in the head and the black digestive tract. Remove and reserve the dark green (tomalley) and light greenish gray (liver) sack from the body. Slice across the tail at each segment of the shell and set aside with meat intact.

Strain tomato mixture through a colander. Puree 1 cup strained vegetables in a blender and add to broth. Discard remaining vegetables. Pour broth into a large steaming pot.

Mash and mix tomalley with liver in a small bowl. Add this mixture to broth. Stir to blend.

Place cod in the bottom of a clean colander. Add shrimp, scallops and mussels, in that order. Top with little-neck clams and lobster tail segments.

Place lobster bodies with claws in broth. Lower colander into the steam pot. Bring to a boil over medium-high heat, cover tightly and steam for 12 to 15 minutes. Be sure clams are opened before serving.

To serve, remove colander from pot and spoon steamed seafood into four large bowls. Then spoon lobster bodies into each bowl of seafood. Spoon broth over fish, sprinkle with remaining parsley and serve.

4 servings
420 calories per serving

Lobster Medallions and Marinated Cucumber Salad with Saffron Dressing

OPTIONS: Shrimp, Crab, Scallops

4 cups water
¼ cup lemon juice
2 frozen lobster tails (8 ounces
  each), thawed
1 seeded cucumber, sliced into
  ¼-inch slices
¼ cup thinly sliced onions
¼ cup rice wine vinegar
1 teaspoon snipped dill or
  ½ teaspoon dried dill
¼ cup Saffron Dressing (recipe
  follows)

In a 4-quart saucepan, combine water and lemon juice. Bring to a boil. Add lobster tails, return to a gentle simmer and cook for 10 to 12 minutes. Remove tails from water and set aside to cool.

In a bowl, toss sliced cucumbers with onions, vinegar and dill. Marinate in the refrigerator for at least 1 hour.

Cut tail shells with sturdy kitchen shears. Remove meat in one piece and slice into ⅜-inch medallions.

Alternate lobster slices with two or three cucumber slices in an overlapping circle around each serving plate. Place a spoonful of Saffron Dressing in the center and garnish with cucumber spears.

> 4 servings
> 141 calories per serving

~~~~~~~~~~~~~~~~~~

Saffron Dressing

> 1½ teaspoons lemon juice
> 1½ teaspoons olive oil
> 2 or 3 saffron threads
> ¼ cup reduced-calorie mayonnaise

In a small saucepan, heat lemon juice and oil. Add saffron, remove from heat and allow to steep for 2 hours at room temperature.

Strain saffron liquid and discard threads. Blend liquid with mayonnaise and serve.

> Makes ¼ cup

Baked Whole Lobster with Lobster Claw Pilaf

> 2 live female lobsters (1 pound each)
> ½ cup chopped onions
> 2 tablespoons olive oil
> ¾ cup rice
> 1⅓ cups chicken stock
> 1 tablespoon minced fresh parsley
> ½ teaspoon dried thyme leaves
> 3 tablespoons orange juice
> ¼ cup bread crumbs

Drop lobsters in a large pot of boiling water and cook for 3 to 5 minutes (page 224).

Cool, then remove and discard gritty sack from the head and the digestive tract. Detach claw arms and claws. Crack the shells, remove meat and cut into small pieces. Set aside.

Remove all meat from the bodies of the lobsters. Gently loosen the meat in each tail and lift it out whole. Cut into pieces and set aside.

In a small saucepan, sauté onions in 1 tablespoon oil for 2 to 3 minutes. Add rice, chicken stock, parsley, thyme and claw meat. Bring to a boil. Cover, reduce heat to low and cook for 20 to 25 minutes.

Mound claw pilaf into cavity of each lobster. Spoon tail meat back into tails.

In a small bowl, combine orange juice and remaining oil. Brush mixture on each lobster, coating tail and pilaf. Sprinkle bread crumbs over pilaf, place lobsters on a large baking sheet and bake in a 400°F oven for 10 to 12 minutes, or until bread crumbs are lightly browned. Serve with orange wedges if desired.

> 2 servings
> 580 calories per serving

Suzy's Lobster Dumplings with Saffron-Parsley Sauce

OPTIONS: Shrimp, Sole, Pike

My sister will eat lobster in any way, shape or form. She often uses this recipe as an elegant appetizer or entrée for her frequent dinner parties.

2 frozen lobster tails (8 ounces each), thawed
¼ cup sliced scallions
2 egg whites
1 cup low-fat cottage cheese
dash of ground nutmeg
dash of ground white pepper
4 cups water
¾ cup Saffron-Parsley Sauce (recipe follows)

Place metal processor blade in freezer 30 minutes before preparation. Meanwhile, keep ingredients chilled.

Cut lobster tail shells with sturdy kitchen shears and remove meat from lobster tails. Place in a food processor and process for 30 seconds. Scrape down sides of bowl.

Add scallions, egg whites, cottage cheese, nutmeg and pepper. Puree all ingredients until a smooth paste forms, about 1 minute, scraping down sides of bowl as necessary.

In a skillet, bring water to a simmer over medium heat. Slide about 1 tablespoonful lobster paste into simmering water, poaching eight dumplings at a time. (Keep remaining portion in the refrigerator.) Poach for 2 minutes. Turn over and poach for another 3 minutes. Then turn dumplings over again and poach for 1 to 2 minutes more. Transfer to a platter with a slotted spoon and keep warm in a 200°F oven. Repeat procedure for remaining eight dumplings.

To serve, spoon Saffron-Parsley Sauce over dumplings and garnish with parsley sprigs.

4 servings
173 calories per serving

~~~~~~~~~~~~~~~~

Saffron-Parsley Sauce

¼ cup boiling chicken stock or water
¼ cup coarsely chopped fresh parsley
4 or 5 saffron threads
2 teaspoons safflower oil
1 tablespoon flour
½ cup hot milk
1 tablespoon minced fresh parsley
dash of ground white pepper
2 teaspoons lemon juice

In a cup, pour chicken stock or water over chopped parsley and saffron. Set aside to steep for 10 minutes.

In a saucepan, combine oil and flour. Cook over medium heat for 2 to 3 minutes, stirring constantly to keep flour from browning.

Strain parsley and saffron mixture into milk. Press parsley to drain. Discard parsley and saffron threads.

Over medium-high heat, add milk to flour and stir or whisk briskly until blended. Stir in minced parsley, pepper and lemon juice. Bring to a boil, stir and remove from heat. Serve hot.

Makes ¾ cup

Sautéed Lobster and Snow Peas

OPTIONS: Shrimp, Crab, Scallops

---

2 frozen lobster tails (8 ounces each), thawed
1 tablespoon peanut oil
4 thin slices gingerroot
½ cup sliced scallions
½ cup julienne of sweet red peppers
2 cups fresh snow peas
¼ cup orange juice

Cut lobster tail shells with sturdy kitchen shears. Remove meat in one piece and cut into ¼-inch slices.

In a large skillet, heat oil. Add ginger and sauté over medium heat for 4 to 5 minutes. Remove and discard ginger. Add scallions, peppers and peas and sauté over medium-high heat for 4 to 5 minutes.

Stir in lobster and cook for 2 minutes. Pour in orange juice, stir and serve, garnished with orange slices and sweet red pepper rings.

4 servings
148 calories per serving

Danny's Lobster Chowder

OPTIONS: Shrimp, Crab, Scallops

This recipe combines hot milk with savory chowder ingredients. My friend Danny loves to heat up a pot of this lobster chowder for lunch at his dairy.

2 tablespoons olive oil
1 cup sliced leeks
1 cup thinly sliced celery
½ cup chopped watercress
1 cup small diced potatoes
dash of ground white pepper
dash of ground nutmeg
2 cups chicken stock
1 cup clam juice
2 frozen lobster tails (8 ounces each), thawed, shell removed and reserved
3 cups hot milk
2 cups Mustard Croutons (page 266)

In a 6- to 8-quart heavy-bottom pot, heat oil. Add leeks and celery and sauté over medium heat for 2 to 3 minutes. Add watercress, potatoes, pepper, nutmeg, chicken stock, clam juice and lobster shells. Stir to blend. Bring to a boil over medium-high heat. Cover, reduce heat to low and simmer for 20 minutes. Remove and discard lobster shells.

Slice lobster meat and add to pot along with milk. Stir, remove from heat and let stand for 5 minutes. Serve in shallow bowls, garnished with paprika and watercress. Top with Mustard Croutons.

4 servings
318 calories per serving

Crawfish
and Squid

~~~~~~~~~~~~~~~~~~~~~~~~~~~~~~~~

Crawfish looks a lot like shrimp but is really more akin to the spiny lobsters that swim in warm ocean waters. Squid looks like nothing else, although it's part of the same family that also lays claim to clams, oysters and mussels. Crawfish and squid quite possibly are two of the strangest sea creatures that make it to the dinner table. But there's no doubt about it: Both are truly delicious.

Crawfish is hot today and getting hotter since Cajun cuisine, in which it stars, hit the culinary scene. And squid, despite its ugly name and unearned seamy reputation, is enjoying new popularity since it adopted its Italian moniker, calamari.

Talking to Your Fishmonger

Most often you will find crawfish whole in the marketplace. Sometimes it is alive and kickin', but usually it is cooked and sold either fresh or frozen. A bright red color is the sure sign of cooked crawfish. Whole crawfish varies in size from 3½ to 8 inches, although the tail holds the only worthwhile morsel of meat. If you're adventuresome, reach inside the body when you separate it from the tail to obtain the tasty orange fat deposit you'll find there, and reserve it to enrich a spicy Creole sauce.

Whole crawfish takes some time to clean, so I recommend that you buy peeled and deveined tail meat that is either raw or cooked. As with other crustaceans, you must work for your meal when it comes to cleaning crawfish. It takes 7 pounds of whole crawfish to produce 1 pound of cleaned tail meat, or a 14 percent yield.

Among squid, loligo is the premium species. On the East Coast it is known as long-fin squid,

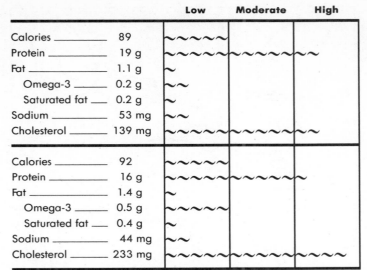

		Low	Moderate	High
Calories	89			
Protein	19 g			
Fat	1.1 g			
Omega-3	0.2 g			
Saturated fat	0.2 g			
Sodium	53 mg			
Cholesterol	139 mg			
Calories	92			
Protein	16 g			
Fat	1.4 g			
Omega-3	0.5 g			
Saturated fat	0.4 g			
Sodium	44 mg			
Cholesterol	233 mg			

School of Nutrients

Crawfish
3½ oz. raw

Squid
3½ oz. raw

Source: Adapted from Agriculture Handbook No. 8-15 (Washington, D.C.: U.S. Department of Agriculture).

winter squid or Boston squid. On the West Coast, California squid or Monterey squid is the premium.

Squid is a hardy seafood that can be thawed and refrozen more than once. Most squid is frozen for the marketplace, but only imported squid is cleaned. If you buy frozen domestic squid, you will have to do the honors.

Unlike crawfish, almost 80 percent of whole squid is edible. The tube, fins and tentacles are all tasty and tender if cooked properly.

The Fillet Board

Let's jump right in on cleaning squid.

Pull the head from the body. If you're lucky, the guts and/or quill will follow, but they seldom do. You must get your finger up into the body to clean everything out. Peel the thin gray skin from the tube to expose the white flesh. Cut the tentacles from the head. Discard the quill, guts, head and skin.

I usually remove the fins and cut them in strips. You can leave the body tube whole to be stuffed or crosscut it into ¼-inch rings. The tentacles can be finely chopped for stuffing or left whole to curl up when they're cooked.

Squid	
Market form	**Amount per person (lb.)**
Cleaned tubes and rings	¼–⅓
Whole	⅓–½

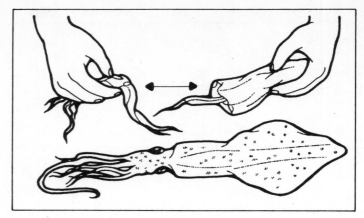

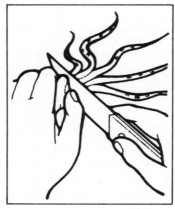

To clean crawfish, you need only to separate the tail from the body and pull the meat from the tail, as you do with shrimp. This procedure is simple, once the crawfish is cooked.

Cooking the Catch

Raw, live crawfish needs to be cooked for only 5 to 7 minutes in a rolling boil of spicy water. You can make up your own blend of spices (include lots of cayenne pepper) or you can use a commercial blend of shrimp boil or crab boil.

The trick to cooking squid is to hardly cook it at all—no more than a few minutes over low heat. Otherwise the snowy white flesh turns tire tough. If you overcook squid by even 5 minutes, you'll have to cook it for another ½ hour to get it soft again.

Crawfish	
Market form	**Amount per person**
Tail meat	¼–⅓ lb.
Whole	6-12

~~~~~~ **Galley Tips**

~~~~~~ Crawfish (1 lb.)

Technique Market form	Directions	Time (min.)	Temp.
Boil Whole	Boil spicy stock for 10–15 minutes; add crawfish, return to boil, remove from heat and let stand for 5 minutes.	5–8	High

~~~~~~ **Galley Tips**

~~~~~~ Squid (1 lb.)

Technique Market form	Directions	Time (min.)	Temp.
Broil Cleaned tubes and rings	Use a flat nonstick pan; brush lightly with vegetable oil/juice mixture; broil 4 inches or less from heat.	1–2	High
Poach Cleaned tubes and rings	Use a deep skillet or large saucepan; bring 1 quart of water to boil; add squid and stir; return to boil and cook for 1 minute.	1–2	Med.-high
Sauté Cleaned tubes and rings	Use a nonstick skillet; sauté in small amount of vegetable oil and citrus juice; stir often.	1–2	Med.-high

Crawfish and Corn Salad

OPTIONS: Shrimp, Lobster meat

¼ cup minced celery
¼ cup minced scallions
1 tablespoon minced fresh parsley
1 tablespoon paprika
  dash of cayenne pepper
1 tablespoon Dijon mustard
2 tablespoons white wine vinegar
¼ cup olive oil
¾ cup corn kernels
1 cup sliced, seeded cucumbers
½ cup thinly sliced celery
1 tablespoon minced pimientos
1 pound crawfish tails, peeled, deveined and cooked
¼ pound fresh spinach leaves

In a large bowl, combine celery, scallions, parsley, paprika, cayenne, mustard and vinegar. In a slow, steady stream, pour oil into mixture while beating with a whisk.

Add corn, cucumbers, celery, pimientos and crawfish. Toss to coat with dressing. Cover and refrigerate for 1 hour.

To serve, spoon salad onto a bed of fresh spinach leaves.

4 servings
241 calories per serving

Louisiana Crawfish Boil with Peppy Peppersauce

OPTIONS: Crab, Shrimp

4 quarts water
2 tablespoons paprika
1 tablespoon crushed dried red pepper
2 tablespoons red-hot pepper sauce
1 tablespoon dry mustard
1 teaspoon garlic powder
¼ cup lemon juice
4 bay leaves
4 dozen whole crawfish, washed
1 cup Peppy Peppersauce (recipe follows)

In a 6- to 8-quart pot, combine water, paprika, dried pepper, hot pepper sauce, mustard, garlic powder, lemon juice and bay leaves. Bring to a boil, cover and simmer for 15 minutes.

Add crawfish to pot. Stir, return to a boil, cover and cook for 5 minutes. Drain and serve crawfish on a large platter with Peppy Peppersauce and, if desired, lemon wedges.

4 servings
73 calories per serving

~~~~~~~~~~~~~~~~

Peppy Peppersauce

1 tablespoon olive oil
⅓ cup chopped onions
1 tablespoon minced fresh chili peppers
1 clove garlic, minced
¾ cup chopped roasted sweet red peppers or pimientos
1 teaspoon paprika
½ teaspoon red-hot pepper sauce
1 teaspoon Worcestershire sauce
1 teaspoon prepared mustard
1 teaspoon red wine vinegar
1 tablespoon chopped, seeded lemon sections

In a small skillet, heat oil. Add onions, chili peppers and garlic and sauté over medium heat for 4 to 5 minutes.

In a blender, combine sautéed vegetables, red peppers or pimientos, paprika, hot pepper sauce, Worcestershire sauce, mustard, vinegar and lemons. Puree until smooth, about 1 minute on high, stopping to scrape down sides.

Cover and refrigerate overnight to blend flavors.

Makes 1 cup

Sautéed Crawfish with Asparagus

OPTIONS: Shrimp, Lobster meat, Scallops

---

2 teaspoons olive oil
¼ cup minced scallions
¼ cup minced watercress leaves
1 tablespoon flour
¾ cup hot milk
   dash of ground white pepper
1 tablespoon butter
1 pound fresh asparagus spears, trimmed
1 pound crawfish tails, peeled and deveined
1 tablespoon lemon juice

In a saucepan, heat oil. Add scallions and watercress and sauté over medium-high heat for 1 to 2 minutes. Stir in flour and cook for 2 minutes, stirring frequently to keep flour from browning. Add milk and stir or whisk quickly until blended. Add pepper, stir and bring to a boil. Stir and remove from heat.

In a large nonstick skillet, melt butter over medium heat. Add asparagus and sauté for 2 minutes and remove to a warm platter.

Add crawfish to skillet and sauté for 3 minutes. Drizzle lemon juice over crawfish and stir.

Pour sauce over asparagus and spoon crawfish onto the platter. Serve immediately.

   4 servings
   169 calories per serving

Peppered Crawfish over Bow Tie Noodles

OPTIONS: Shrimp, Lobster meat

---

1 tablespoon peanut oil
⅔ cup julienne of green peppers
⅔ cup julienne of sweet red peppers
⅔ cup julienne of sweet yellow peppers
½ cup sliced leeks
1 clove garlic, minced
½ cup diced plum tomatoes
¼ cup minced fresh parsley
1 pound crawfish tails, peeled and deveined
½ cup chicken stock
½ pound bow tie noodles, cooked

In a 6- to 8-quart heavy pot, heat oil. Add peppers and leeks and sauté over medium-high heat for 5 minutes. Stir in garlic, tomatoes, parsley and crawfish and sauté for 3 minutes.

Add chicken stock, stir, cover and cook for 3 to 4 minutes. Serve over bow tie noodles and garnish with parsley sprigs.

   4 servings
   343 calories per serving

Crawfish Tails
over Bayou Rice

OPTIONS: Shrimp, Crabmeat,
Lobster meat

1	tablespoon peanut oil
1	cup sliced celery
½	cup sliced scallions
½	cup diced green peppers
½	cup diced sweet red peppers
1	clove garlic, minced
1	teaspoon paprika
⅛	teaspoon cayenne pepper
½	cup chicken stock
1	pound crawfish tails, peeled and deveined
2	cups Bayou Rice (page 262)

In a large nonstick skillet, heat oil. Add celery, scallions, green peppers and red peppers and sauté over medium heat for 5 minutes. Add garlic, paprika, cayenne and chicken stock. Bring to a simmer, cover and cook for 10 minutes.

Add crawfish, stir, cover and cook for 5 minutes. Serve over Bayou Rice, garnished with celery leaves.

4 servings
340 calories per serving

Sautéed Squid Rings

OPTIONS: Clams, Oysters, Mussels

1½	pounds whole squid
½	cup flour
1	teaspoon paprika
¼	teaspoon ground white pepper
¼	teaspoon ground nutmeg
¼	teaspoon garlic powder
1	egg white, slightly beaten
¼	cup plain low-fat yogurt
½	to ⅔ cup bread crumbs
1	teaspoon dried oregano
¼	cup olive oil

Clean squid (page 233). Slice body into ½-inch rings and leave tentacles whole. Set aside.

In a shallow bowl, mix together flour, paprika, pepper, nutmeg and garlic powder. In another shallow bowl, combine egg white and yogurt and whisk with a fork to blend thoroughly. In a third shallow bowl, blend together ½ cup bread crumbs and oregano.

Dredge squid rings and tentacles in seasoned flour. Dip into egg white/yogurt mixture, then into bread crumbs. Add more bread crumbs, if necessary.

In a large skillet, heat oil over medium heat for 1 to 2 minutes. Quickly sauté squid for 2 minutes, turning once. Attempt only a small amount at a time. Drain on paper towels and transfer to a warm platter. Serve with lemon and lime wedges, if desired.

4 servings
374 calories per serving

Calamari Salad

OPTIONS: Clams, Oysters, Mussels

1½	pounds whole squid
2	cups water
2	tablespoons lemon juice
1	cup diced plum tomatoes
1	cup thinly sliced celery
¼	cup sliced scallions
1	clove garlic, cut in half
2	tablespoons red wine vinegar
¼	cup olive oil
¼	teaspoon dried oregano
1	tablespoon minced fresh parsley
4	romaine lettuce leaves
1	tablespoon shredded Romano cheese

Clean squid (page 233). Slice body into ¼-inch rings and tentacles into small pieces.

In a saucepan, combine water and lemon juice and bring to a boil. Blanch squid pieces for 1 minute. Drain and cool quickly.

In a large bowl, combine blanched squid, tomatoes, celery and scallions and toss to mix.

Rub the inside of a small bowl with garlic halves and discard. Add vinegar, oil, oregano and parsley and whisk with a fork. Pour dressing over salad. Toss to coat, cover and refrigerate for 1 hour.

To serve, spoon calamari salad onto lettuce leaves, sprinkle with Romano and garnish with lemon slices.

4 servings
269 calories per serving

Spaghetti with Calamari, Garlic and Parsley

OPTIONS: Clams, Oysters, Mussels

1½ pounds whole squid
 1 pound thin spaghetti
 4 quarts water
 ½ cup diced onions
 2 cloves garlic, thinly sliced
 1 tablespoon olive oil
 1 tablespoon butter
 ½ cup minced fresh parsley
 1 cup clam juice
 1 tablespoon grated Parmesan cheese

Clean squid (page 233). Slice body into ¼-inch rings and leave tentacles whole. Set aside.

In a 6-quart pot, cook spaghetti in boiling water for 9 to 11 minutes.

Meanwhile, in a large nonstick skillet, sauté onions and garlic in oil over medium heat for 3 to 4 minutes. Add butter and melt. Add parsley and sauté for 3 minutes. Add clam juice and bring to a boil. Stir in squid and cook for 1 minute.

Drain spaghetti and place in a large bowl. Spoon squid mixture over spaghetti and toss to blend. Sprinkle with Parmesan and serve.

4 servings
625 calories per serving

Portuguese Squid

OPTIONS: Clams, Oysters, Shrimp

1½ pounds whole squid
 1 tablespoon olive oil
 ½ cup sliced red onions
 1 large sweet red pepper, cut into ¾-inch wedges
 4 black olives, sliced
 1 pound small red-skin potatoes, sliced into ½-inch wedges
 ¼ teaspoon freshly ground black pepper
 2 cups chicken stock
 1 tablespoon lemon juice
 2 tablespoons orange juice
 2 tablespoons minced fresh parsley

Clean squid (page 233). Slice body into ½-inch rings and leave tentacles whole. Set aside.

In a large skillet, heat oil. Add onions, peppers and olives and sauté over medium heat for 3 to 4 minutes. Add potatoes, black pepper, chicken stock, lemon juice and orange juice. Bring to a simmer, cover and cook for 15 minutes, or until potatoes are tender.

Stir in parsley and squid. Return to a simmer and cook for 1 minute.

To serve, spoon stew into a large serving bowl. Garnish with hard-cooked egg slices and orange slices arranged around the edge of the bowl.

4 servings
292 calories per serving

Sportfish

~~~~~~

I'm delighted to share some of my favorite recipes for sportfish—namely, bass, perch, pike, marlin, shad, sunfish, walleye and whitefish. For one thing, anglers who bring them home often have limited ideas on how to cook their catch. Also, these gamefish show up in the fish market now and then. That gives nonfishermen the opportunity to taste the rewards of sportfishing without the expense of costly tackle and the annoyance of wet clothing. So this section is for those who love the splash of a white-water creek or ocean spray—and for those who prefer to enjoy the bounty without the hunt.

Bass, large mouth, small mouth or other fresh-water type, is a prize gamefish throughout the United States and Canada. Bass has lean meat and the taste will be sweet and light as long as you skin the fillets. The skin usually has an off-flavor that overpowers the subtle-tasting flesh. You won't find a freshwater bass in the seafood case at the market. It is a special treat that you or a friend can find only with a rod and reel.

Yellow perch is a small (usually under 1 pound in the United States), widely available sportfish. It is a highly desirable lake fish with firm, white flesh. It is usually sold as fillets, but a fresh-caught perch can be pan-dressed and pan-fried for perfect eating.

Northern pike is fished from lakes and rivers throughout the northern United States and Canada. Dip the fish in boiling water for 30 to 40 seconds to prep it for an easy scaling. Cut steaks and larger cross sections from the body for convenient cooking. The flesh is lean and snow white when cooked. Be

	Black bass	Striped bass	Yellow perch	Northern pike	Shad	Sunfish	Wall-eye	White-fish
Calories	114	97	91	88	197	89	93	134
Protein (g)	19	18	19	19	17	19	19	19
Fat (g)	3.7	2.3	0.9	0.7	13.8	0.7	1.2	5.9
Omega-3 (g)	0.7	0.8	0.3	0.1	—	0.1	0.3	1.4
Saturated fat (g)	0.8	0.5	0.2	0.1	—	0.1	0.2	0.9
Sodium (mg)	70	69	62	39	51	80	51	51
Cholesterol (mg)	68	80	90	39	—	67	86	60

School of Nutrients

Source: Adapted from Agriculture Handbook No. 8–15 (Washington, D.C.: U.S. Department of Agriculture).

Notes:
Information is based on 3½-oz., raw portions.
Information for marlin is not available.

careful to remove the rows of Y-shaped bones from the flesh.

You might chance upon pike on ice in your fishmonger's case. Fresh from the water, pike is a prize delicacy for the angler and some close friends.

Marlin is a large, ocean gamefish primarily hunted for the sport and released by fishermen after the catch. Marlin steaks, however, are showing up at the fish market, probably because of the recent popularity of fresh shark and fresh tuna steaks.

You can substitute marlin for swordfish, tuna and shark in any recipe. Marlin is lean, so it dries out quickly. I like to marinate marlin steaks for a short time. Then, I follow the recipe precisely to avoid overcooking.

Shad, the largest member of the herring family, is anadromous. That means the shad swims madly from the Atlantic Ocean up the rivers of the Eastern seaboard in spawning runs that start in Florida in December and peak in New England by April.

The sweet, delicate meat is oily and carries a reputation for the rows of Y-shaped pin bones in each fillet. Some fishmongers can remove these bones with a few quick passes of the fillet knife. Nevertheless, grilled, pan-fried or broiled shad is a marvelous spring tonic for regenerating your palate after the winter season.

Sunfish—bluegills, crappies and other panfish—are easy to catch, cook and eat. Most of the time, they are only large enough to pan-dress. Yet, large bluegill can offer some practice for your filleting techniques. Either form needs only some dusting with seasoned flour before simple pan or broiler cooking.

Walleye is not a pike but a member of the freshwater perch family. It is the most versatile of the freshwater white-fleshed fish. It can be adapted to cod, haddock and flounder recipes and is readily available in the northern U.S. and Canadian markets. The flesh is flaky and white and you won't be bothered with a complex bone structure. Dressing and eating walleye are easy and satisfying.

Whitefish, a white-fleshed cousin of salmon and trout, is fished primarily in the Great Lakes region. Smoked whitefish is commonly available throughout the United States. Fresh whitefish can be found in northern markets and is used, along with walleye, in the preparation of gefilte fish.

Black Bass Fillets Barbequed on Tiles

OPTIONS: Striped bass, Red snapper, Black sea bass

---

  1 tablespoon lemon juice
  2 tablespoons tomato paste
  1 tablespoon safflower oil
  1 tablespoon minced shallots or scallions
  1 tablespoon chopped capers
1¼ pounds black bass fillets, skinless, cut into 4 equal pieces
  1 lemon, sliced into 8 equal slices

In a bowl, combine lemon juice, tomato paste, oil, shallots or scallions and capers. Stir to blend.

Place fillets in a gallon-size, plastic food-storage bag. Pour marinade into bag and twist-tie shut. Knead gently with fingertips to coat fillets evenly. Place in refrigerator for no more than 1 hour.

Remove fish fillets from the bag (reserving marinade) and lay flat on four quarry tiles coated with vegetable cooking spray. Place two lemon slices on each fish portion. Place tiles on the rack of a barbecue grill directly over the heat. Cover and grill over high heat for 8 to 10 minutes. Baste with remaining marinade. Serve fillets on a plate or serve tiles directly on a finished plank of wood to each guest.

  4 servings
  182 calories per serving

Lime-Broiled Striped Bass Fillet

OPTIONS: Red snapper, Salmon

  ¼ cup finely chopped, seeded lime sections
  1 teaspoon grated lime peel
  1 tablespoon peanut oil
  ¼ teaspoon paprika
  1 clove garlic, minced
1¼ pounds striped bass fillet, cut into 4 equal pieces
  1 cup Peppered Onions (page 262)

In a small bowl, combine lime sections, lime peel, oil, paprika and garlic. Stir to blend.

Place fillets, skin side down, on a broiling pan that has been coated with vegetable cooking spray. Spoon lime mixture over fillets and broil 4 inches from heat for 6 to 8 minutes, or until fish is cooked through. Serve hot with Peppered Onions and, if desired, lime slices on the side.

  4 servings
  219 calories per serving

Pan-Fried Yellow Perch with Scallion Relish

OPTIONS: Freshwater trout, Sunfish

1 tablespoon orange juice
1 tablespoon honey
1 tablespoon white wine vinegar
1 teaspoon safflower oil
1 teaspoon minced gingerroot or
　½ teaspoon ground ginger
⅓ cup thinly sliced scallions
2 tablespoons minced celery
2 tablespoons chopped pimientos
1 egg white, slightly beaten
¼ cup skim milk
¼ cup cornmeal
¼ cup bread crumbs
1 teaspoon rubbed sage
4 small yellow perch, pan-dressed
2 tablespoons peanut oil

In a saucepan, combine orange juice, honey, vinegar, safflower oil and ginger. Heat to the boiling point and remove from heat.

Add scallions, celery and pimientos. Stir to blend. Let stand for 1 hour before serving. (Serve chilled or at room temperature.)

In a shallow bowl, combine egg white and milk. Whisk with a fork. In another shallow bowl, mix together cornmeal, bread crumbs and sage.

Dip fish into egg white mixture, then dredge in cornmeal mixture to coat evenly.

In a large nonstick skillet, heat peanut oil. Add fish and sauté over medium-high heat for 2 to 3 minutes on each side. Garnish with julienne of scallions and pimientos and serve with scallion relish.

4 servings
381 calories per serving

Northern Pike Steaks with Snow Peas and Asparagus

OPTIONS: Walleye, Striped bass

1 tablespoon white wine
　Worcestershire sauce
1 tablespoon safflower oil
4 northern pike steaks (about 1½
　pounds)
1 clove garlic, cut in half
1 tablespoon olive oil
¾ pound fresh or frozen asparagus
½ pound fresh or frozen snow peas
½ cup sliced scallions
1 teaspoon fresh thyme leaves or
　¼ teaspoon dried thyme leaves
1 tablespoon lime juice

In a cup, combine Worcestershire sauce and safflower oil. Place fish steaks on a broiling pan that has been coated with vegetable cooking spray. Brush tops of steaks with oil mixture and broil 4 inches from heat for 6 to 8 minutes, or until done. Remove from broiler and let stand for 2 minutes before serving.

In a large nonstick skillet, sauté garlic halves in olive oil over medium-high heat for 2 to 3 minutes. Remove and discard garlic. Add asparagus, snow peas, scallions and thyme to the skillet and sauté for 5 to 6 minutes, stirring occasionally. Drizzle lime juice over vegetables and stir. Arrange vegetables on a serving platter and top with fish steaks. Garnish with cherry tomatoes and lime wedges and serve.

4 servings
237 calories per serving

Island Marlin Steak
with Mango–Lime Marinade

OPTIONS: Swordfish, Mako shark, Tuna

¼ mango
2 tablespoons lime juice
1 tablespoon minced fresh cilantro
   or 1 teaspoon dried parsley
   flakes
1 small fresh chili pepper, minced
1 clove garlic, minced
2 tablespoons olive oil
1¼ pounds marlin steak, cut into
   4 equal pieces

In a bowl, mash mango with a fork. Add lime juice, cilantro or parsley, chili peppers, garlic and oil. Stir briskly with a fork to blend.

Place fish in a gallon-size, plastic food-storage bag. Pour marinade into bag and twist-tie shut. Knead with fingertips to coat steaks evenly. Place bag in refrigerator for no more than 1 hour.

Arrange steaks on a broiling pan that has been coated with vegetable cooking spray, and broil 4 inches from heat for 6 to 8 minutes, basting with marinade. Do not overcook; it dries out quickly.

Serve hot, garnished with mango and lime slices.

   4 servings
   231 calories per serving

Sautéed Shad
with Shallots
and Mushrooms

OPTIONS: Sea trout, Red snapper, Whitefish

1¼ pounds boneless shad fillets,
   cut into 4 equal pieces
½ cup flour
2 teaspoons peanut oil
1 tablespoon butter
¼ cup minced shallots
1 cup chopped fresh mushrooms
1 tablespoon chopped fresh
   parsley
1 tablespoon bread crumbs

Dredge fillets in flour, coating both sides.

Heat oil in a large nonstick skillet over medium heat. Place fillets in hot oil, skin side up, and cook for 4 minutes. Turn over and cook for 6 to 8 minutes. Transfer fillets to a warm platter.

Quickly melt butter. Add shallots, mushrooms and parsley and sauté for 2 to 3 minutes. Stir in bread crumbs and cook for 1 minute. Spoon mushroom mixture over fish fillets. Garnish with raw or quickly sautéed mushroom caps and serve.

   4 servings
   404 calories per serving

Plank-Roasted Sunfish

OPTIONS: Freshwater trout, Yellow perch, Freshwater bass

---

    4 sunfish, split (page 41)
    ¼ cup orange juice
    2 tablespoons lemon juice
    2 tablespoons lime juice
    2 tablespoons safflower oil

Wash 12 nails. Using 2 hardwood planks (2 × 4 × 12 inches), nail two split fish, skin side down, to each plank with 3 nails for each fish.

In a small bowl, combine orange juice, lemon juice, lime juice and oil. Brush some basting juice on each fish. Place planks on a hot grill with fish standing upright, tail end up. Cover and grill for 10 to 15 minutes. Baste occasionally. Serve hot from the plank, garnished with orange wedges.

    4 servings
    174 calories per serving

Baked Walleye with Sweet-and-Sour Raspberry Butter

OPTIONS: Perch, Flounder

---

    2 tablespoons butter, softened
    1 tablespoon seedless raspberry
       preserves or jam
    1 teaspoon raspberry vinegar
    1 teaspoon Dijon mustard
    1¼ pounds walleye fillets, skinless,
       cut into 4 equal pieces
    ½ cup fresh whole raspberries

In a small bowl, combine butter, preserves or jam, vinegar and mustard. Stir to blend.

Place fillets in a large baking dish that has been coated with vegetable cooking spray. Spread with sweet-and-sour raspberry butter and bake in a 400°F oven for 10 to 12 minutes. Top with fresh raspberries and serve, garnished with fresh chive spikes.

    4 servings
    77 calories per serving

Poached Whitefish with Red Beet Horseradish Mayonnaise

OPTIONS: Sea trout, Salmon, Freshwater trout

---

    3 cups chicken stock
    1 cup shredded carrots
    ½ cup chopped onions
    ½ teaspoon dried thyme leaves
    1¼ pounds whitefish fillets, cut
       into 4 equal pieces
    2 tablespoons horseradish with
       beets
    2 cups reduced-calorie
       mayonnaise

In a large, deep skillet, combine chicken stock, carrots, onions and thyme. Bring to a boil. Reduce heat to low, cover and simmer for 15 minutes.

Add fillets to poaching bouillon. Return to a simmer over medium heat and poach for 10 to 12 minutes.

In a small bowl, combine horseradish and mayonnaise. Stir to blend.

Garnish fish with carrot curls and serve hot with red beet horseradish mayonnaise.

    4 servings
    214 calories per serving

California Crabmeat Cocktail
page 204

Steamed Shellfish Combo
page 215

***Baked Whole Lobster
with Lobster Claw Pilaf***
page 229

Sautéed Crawfish with Asparagus
page 237

250

Future Fish

~~~~~~~~~~~~~~~~~~~~~~~~~~~~~~

All these "future fish" are here right now and have always been available, but mostly in their native areas. Because of better distribution channels, improved technology and an increased interest in fresh fish variety, they have surfaced on iced seafood displays nearly everywhere.

Taste test these fish when you see them at your fish market. Most tend to be inexpensive, so they offer a bargain opportunity for dining pleasure. They deserve your attention.

Cusk is so similar to cod that some people think they're interchangeable. The telltale sign is the long row of pin bones on the cusk fillet. They can easily be cut out in a thin strip. The remaining flesh is firm and cooks up white.

Drum is well appreciated on the southeast Atlantic and Gulf coasts. It is highly prized as a chowder fish in the Carolinas.

Eel is an excellent-tasting fish that is quite adaptable to most cooking methods. Its snakelike appearance has kept it from achieving the popularity in America that it enjoys elsewhere. Eel has tender, moist meat that separates easily from the simple bone structure. There are no small bones in this fish. Eels should be skinned before they are cooked.

Mahimahi, also known as dolphinfish, is a great-tasting fish that is growing in popularity. Here is another case where a new name made the difference in the marketplace. Our supply is landed in the 50th state, Hawaii, and shipped to the mainland. Mahimahi is a hardy fish with an excellent shelf life.

	Cusk	Drum	Eel	Mahi-mahi	Ocean pout	Sable-fish	Skate	Tile-fish	Wolf-fish
Calories	87	119	184	85	79	195	97	96	96
Protein (g)	19	18	18	19	17	13	20	18	17.5
Fat (g)	0.7	4.9	11.7	0.7	0.9	15.3	1.3	2.3	2.4
Omega-3 (g)	—	0.6	0.6	0.1	—	1.5	0.6	0.4	0.6
Saturated fat (g)	—	1.1	2.4	0.2	0.3	3.2	0.3	0.4	0.4
Sodium (mg)	31	75	51	88	61	56	90	53	85
Cholesterol (mg)	41	64	126	73	52	49	56	—	46

Source: Adapted from Agriculture Handbook No. 8-15 (Washington, D.C.: U.S. Department of Agriculture).

Notes:
Information is based on 3½-oz., raw portions.
Information for orange roughy is not available.

Ocean pout is a sleeper, a great value whose time has come. Fillets are long and thin, and its mild-flavored flesh cooks up snowy white.

Orange roughy, an import from New Zealand, arrives frozen as a mild-tasting, boneless fillet that is snowy white.

Sablefish is a familiar fish, usually marketed in smoked form. This fatty fish is known also as black cod on the West Coast.

Skate is low in cost and easy to prepare. Have the fishmonger skin the skate wing before you accept it. When cooked, the firm white flesh separates easily from the wing cartilage.

Tilefish was unknown to me until I was already managing a seafood restaurant on the New Jersey shore. What impressed me when I first tasted it was the firmness of the cooked, white flesh. I immediately started using tilefish in fish salads. Try the fillet of this large, inexpensive white fish at your first opportunity. Buy more than you need for a meal, but cook it all. Refrigerate the leftover portion and prepare a salad the next day using your favorite tuna fish salad recipe or Taffi's Tilefish Tossed Salad (page 257).

Wolffish, better known as ocean catfish, is a mild-tasting, white-fleshed fish that finds its way into the trawler's catch. If you like cod and haddock, give wolffish a try.

Cusk Kabobs Niçoise

OPTIONS: Cod, Haddock, Pollack

- 1 small zucchini
- 1 pound cusk fillets, cut into 16 cubes
- 4 shallot bulbs, peeled
- 2 cups canned crushed plum tomatoes
- 8 black olives
- 2 teaspoons minced fresh rosemary or ½ teaspoon crushed dried rosemary

Soak four 9-inch skewers in water for 1 hour.

Slice zucchini into eight 1-inch pieces discarding ends. Alternate fish and zucchini on skewers with shallots in the center.

Coat a baking dish with vegetable cooking spray. Place skewers in the dish. Pour tomatoes over skewers and sprinkle with olives and rosemary. Cover with foil and bake in a 400°F oven for 20 to 25 minutes. Garnish each with a sprig of rosemary and serve with sauce spooned over kabobs.

    4 servings
    144 calories per serving

Dolbin's Drum Chowder with Peanuts

OPTIONS: Red snapper, Grouper

My brother-in-law's family, the Dolbins, import fresh roasted peanuts from Virginia for this flavorful chowder from the South.

- 1 tablespoon peanut oil
- 1 cup diced onions
- 1 cup diced sweet red peppers
- 3½ cups chicken stock
- ¼ cup rice
- 1 tablespoon peanut butter
- 1 tablespoon Dijon mustard
- ⅛ teaspoon freshly grated nutmeg dash of ground white pepper
- 1 pound red drum or black drum fillet, cut into 1-inch cubes
- 2 cups hot milk
- 2 tablespoons chopped roasted peanuts

In a large, heavy pot, heat oil. Add onions and peppers and sauté over medium-high heat for 2 to 3 minutes, stirring frequently. Add chicken stock, rice, peanut butter, mustard, nutmeg and white pepper. Stir to blend and bring to a boil. Cover, reduce heat to low and simmer for 17 to 20 minutes.

Add fish to pot, stir and remove from heat. Cover and steep fish for 5 minutes. Stir in milk. Serve in shallow bowls, sprinkled with chopped peanuts.

    4 servings
    396 calories per serving

Irish-Style Eel Stew

OPTIONS: Ocean pout, Catfish, Tilefish

This stew embodies the spirit of the Emerald Isle. The firm-fleshed eel marries perfectly with the potatoes, carrots and green cabbage—possibly the next St. Patrick's Day tradition.

- 1½ pounds eel, cut into 2-inch steaks
- ½ cup flour
- 2 teaspoons safflower oil
- 2 large or 3 medium potatoes, peeled and cut into large chunks
- 2 large carrots, cut in 2-inch lengths
- 1 onion, cut into 8 wedges
- 1 cup coarsely cut cabbage
- 5 cups fish stock or chicken stock
- ⅛ teaspoon ground white pepper
- ½ cup peas
- 1 tablespoon chopped fresh parsley

Dredge steaks in flour.

In a large, heavy pot, heat oil. Add steaks and sauté over medium-high heat for 3 to 4 minutes, browning lightly. Add potatoes, carrots, onions, cabbage, fish stock or chicken stock and pepper. Bring to a boil. Cover, reduce heat to low and simmer for 20 to 25 minutes.

Stir in peas and chopped parsley. Cover, remove from heat and let stand for 10 minutes. Serve in shallow bowls, garnished with parsley sprigs.

4 servings
464 calories per serving

Mahimahi with Banana and Cilantro

OPTIONS: Pollack, Bluefish

- 1½ pounds mahimahi fillet, cut into 4 equal pieces
- 1 large banana, cut into ¼-inch slices
- 1 cup thinly sliced onions
- 1 tablespoon chopped fresh cilantro or 1 teaspoon dried parsley flakes

Place each fillet in the center of a large sheet of aluminum foil. Place banana slices on top of fillets, mound onions on top of bananas and sprinkle with cilantro or parsley. Wrap foil to enclose fish.

Place wrapped fish, top down, directly on hot coals of a barbecue grill or in a 500°F oven for 6 to 8 minutes. Serve fillets on a platter, garnished with cilantro sprigs.

4 servings
191 calories per serving

Mom's Ocean Pout with Pistachios

OPTIONS: Flounder, Orange roughy, Sole

When I dressed up these mild-tasting ocean pout fillets with bread crumbs and nuts, my mother adopted this fish dish as a member of the family favorites.

- 1 egg white, slightly beaten
- ¼ cup plain low-fat yogurt
- 1 teaspoon honey
- ½ cup unsalted shelled pistachio nuts
- ¼ cup bread crumbs
- ½ teaspoon paprika
- 1¼ pounds ocean pout fillets, cut into 4 equal pieces

In a shallow bowl, combine egg white, yogurt and honey. Whisk with a fork to blend.

In a blender, finely chop pistachios. Then mix with bread crumbs and paprika in another shallow bowl.

Dip fillets in egg white mixture and then dredge in pistachio mixture. Lay fillets flat on a baking sheet that has been coated with vegetable cooking spray. Place in refrigerator for 15 minutes.

Remove from refrigerator and bake in a 425°F oven for 5 minutes. Turn fillets over and continue baking for another 5 to 7 minutes. Serve, garnished with pistachios.

    4 servings
    268 calories per serving

Tom's Orange Roughy with Green Chili Salsa

OPTIONS: Flounder, Sole, Whitefish

My friend took to orange roughy as soon as it arrived on our shores from New Zealand. He also prides himself on his fireproof palate. This recipe suits both tastes.

  ½ cup flour
  1 teaspoon paprika
  ½ teaspoon ground cumin
  ¼ teaspoon garlic powder
1¼ pounds orange roughy fillets, cut into 4 equal pieces
  2 teaspoons olive oil
  1 cup Green Chili Salsa (recipe follows)

In a shallow bowl, combine flour, paprika, cumin and garlic powder. Dredge fillets in seasoned flour.

In a large nonstick skillet, heat oil over medium heat for 2 minutes.

Lay fillets flat in hot oil and sauté for 4 minutes. Turn fillets over and sauté for 6 to 8 minutes. Remove fillets and pat dry with paper towel. Garnish with cilantro sprigs and serve with Green Chili Salsa on the side.

    4 servings
    282 calories per serving

Green Chili Salsa

  1 teaspoon olive oil
  ⅓ cup diced green peppers
  ¼ cup sliced scallions
  1 clove garlic, minced
  ⅓ cup sliced canned mild green chili peppers
  ¼ cup chopped fresh cilantro or 1 tablespoon dried parsley flakes
  ¼ cup canned crushed tomatoes
  ¼ teaspoon chili powder
  1 teaspoon red wine vinegar

In a saucepan, heat oil. Add green peppers, scallions and garlic and sauté over medium heat for 2 minutes. Stir in chili peppers, cilantro or parsley, tomatoes, chili powder and vinegar, cover and cook for 10 minutes, stirring occasionally. Serve hot.

    Makes 1 cup

Taffet's Diced Orange Roughy in Filo Pastry

OPTIONS: Flounder, Sole

I served this to my wife's family for a holiday dinner. Now it is a culinary tradition at their house for our annual family gathering.

1¼ pounds orange roughy fillets, diced
1 tablespoon white wine Worcestershire sauce
1 clove garlic, minced
1 teaspoon safflower oil
1 cup diced carrots
1 cup corn kernels
1 cup peas
¼ cup minced onions
9 sheets filo dough, thawed and covered with a damp cloth
1 tablespoon olive oil

Toss fish in a small bowl and mix with Worcestershire sauce and garlic. In a large nonstick skillet, heat safflower oil. Add carrots, corn, peas and onions and sauté for 5 to 6 minutes. Set aside.

Coat a 9-inch glass pie dish with vegetable cooking spray. Removing one at a time, lightly brush three sheets of dough with olive oil and press gently into the bottom of the dish. Spoon sautéed vegetables evenly over dough. Remove three more sheets, brush each with olive oil and place over vegetables. Top second layer of dough with fish. Brush last three sheets with oil and place over fish. Brush remaining oil on top layer. Mold overhanging edges of dough gently with fingertips to fit into the dish and bake in a 400°F oven for 15 to 17 minutes, or until golden brown.

To serve, cut into wedges and garnish with lemon.

4 servings
455 calories per serving

Alice Anne's Smoked Sablefish Wrap with Soy Dipping Sauce

OPTIONS: Smoked salmon, Smoked whitefish

This tasty finger-food method for preparing sablefish fits the dainty grasp of my favorite niece to a tee.

¾ pound smoked sablefish fillet
½ cup thinly sliced scallions
1 small clove garlic, minced
1 hard-cooked egg, coarsely chopped
1 teaspoon sesame oil
12 egg roll wrappers
1½ teaspoons peanut oil
½ cup Soy Dipping Sauce (recipe follows)

In a bowl, flake fish into small pieces with a fork. Add scallions, garlic, eggs and sesame oil. Stir with a fork to blend.

Lay each egg roll wrapper flat and brush lightly with water. Place two heaping tablespoons of fish mixture in the center of each wrapper. Fold wrapper in thirds over fish and brush top lightly with water. Fold ends on top to meet in the middle.

In a large nonstick skillet, heat peanut oil over medium heat for 2 minutes. Sauté fish wraps about 3 minutes on each side, or until browned. Serve hot with Soy Dipping Sauce. Garnish plates with scallion brushes.

4 servings
480 calories per serving

Soy Dipping Sauce

½ cup low-sodium soy sauce
1 teaspoon sesame oil
2 tablespoons thinly sliced
   scallions
¼ teaspoon wasabi green
   horseradish powder (optional)

In a small bowl, combine all ingredients and stir to blend. Let stand for 1 hour before serving.

    Makes ½ cup

Poached Skate Wings with Black Mustard

OPTION: Scallops

1 quart water
½ lemon, sliced
2 bay leaves
2 sprigs fresh parsley
½ teaspoon dried thyme leaves
10 black peppercorns
2 pounds skate wings
1 tablespoon olive oil
2 teaspoons coarse Dijon mustard
¼ cup milk
2 tablespoons minced fresh
   parsley

In a large pot, combine water, lemon, bay leaves, parsley, thyme and peppercorns. Bring to a boil, reduce heat and simmer for 10 minutes.

Cut skate wings into four equal pieces. Add wings to bouillon and cook for 10 minutes. Remove bay leaves.

In a heavy saucepan, combine oil and mustard. Cook over medium-high heat, stirring constantly until the mustard is incorporated into oil, about 2 to 3 minutes. Add milk and stir briskly. Remove from heat.

To serve, drizzle mustard sauce over wings and sprinkle with minced parsley.

    4 servings
    339 calories per serving

Taffi's Tilefish Tossed Salad

OPTIONS: Catfish, Red snapper

My wife, taffi, prepares the perfect tossed salad. The tilefish in it is the big attraction because this flavorful fish holds its bite-size shape through the brisk tossing.

1 pound tilefish fillets
2 tablespoons plus 1 teaspoon
   safflower oil
1 cup thin tomato wedges
1 cup sliced, seeded cucumbers
¼ cup julienne of scallions
¼ cup julienne of carrots
1 tablespoon sliced fresh basil or
   ½ teaspoon dried basil
1 tablespoon chopped fresh
   parsley
¼ teaspoon dried oregano
   dash of garlic powder
⅛ teaspoon freshly ground black
   pepper
1 tablespoon grated Parmesan
   cheese
2 tablespoons white wine vinegar
2 cups sliced iceberg lettuce

Rub fillets with 1 teaspoon oil. Place in a baking dish and bake in a 350°F oven for 12 to 14 minutes. Remove from oven and let stand for 15 minutes. Then chill for 30 minutes.

In a large bowl, combine tomatoes, cucumbers, scallions, carrots, basil, parsley, oregano, garlic powder, pepper, Parmesan, remaining oil and vinegar. Toss to coat all vegetables thoroughly.

When chilled, break fish into bite-size pieces and fold into vegetables. Serve on a bed of sliced lettuce, garnished with radishes.

    4 servings
    209 calories per serving

Wolffish in a Wink

OPTIONS: Tilefish, Ocean pout,
Catfish

This quick and delicious ocean cat-fish dish is a favorite of my buddy Wink Purcell — probably because slic-ing the fish into thin cutlets gets you out of the kitchen in a short time so you can take all the bows.

⅓ cup flour
1 heaping teaspoon curry powder
1¼ pounds wolffish fillet, cut into
⅟₂-inch cutlets
1 tablespoon peanut oil

In a shallow bowl, combine flour and curry powder. Stir to blend.

Dredge cutlets in seasoned flour.

In a large non-stick skillet, heat oil over medium heat for 2 minutes. Sauté cutlets 2 to 3 minutes on each side, or until lightly browned. Serve hot with lemon or lime wedges.

4 servings
210 calories per serving

Accompaniments

~~~~~~~~~~~~~~~~~~~~~~~~~~~~~~~~

When I think of a fish dinner, I see the whole picture—a platter with a perfect piece of fish and the accompaniments that round out the meal and make it memorable. I guess it comes from having been in the restaurant business, but I think in terms of full menus—appetizing combinations. I visualize herbed Roasted Sweet Onions with a broiled shark steak, colorful Pickled Beets enhancing a baked bluefish, spicy Bayou Stewed Tomatoes as a tasty match for catfish, tangy Marinated Cucumbers with fresh-caught trout.

I'm sure you have your favorite combinations, too. Family traditions, local availability, fortunate discoveries or trips to another state or another country all contribute indelible taste impressions that we want to experience again and again.

This chapter includes a selection of my favorite fish accompaniments. They all have my personal touch. I know they'll add to your enjoyment of the fine fish dishes in this book.

Pickled Cabbage

A natural match for simply prepared fish—grilled, broiled or baked. Try it with a grilled tuna steak.

¼ cup cider vinegar
2 teaspoons honey
1 tablespoon safflower oil
⅛ teaspoon celery seeds
¼ cup shredded carrots
¼ cup minced sweet red peppers
1½ cups chopped cabbage

In a saucepan, cook vinegar and honey over medium heat for 1 to 2 minutes, stirring until honey dissolves. Remove from heat and add oil.

In a bowl, mix together celery seeds, carrots, peppers and cabbage. Pour vinegar mixture over cabbage and toss. Let stand at room temperature for 1 hour, tossing twice.

Chill for at least 30 minutes before serving.
4 servings
54 calories per serving

Coleslaw

This lightly sweetened version really works magic with monkfish.

6 cups thinly sliced cabbage
½ cup shredded carrots
½ cup shredded green apple
¼ cup lemon juice
¾ cup plain low-fat yogurt, drained
    1 to 2 hours
¼ cup reduced-calorie mayonnaise
1 teaspoon honey
¼ cup skim milk
¼ teaspoon dry mustard
    dash of ground white pepper

In a large bowl, mix together cabbage, carrots and apples. Pour lemon juice over vegetables and toss to coat.

In a small bowl, combine yogurt, mayonnaise, honey, milk, mustard and pepper. Stir to blend thoroughly.

Pour dressing over cabbage and toss to coat. Cover and refrigerate for at least 1 hour, or preferably overnight. Stir before serving.
6 servings
86 calories per serving

Sweet-and-Sour Pickled Napa Cabbage

The sweet, firm meat of shrimp matches this Orient-accented raw cabbage as though they were made for each other.

1 tablespoon peanut oil
4 cups thinly sliced napa cabbage, packed
1 clove garlic, minced
¼ cup rice wine vinegar
1 tablespoon honey

In a wok, heat oil over medium-high heat for 1 minute. Add cabbage and stir-fry for 2 minutes. Add garlic and stir-fry for 1 minute more. Remove cabbage to a large bowl.

Warm vinegar in a small saucepan over medium heat for 1 to 2 minutes. Add honey and stir until dissolved.

Pour vinegar/honey mixture over cabbage. Toss to blend. Cover and refrigerate for at least 1 hour, or preferably overnight, before serving.
4 servings
71 calories per serving

Pottsville Pepper Relish

When the locals in my hometown, Pottsville, Pennsylvania, get together for a trout supper in the spring, this special relish has an honored spot on every table.

    2 tablespoons olive oil
    1 cup thinly sliced fresh chili
          peppers
    1 cup thinly sliced sweet red
          peppers
    1 cup thinly sliced green peppers
    1 cup thinly sliced red onions
    ¼ cup red wine vinegar
    2 tablespoons honey
    1 teaspoon mustard seeds, ground

In a 6- to 8-quart pot, heat oil. Add peppers and onions and sauté over medium heat for 10 minutes.

Stir in vinegar, honey and mustard seeds until blended. Cover, reduce heat to low and cook for 30 minutes. Stir frequently. Remove from heat to cool.

Makes 1½ cups
182 calories per ½-cup serving

Pickled Beets

It's the touch of clove that brings a special distinction to this colorful accompaniment. Serve with blue-fish and other fish that have an asser-tive flavor.

    1 can (8 ounces) whole baby beets
    ½ cup cider vinegar
    1 teaspoon honey
    ½ cup sliced onions
    1 whole clove

Drain beets and reserve juice. Slice beets ¼ inch thick and place in a bowl.

In a saucepan, combine beet juice, vinegar, honey, onions and clove. Bring to a boil over medium-high heat, then remove from heat. Pour over beets and allow to cool for 1 hour. Cover and refrigerate for at least 1 hour, or preferably overnight, before serving.

4 servings
45 calories per serving

Carolina Corn Relish

The herb-and-spice combination in this recipe brings a new dimension to down-home corn. I like it with Carolina's own red snapper.

    ¼ cup white vinegar
    1 teaspoon crab boil mix
    ¼ teaspoon dried thyme leaves
    1 teaspoon honey
    1 cup slightly cooked corn kernels
    ½ cup finely chopped celery
          (including leaves)
    ¼ cup thinly sliced scallions
    1 tablespoon chopped pimientos
    1 tablespoon minced fresh parsley

In a small saucepan, combine vinegar, crab boil mix, thyme and honey. Bring to a boil, remove from heat and let stand for 10 minutes.

In a bowl, mix together corn, cel-ery, scallions, pimientos and parsley.

Strain vinegar over vegetables and discard crab boil mix and thyme. Toss corn to coat evenly. Cover and refrigerate for at least 1 hour, or preferably overnight, before serving.

Makes 1½ cups
30 calories per ¼-cup serving

Peppered Onions

2½ cups sliced sweet onions
1 tablespoon olive oil
2 tablespoons chicken stock
1 teaspoon freshly ground black
    pepper
1 tablespoon tarragon vinegar

In a large nonstick skillet, sauté onions in oil and chicken stock over medium heat for 4 minutes. Add pepper. Stir, cover, reduce heat to low and cook the onions for 15 minutes. Do not brown onions.

Add vinegar, stir and serve hot (can be served chilled or at room temperature).

Makes 1 cup
72 calories per ¼-cup serving

Roasted Sweet Onions

Serve these as a pleasant surprise with any firm-fleshed fish, such as shark or tuna, simply cooked.

2 large onions, cut in half
    crosswise
1 tablespoon olive oil
½ teaspoon dried thyme leaves
½ cup hot chicken stock
¼ teaspoon mustard seeds, ground

Place onion halves in a small baking dish, cut side up. Rub surface with oil and sprinkle with thyme. Pour chicken stock into baking dish. Sprinkle onions with mustard seeds, cover dish with foil and bake in a 400°F oven for 15 minutes. Remove foil and continue to roast for another 15 to 20 minutes. Serve immediately.

4 servings
55 calories per serving

"Dirty" Rice

This creole classic is a perfect partner for the fish dishes that made lower Dixie famous — shrimp creole, for example.

2 teaspoons olive oil
¼ pound chicken livers, sliced into
    small pieces
¼ cup diced onions
1 clove garlic, minced
1 tablespoon chopped fresh
    parsley
1 cup rice
1¾ cups chicken stock

In a small saucepan, heat oil. Add livers and onions and sauté over medium-high heat for 2 minutes, stirring briskly to break up livers. Add garlic and parsley, stir and cook for 1 minute.

Stir in rice and chicken stock and bring to a boil. Cover, reduce heat to low and cook for 20 minutes. Serve hot.

4 servings
235 calories per serving

Bayou Rice

1 clove garlic, minced
1 tablespoon olive oil
½ teaspoon celery seeds
¼ teaspoon freshly ground black
    pepper
¼ cup chopped fresh parsley
1 cup rice
1¾ cups chicken stock
1 tablespoon lemon juice
1 teaspoon butter

In a heavy saucepan, sauté garlic in oil over medium heat for 2 minutes.

Add celery seeds, pepper, parsley, rice, chicken stock and lemon juice. Stir and bring to a boil over high heat. Cover, reduce heat to low and cook, undisturbed, for 17 to 20 minutes. Remove from heat, add butter and fluff with a fork before serving.

Makes 2 cups

217 calories per ½-cup serving

Bayou Stewed Tomatoes

Some folks can't imagine serving catfish without this Louisiana specialty on the side — you might become one of those folks once you taste it.

½ cup sliced scallions
1 tablespoon olive oil
1 tablespoon red wine vinegar
1 whole clove
½ cup thinly sliced fresh okra
1 teaspoon minced fresh chili peppers
3 cups canned plum tomatoes (including juice)
1 tablespoon chopped fresh parsley

In a saucepan, sauté scallions in oil over medium heat for 1 minute. Add vinegar and clove. Stir, cover and cook for 3 minutes. Remove and discard clove.

Stir in okra, chili peppers, tomatoes (with juice) and parsley. Bring to a simmer, cover and cook for 10 minutes. Serve immediately.

Makes 3½ cups

39 calories per ½-cup serving

Marinated and Grilled Zucchini Steaks

Nobody will accuse you of serving the same old thing when these tasty, chunky disks turn up next to a swordfish steak or a bluefish fillet.

1 tablespoon lemon juice
2 teaspoons low-sodium soy sauce
1 teaspoon honey
1 teaspoon sesame oil
1 clove garlic, minced
2 zucchinis (9 inches each), sliced diagonally into 1-inch steaks

In a cup, combine lemon juice, soy sauce, honey, oil and garlic. Stir to blend.

Place zucchini steaks in a gallon-size, plastic food-storage bag. Pour marinade over zucchini and twist-tie shut. Knead bag gently to coat squash evenly. Marinate in refrigerator for 1 hour.

Lay zucchini steaks flat on a hot grill and barbecue for 2 to 3 minutes on each side, basting with marinade. Serve hot or chilled in a salad.

4 servings

34 calories per serving

Fresh Okra
in Creole Sauce

In the Carolinas and on the Gulf, okra is a big favorite and this dish is perfect on a menu with crawfish and red snapper.

1 tablespoon olive oil
¼ cup sliced scallions
½ cup diced green peppers
1 clove garlic, minced
¼ cup chopped fresh parsley
1 cup diced plum tomatoes
½ cup tomato puree
1 pound fresh okra, cut into 1-inch pieces

In a 4-quart saucepan, heat oil. Add scallions and peppers and sauté over medium heat for 2 to 3 minutes. Stir in garlic, parsley and tomatoes and sauté 1 minute more. Add tomato puree and stir. Cover, reduce heat to low and simmer for 10 minutes.

Add okra to sauce. Cover and simmer for 10 minutes. Stir and serve.

4 servings
99 calories per serving

Cheese-Stuffed
Baked Potatoes

I feature this sure-fire favorite at an annual trout roast I cater. The cottage cheese cuts out the butter that usually zooms the fat level and calorie count when baked potatoes are served.

4 baking potatoes
½ cup low-fat cottage cheese
1 tablespoon freshly grated Parmesan cheese
1 tablespoon snipped chives
⅛ teaspoon paprika

Bake potatoes in a 400°F oven for 45 to 55 minutes.

Slice potatoes in half and scoop out most of the pulp. Reserve skins.

In a bowl, combine potato pulp, cottage cheese, Parmesan and chives. Whisk with a fork to blend. Spoon mixture into skins and place on a baking sheet. Sprinkle potatoes with paprika and bake in a 450°F oven for 8 to 10 minutes, or until lightly browned on top. Serve piping hot.

4 servings
248 calories per serving

Pickled Carrot Slices

The Pennsylvania Dutch specialize in sweet-tart relishes like this. I get cheers when I pair it with grilled shrimp.

4 cups diagonally sliced carrots
1 cup thinly sliced onions
1 cup cider vinegar
¼ cup orange marmalade
1 tablespoon prepared horseradish
½ cup orange juice

In a saucepan, combine carrots, onions and vinegar. Bring to a simmer over medium heat. Stir, cover, reduce heat to low and cook for 5 minutes. Drain and reserve vinegar.

In a large bowl, combine ¼ cup reserved vinegar, marmalade, horseradish and orange juice. Stir to blend. Discard remaining vinegar. Add carrots and onions and toss to coat evenly. Cover and refrigerate for at least 1 hour. Toss carrots once or twice while marinating.

> 4 servings
> 132 calories per serving

Marinated Cucumbers

Cool cucumber, enlivened with a tangy but smooth marinade, is ideal for a summer flounder feast.

> 1 sliced, seeded cucumber
> ¼ cup white vinegar
> 1 tablespoon Dijon mustard
> 1 clove garlic, minced
> ¾ cup plain low-fat yogurt, drained
>   1 to 2 hours
> 2 tablespoons snipped dill or
>   2 teaspoons dried dill

Split cucumber lengthwise. Remove and discard seeds. Slice cucumber halves into ¼-inch slices.

In a shallow bowl, combine vinegar, mustard and garlic. Stir to blend. Add cucumber slices and toss to coat evenly. Cover and let stand for 1 to 2 hours.

Drain and discard marinade. Stir in yogurt and dill. Refrigerate for at least 1 hour before serving.

> 4 servings
> 43 calories per serving

New Red-Skin Potato Salad

It's raves for this unusual red-skin version of a patio tradition. I use it as a color accent with a white fish steak, such as haddock.

> 1 pound unpeeled new red-skin
>   potatoes, cut into ½-inch slices
> 2 cups chicken stock
> 1 clove garlic, minced
> 1 tablespoon olive oil
> ¼ cup red wine vinegar
> 1 teaspoon fresh thyme leaves or
>   ¼ teaspoon dried thyme leaves
> 1 tablespoon minced fresh parsley
> ⅛ teaspoon freshly ground black
>   pepper
> 1 cup sliced plum tomatoes
> ½ cup thinly sliced celery
> ¼ cup thinly sliced scallions

In a 4-quart saucepan, combine potatoes and chicken stock and bring to a boil over medium-high heat. Cover, reduce heat to low and simmer gently for 10 minutes. Remove potatoes from pot, reserving liquid. Cool potatoes under cold running water, drain and let stand at room temperature. Reduce cooking liquid by half at a rolling boil.

In a small skillet, sauté garlic in oil over medium heat for 1 to 2 minutes. Do not brown. Strain, reserving oil and discarding garlic.

In a large bowl, combine ¼ cup reduced cooking liquid, strained oil, vinegar, thyme, parsley and pepper. Whisk with a fork. Add tomatoes, celery and scallions and toss to coat evenly. Stir in potatoes. Cover and refrigerate for at least 1 hour before serving.

> 4 servings
> 135 calories per serving

Ratatouille

A nice addition to broiled scallops or any firm-fleshed, unsauced fish.

2 teaspoons olive oil
½ cup diced onions
½ cup diced green peppers
1 clove garlic, minced
3 cups cubed eggplant
1 can (15 ounces) whole plum tomatoes (including juice), coarsely chopped
1 teaspoon fresh thyme leaves or ¼ teaspoon dried thyme leaves
1 tablespoon sliced fresh basil or 1 teaspoon dried basil
1 zucchini, sliced into ½-inch slices

In a 4-quart saucepan, heat oil. Add onions and peppers and sauté over medium heat for 3 or 4 minutes. Stir in garlic and eggplant and sauté for 1 minute. Add tomatoes (with juice), thyme and basil and stir. Cover, reduce heat to low and simmer for 10 minutes.

Add zucchini to saucepan. Stir, cover and simmer for 5 minutes. Serve hot or chilled.

4 servings
77 calories per serving

Caesar Salad

If it's a touch of class you want with your next fish dinner, look no further.

1 clove garlic, cut in half
1 anchovy
2 tablespoons olive oil
1 egg
1 cup hot water
2 tablespoons lemon juice
1 head romaine lettuce broken into bite-size pieces
1 tablespoon grated Parmesan cheese
¼ teaspoon freshly ground black pepper
2 cups Mustard Croutons (recipe follows)

Rub the inside of a wooden salad bowl with cut surfaces of garlic halves, pressing to extract juices. Discard garlic. Combine anchovy and oil in the bowl, mashing anchovy with a fork.

Allow egg to stand in water for 2 minutes. Separate egg white from yolk, break egg white into a small bowl and whisk with the fork. Add to anchovy paste along with lemon juice. Whisk to blend dressing.

Add romaine and toss to coat with dressing. Sprinkle with Parmesan and black pepper. Toss and serve with Mustard Croutons.

6 servings
80 calories per serving

~~~~~~~~~~~~~~~~

Mustard Croutons

2 thick slices of seedless rye bread
1 tablespoon brown mustard
2 teaspoons olive oil

Spread rye bread evenly with mustard. Cut bread into 1-inch cubes with a sharp knife.

Heat oil in a skillet over medium heat for 2 to 3 minutes. Add bread cubes and sauté for 6 to 8 minutes, browning both sides. Use immediately.

Makes 2 cups
28 calories per ¼-cup serving

Risotto with Peas and Beans

A nice complement to sautéed monkfish or steamed cod.

- ¼ cup sliced scallions
- 1 tablespoon olive oil
- 1 cup short grain Italian rice (arborio)
- 2 cups chicken stock
- ½ cup fresh peas, slightly steamed
- ½ cup cooked red kidney beans
- 4 pimiento-stuffed green olives, sliced

In a saucepan, sauté scallions in oil over medium heat for 2 minutes. Do not brown. Add rice and stir until oil is absorbed, about 2 minutes.

Gradually add chicken stock, ½ cup at a time, stirring constantly. Then allow rice to absorb each ½ cup of stock before you add the next. Total cooking time should be about 20 minutes.

Add peas, beans and olives. Stir, cover and remove from heat. Let stand for 5 minutes and serve.

4 servings
270 calories per serving

Rice–Barley Pilaf

Shrimp and rice is a classic coupling, but here is a variation that adds an exotic dimension.

- ½ cup diced onions
- 2 teaspoons olive oil
- ½ cup rice
- ½ cup pearled barley
- 1¾ cups chicken stock
- 1 teaspoon fresh thyme leaves or ¼ teaspoon dried thyme leaves
- ¼ teaspoon mustard seeds, ground dash of freshly ground black pepper

In a medium saucepan, sauté onions in oil over medium heat for 2 minutes. Stir in rice and barley and sauté until grains are slightly toasted, 4 to 5 minutes. Add chicken stock, thyme, mustard seeds and pepper and bring to a boil. Reduce heat to low and cook for 17 to 20 minutes without removing the cover. Fluff with a fork and serve.

4 servings
206 calories per serving

Scalloped Sweet Potatoes

As a winter warm-up with a baked cod or haddock dish, you can't go wrong with this specialty of mine.

4 sweet potatoes sliced
3 quarts water
1 cup thinly sliced onions
½ cup bread crumbs
1 cup milk
1 tablespoon maple syrup
½ teaspoon dry mustard
¼ teaspoon paprika
dash of ground white pepper

Place sweet potatoes in a 4-quart saucepan, and cover with water. Bring to a boil, reduce heat and simmer for 8 minutes. Drain.

Coat a 1½-quart, shallow casserole dish with vegetable cooking spray. Arrange sweet potatoes in the dish in four layers spreading onions and 2 tablespoons bread crumbs between each layer, end with a top layer of sweet potatoes.

In a saucepan, combine milk, syrup, mustard, paprika and pepper. Bring to a simmer over medium heat, stirring constantly. Pour mixture over sweet potatoes. Sprinkle remaining bread crumbs on top. Cover and bake in a 350°F oven for 25 minutes.

Remove the cover and bake 10 to 15 minutes more, or until lightly browned. Remove from oven and let stand 5 minutes before serving.

4 servings
250 calories per serving

Wild and Brown Rice Stuffing

2½ cups chicken stock
¼ cup wild rice
¾ cup brown rice
1 tablespoon vegetable oil
2 shallots, minced
½ cup sliced fresh mushrooms
¼ cup diced green peppers or
   sweet red peppers
½ cup peas
¼ cup diced carrots
1 teaspoon low-sodium soy sauce

In a 2-quart saucepan, bring chicken stock to a boil. Add wild rice and brown rice and reduce heat to medium. Cover and simmer for 30 to 35 minutes, or until rice is tender.

Meanwhile, in a medium nonstick skillet, heat oil over medium heat. Add shallots and mushrooms and sauté until softened. Add peppers, peas, carrots and soy sauce. Sauté for another 5 to 6 minutes. Remove from heat. Toss with rice until well combined and serve.

Makes 4 cups
113 calories per ½-cup serving

Wasabi White Sauce

½ teaspoon wasabi green
   horseradish powder
1 teaspoon water
¼ cup sour cream
¼ cup reduced-calorie mayonnaise

In a small bowl, combine wasabi powder with water. Stir in sour cream and mayonnaise and blend thoroughly before serving.

Makes ½ cup
36 calories per tablespoon

Marinara Sauce

2 tablespoons olive oil
½ cup minced celery
½ cup minced onions
2 cloves garlic, minced
2 cups canned plum tomatoes
    (including juice)
2 cups tomato puree
1 cup water
2 tablespoons minced fresh
    parsley
½ teaspoon dried basil

In a saucepan, heat oil. Add celery, onions and garlic and sauté over medium heat for 3 minutes. Stir in tomatoes (with juice), tomato puree, water, parsley and basil, cover, reduce heat to low and simmer for 30 minutes, stirring frequently. Serve hot.
    Makes approximately 4 cups
    67 calories per ½-cup serving

Guacamole

1 avocado
½ cup minced fresh tomatoes
3 tablespoons lemon juice
¼ cup minced onions
2 tablespoons minced green chili
    peppers
2 teaspoons minced fresh cilantro
¾ teaspoon chili powder

In a bowl, mash avocado pulp with a fork. Whisk in remaining ingredients and blend thoroughly before serving.
    Makes 1¼ cups
    71 calories per ¼-cup serving

Cocktail Sauce

½ cup chili sauce
1 tablespoon minced onions
1 tablespoon prepared horseradish
1 tablespoon lemon juice
½ teaspoon Worcestershire sauce

In a small bowl, combine all ingredients. Whisk with a fork to blend thoroughly. Cover and refrigerate for at least 1 hour before serving.
    Makes ⅔ cup
    23 calories per tablespoon

Italian Catsup

¼ cup minced onions
1 small clove garlic, minced
1 teaspoon olive oil
½ cup tomato puree
1 teaspoon red wine vinegar
1 teaspoon honey

In a small saucepan, sauté onions and garlic in oil over medium-low heat for 5 minutes. Do not brown.
    Add tomato puree, vinegar and honey, stirring to blend. Cover, remove from heat and let stand for 5 minutes.
    Spoon catsup into a jar, cover and chill for at least 1 hour before serving.
    Makes ¾ cup
    11 calories per tablespoon

Note: If you want a smooth catsup, puree mixture in a blender before chilling.

INDEX

Page references in *italic* indicate tables.